The Rising Tide of Color Against White World-Supremacy

Lothrop Stoddard

The Rising Tide of Color Against White World-Supremacy

For information and contact visit our website at:
IndoEuropeanPublishing.com

The present edition is a revised version of 1927 of this work published by Scribners publishing, produced in the current edition with completely new, easy to read format, and is set and proofread by Alfred Aghajanian for Indo-European Publishing.

Cover Design by Indo-European Design Team

ISBN: 978-1-60444-443-8

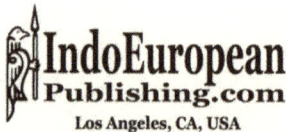

IndoEuropean
Publishing.com
Los Angeles, CA, USA

CONTENTS

PREFACE

More than a decade ago I became convinced that the key-note of twentieth-century world-politics would be the relations between the primary races of mankind. Momentous modifications of existing race-relations were evidently impending, and nothing could be more vital to the course of human evolution than the character of these modifications, since upon the quality of human life all else depends.

Acordingly, my attention was thenceforth largely directed to racial matters. In the preface to an historical monograph ("The French Revolution in San Domingo ") written shortly before the Great War, I stated: "The world-wide struggle between the primary races of mankind - the 'conflict of color,' as it has been happily termed - bids fair to be the fundamental problem of the twentieth century, and great communities like the United States of America, the South African Confederation, and Australasia regard the 'color question' as perhaps the gravest problem of the future."

Those lines were penned in June, 1914. Before their publication the Great War had burst upon the world. At that time several reviewers commented upon the above dictum and wondered whether, had I written two months later, I should have held a different opinion.

As a matter of fact, I should have expressed myself even more strongly to the same effect. To me the Great War was from the first the White Civil War, which, whatever its outcome, must gravely complicate the course of racial relations.

Before the war I had hoped that the readjustments rendered inevitable by the renascence of the brown and yellow peoples of Asia would be a gradual, and in the main a pacific, process, kept within evolutionary bounds by the white world's inherent strength and

1

fundamental solidarity. The frightful weakening of the white world during the war, however, opened up revolutionary, even cataclysmic, possibilities.

In saying this I do not refer solely to military "perils." The subjugation of white lands by colored armies may, of course, occur, especially if the white world continues to rend itself with internecine wars. However, such colored triumphs of arms are less to be dreaded than more enduring conquests like migrations which would swamp whole populations and turn countries now white into colored man's lands irretrievably lost to the white world. Of course, these ominous possibilities existed even before 1914, but the war has rendered them much more probable.

The most disquieting feature of the present situation, however, is not the war but the peace. The white world's inability to frame a constructive settlement, the perpetuation of intestine hatreds, and the menace of fresh white civil wars complicated by the spectre of social revolution, evoke the dread thought that the late war may be merely the first stage in a cycle of ruin.

In fact, so absorbed is the white world with its domestic dissensions that it pays scant heed to racial problems whose importance for the future of mankind far transcends the questions which engross its attention to-day.

This relative indifference to the larger racial issues has determined the writing of the present book. So fundamental are these issues that a candid discussion of them would seem to be timely and helpful.

In the following pages I have tried to analyze in their various aspects the present relations between the white and non-white worlds. My task has been greatly aided by the Introduction from the pen of Madison Grant, who has admirably summarized the biological and historical background. A life-long student of biology, Mr. Grant approaches the subject along that line. My own avenue of approach being world-politics, the resulting convergence of different viewpoints has been a most useful one.

For the stimulating counsel of Mr. Grant in the preparation of this book my thanks are especially due. I desire also to acknowledge my indebtedness for helpful suggestions to Messrs. Alleyne Ireland, Glenn Frank, and other friends.

LOTHROP STODDARD
NEW YORK CITY,
February 28, 1920

PART I

The Rising Tide of Color

CHAPTER I
THE WORLD OF COLOR

THE man who, on a quiet spring evening of the year -1914, opened his atlas to a political map of the world and pored over its many-tinted patterns probably got one fundamental impression: the overwhelming preponderance of the white race in the ordering of the world's affairs. Judged by accepted canons of statecraft, the white man towered the indisputable master of the planet. Forth from Europe's teeming mother hive the imperious Sons of Japhet had swarmed for centuries to plant their laws, their customs, and their battle-flags at the uttermost ends of the earth. Two whole continents, North America and Australia, had been made virtually as white in blood as the European motherland; two other continents, South America and Africa, had been extensively colonized by white stocks; while even huge Asia had seen its empty northern march, Siberia, pre-empted for the white man's abode. Even where white populations had not locked themselves to the soil few regions of the earth had escaped the white man's imperial sway, and vast areas inhabited by uncounted myriads of dusky folk obeyed the white man's will.

4

Beside the enormous area of white settlement or control, the regions under non-white governance bulked small indeed. In eastern Asia, China, Japan, and Siam; in western Asia, Turkey, Afghanistan, and Persia; in Africa, Abyssinia, and Liberia; and in America the minute state of Haiti: such was the brief list of lands under non-white rule. In other words, of the 53,000,000 square miles which (excluding the polar regions) constitute the land area of the globe, only 6,000,000 square miles had non-white governments, and nearly two-thirds of this relatively modest remainder was represented by China and its dependencies.

Since 1914 the world has been convulsed by the most terrible war in recorded history. This war was primarily a struggle between the white peoples, who have borne the brunt of the conflict and have suffered most of the losses. Nevertheless, one of the war's results has been a further whittling down of the areas standing outside white political control. Turkey is to-day practically an Anglo-French condominium, Persia is virtually a protectorate of the British Empire, while the United States has thrown over the endemic anarchy of Haiti the aegis of the Pax Americana. Study of the political map might thus apparently lead one to conclude that white world-predominance is immutable since the war's ordeal has still further broadened the territorial basis of its authority.

At this point the reader is perhaps asking himself why this book was ever undertaken. The answer is: the dangerous delusion created by viewing world affairs solely from the angle of politics, The late war has taught many lessons as to the unstable and transitory character of even the most imposing political phenomena, while a better reading of history must bring home the truth that the basic factor in human affairs is not politics, but race. The reader has already encountered this fundamental truth on every page of the Introduction. He will remember, for instance, how west-central Asia, which in the dawn of history was predominantly white man's country, is to-day racially brown man's land in which white blood survives only as vestigial traces of vanishing significance. If this portion of Asia, the former seat of mighty white empires and

5

possibly the very homeland of the white race itself, should have so entirely changed its ethnic character, what assurance can the most impressive political panorama give us that the present world-order may not swiftly and utterly pass away ?

The force of this query is exemplified when we turn from the political to the racial map of the globe. What a transformation! Instead of a world politically nine-tenths white, we see a world of which only four-tenths at the most can be considered predominantly white in blood, the rest of the world being inhabited mainly by the other primary races of mankind - yellows, browns, blacks, and reds. Speaking by continents, Europe, North America to the Rio Grade, the southern portion of South America, the Siberian part of Asia, and Australasia constitute the real white world; while the bulk of Asia, virtually the whole of Africa, and most of Central and South America form the world of color. The respective areas of these two racially contrasted worlds are 22,000,000 square miles for the whites and 31,000,000 square miles for the colored races. Furthermore it must be remembered that fully one-third of the white area (notably Australasia and Siberia) is very thinly inhabited and is thus held by a very slender racial tenure-the only tenure which counts in the long run.

The statistical disproportion between the white and colored worlds becomes still more marked when we turn from surveys of area to tables of population. The total number of human beings alive to-day is about 1,700,000,000. Of these 550,000,000 are white, while 1,150,000,000 are colored. The colored races thus outnumber the whites more than two to one. Another fact of capital importance is that the great bulk of the white race is concentrated in the European continent. In 1914 the population of Europe was approximately 450,000,000. The late war has undoubtedly caused an absolute decrease of many millions of souls. Nevertheless, the basic fact remains that some four-fifths of the entire white race is concentrated on less than one-fifth of the white world's territorial area (Europe), while the remaining one-fifth of the race (some 110,000,000 souls), scattered to the ends of the earth, must protect four-fifths of the white territorial heritage against the pressure of colored races eleven times its numerical strength.

As to the 1,150,000,000 of the colored world, they are divided, as already stated, into four primary categories: yellows, browns, blacks, and reds. The yellows are the most numerous of the colored races, numbering over 500,000,000. Their habitat is eastern Asia. Nearly as numerous and much more wide-spread than the yellows are the browns, numbering some 450,000,000. The browns spread in a broad belt from the Pacific Ocean westward across southern Asia and northern Africa to the Atlantic Ocean. The blacks total about 150,000,000. Their centre is Africa south of the Sahara Desert, but besides the African continent there are vestigial black traces across southern Asia to the Pacific and also strong black outposts in the Americas. Least numerous of the colored race-stocks are the reds-the "Indians" of the western hemisphere. Mustering a total of less than 40,000,000, the reds are almost all located south of the Rio Grande in "Latin America."

Such is the ethnic make-up of that world of color which, as already seen, outnumbers the white world two to one. That is a formidable ratio, and its significance is heightened by the fact that this ratio seems destined to shift still further in favor of color. There can be no doubt that at present the colored races are increasing very much faster than the white. Treating the primary race-stocks as units, it would appear that whites tend to double in eighty years, yellows and browns in sixty years, blacks in forty years. The whites are thus the slowest breeders, and they will undoubtedly become slower still, since section after section of the white race is revealing that lowered birth rate which in France has reached the extreme of a stationary population.

On the other hand, none of the colored races shows perceptible signs of declining birth-rate, all tending to breed up to the limits of available subsistence. Such checks as now limit the increase of colored populations are wholly external, like famine, disease, and tribal warfare. But by a curious irony of fate, the white man has long been busy removing these checks to colored multiplication. The greater part of the colored world is to-day under white political control. Wherever the white man goes he attempts to impose the bases of his ordered civilization. He puts down tribal war, he wages truceless combat against epidemic disease, and he so improves communications that augmented and better distributed food-supplies minimize the blight of famine. In response to these life-saving activities the enormous death-rate which in the past has kept the colored races from excessive multiplication is falling to proportions comparable with the death-rate of white countries. But to lower the colored world's prodigious birth rate is quite another matter. The consequence is a portentous increase of population in nearly every portion of the colored world now under white political sway. In fact, even those colored countries which have maintained their independence, such as China and Japan, are adopting the white man's life-conserving methods and are experiencing the same accelerated increase of population.

Now what must be the inevitable result of all this? It can mean only one thing: a tremendous and steadily augmenting outward thrust of surplus colored men from overcrowded colored homelands. Remember that these homelands are already populated up to the available limits of subsistence. Of course present limits can in many cases be pushed back by better living conditions, improved agriculture, and the rise of modern machine industry such as is already under way in Japan. Nevertheless, in view of the tremendous population increases which must occur, these can be only palliatives. Where, then, should the congested colored world tend to pour its accumulating human surplus, inexorably condemned to emigrate or starve? The answer is: into those emptier regions of the earth under white political control. But many of those relatively empty lands have been definitely set aside by the white man as his own special heritage. The upshot is that the rising flood of color finds itself walled in by white dikes debarring it from many a promised land which it would fain deluge with its dusky waves.

Thus the colored world, long restive under white political

domination, is being welded by the most fundamental of instincts, the instinct of self-preservation, into a common solidarity of feeling against the dominant white man, and in the fire of a common purpose internecine differences tend, for the time at least, to be burned away. Before the supreme fact of white political world-domination, antipathies within the colored world must inevitably recede into the background.

The imperious urge of the colored world toward racial expansion was well visualized by that keen English student of world affairs, Doctor E. J. Dillon, when he wrote more than a decade ago: "The problem is one of life and death-a veritable sphinx-question- to those most nearly concerned. For, no race, however inferior it may be, will consent to famish slowly in order that other people may fatten and take their ease, especially if it has a good chance to make a fight for life." (E. J. Dillon, "The Asiatic Problem," Contemporary Review, February, 1908.)

This white statement of the colored thesis is an accurate reflection of what colored men say themselves. For example, a Japanese scholar, Professor Ryutaro Nagai, writes: "The world was not made for the white races, but for the other races as well. In Australia, South Africa, Canada, and the United States, there are vast tracts of unoccupied territory awaiting settlement, and although the citizens of the ruling Powers refuse to take up the land, no yellow people are permitted to enter. Thus the white races seem ready to commit to the savage birds and beasts what they refuse to intrust to their brethren of the yellow race. Surely the arrogance and avarice of the nobility in apportioning to themselves the most and the best of the land in certain countries is as nothing compared with the attitude of the white races toward those of a different hue." (Ryutaro Nagai in The Japan Magazine. Quoted from The Amer- can Review of Reviews, July, 1913, p. 107.)

The bitter resentment of white predominance and exclusiveness awakened in many colored breasts is typified by the following lines penned by a brown man a British-educated Afghan, shortly before the European War. Inveighing against our "racial prejudice, that cowardly, wretched caste-mark of the European and the American the world over," he exultantly predicts "a coming struggle between Asia, all Asia, against Europe and America. You are heaping up material for a Jehad, a Pan-Islam, a Pan-Asia Holy War, a gigantic day of reckoning, an invasion of a new Attila and Tamerlane who will use rifles and bullets, instead of lances and spears. You are deaf to the voice of reason and fairness, and so you must be taught with the whirring swish of the sword when it is red." (Achmet Abdullah, "Seen Through Mohammedan Spectacles," FORUM, October, 1914.)

Of course in these statements there is nothing either exceptional or novel. The colored races never welcomed white predominance and were always restive under white control. Down to the close of the nineteenth century, however, they generally accepted white hegemony as a disagreeable but inevitable fact. For four hundred years the white man had added continent to continent in his imperial progress, equipped with resistless sea-power and armed with a mechanical superiority that crushed down all local efforts at resistance. In time, therefore, the colored races accorded to white supremacy a fatalistic acquiescence, and, though never loved, the white man was usually respected and universally feared.

During the closing decades of the nineteenth century, to be sure, premonitory signs of a change in attitude began to appear. The yellow and brown races, at least, stirred by the very impact of Western ideas, measured the white man with a more critical eye and commenced to wonder whether his superiority was due to anything more than a fortuitous combination of circumstances which might be altered by efforts of their own. Japan put this theory to the test by going sedulously to the white man's school. The upshot was the Russo-Japanese War of 1904, an event the momentous character of which is even now not fully appreciated. Of course, that war was merely the sign-manual of a whole nexus of forces making for a revivified Asia. But it dramatized and clarified ideas which had been germinating half-unconsciously in millions of colored minds, and both Asia and Africa thrilled with joy and hope. Above all, the legend of white invincibility lay, a fallen idol, in the dust. Nevertheless, though freed from imaginary terrors, the colored world accurately gauged the white man's practical strength and appreciated the magnitude of the task involved in overthrowing white supremacy. That supremacy was no longer acquiesced in as inevitable and hopes of ultimate success were confidently entertained, but the process was usually conceived as a slow and difficult one. Fear of white power and respect for white civilization thus remained potent restraining factors.

Then came the Great War. The colored world suddenly saw the white peoples which, in racial matters had hitherto maintained something of a united front, locked in an internecine death-grapple of unparalleled ferocity; it saw those same peoples put one another furiously to the ban as irreconcilable foes; it saw white race-unity cleft by political and moral gulfs which white men themselves continuously iterated would never be filled. As colored men realized the significance of it all, they looked into each other's eyes and there saw the light of undreamed-of hopes. The white world was tearing itself to pieces. White solidarity was riven and shattered. And fear of white power and respect for white civilization together dropped away like garments outworn. Through the bazaars of Asia ran the sibilant whisper: "The East will see the West to bed! "

The chorus of mingled exultation, hate, and scorn sounded from every portion of the colored world. Chinese scholars, Japanese professors, Hindu pundits, Turkish journalists, and Afro-American editors, one and all voiced drastic criticisms of white civilization and hailed the war as a well-merited Nemesis on white arrogance and greed. This is how the Constantinople TANINE, the most serious Turkish newspaper, characterized the European Powers: "They would not look at the evils in their own countries or elsewhere, but interfered at the slightest incident in our borders; every day they would gnaw at some part of our rights and our sovereignty; they would perform vivisection on our quivering flesh and cut off great pieces of it. And we, with a forcibly controlled spirit of rebellion in our hearts and with clinched but powerless fists, silent and depressed, would murmur as the fire burned within: 'Oh, that they might fall out with one another! Oh, that they might eat one another up!' And lo! to-day they are eating each other up, just as the Turk wished they would." (Quoted from THE LITERARY DIGEST, October 24, 1914, p. 784.)

[he Afro-American author, W. E. Burghardt Dubois, wrote of the colored world: "These nations and races, composing as they do a vast majority of humanity, are going to endure this treatment just as long as they must and not a moment longer. Then they are going to fight, and the War of the Color Line will outdo in savage inhumanity any war this world has yet seen. For colored folk have much to remember and they will not forget." (W. E. Burghardt Dubois `"The African Roots of War," ATLANTIC MONTHLY, May, 1915.)

"What does the European War mean to us Orientals?" queried the Japanese writer, Yone Noguchi "It means the saddest downfall of the so-called western civilization, our belief that it was builded upon a higher and sounder footing than ours was at once knocked down and killed; we are sorry that we somehow overestimated its happy possibility and were deceived and cheated by its superficial glory. My recent western journey confirmed me that the so-called dynamic western civilization was all against the Asiatic belief. And when one does not respect the others, there will be only one thing to come, that is, fight, in action or silence." (Yone Noguchi, "The Downfall of Western Civilization," THE NATION (New York), October 8, 1914.)

Such was the colored world's reaction to the white death-grapple, and as the long struggle dragged on both Asia and Africa stirred to their very depths. To be sure, no great explosions occurred during the war years, albeit lifting veils of censorship reveal how narrowly such explosions were averted. Nevertheless, Asia and Africa are to-day in acute ferment, and we must not forget that this ferment is not primarily due to the war. The war merely accelerated a movement already existent long before 1914. Even if the Great War had been averted, the twentieth century must have been a time of wide-spread racial readjustments in which the white man's present

12

position of political world-domination would have been sensibly modified, especially in Asia. However, had the white race and white civilization been spared the terrific material and moral losses involved in the Great War and its still unliquidated aftermath, the process of racial readjustment would have been far more gradual and would have been fraught with far fewer cataclysmic possibilities. Had white strength remained intact it would have acted as a powerful shock-absorber, taking up and distributing the various colored impacts. As a result, the coming modification of the world's racial equilibrium, though inevitable, would have been so graduated that it would have seemed more an evolution than a revolution. Such violent breaches as did occur might have been localized, and anything like a general race-cataclysm would probably have been impossible.

But it was not to be. The heart of the white world was divided against itself, and on the fateful 1st of August, 1914, the white race, forgetting ties of blood and culture, heedless of the growing pressure of the colored world without, locked in a battle to the death. An ominous cycle opened whose end no man can foresee. - Armageddon engendered Versailles; earth's worst war closed with an unconstructive peace which left old sores unhealed and even dealt fresh wounds. The white world to-day lies debilitated and uncured; the colored world views conditions which are a standing incitement to rash dreams and violent action.

Such is the present status of the world's race-problem, expressed in general terms. The analysis of the specific elements in that complex problem will form the subject of the succeeding chapters.

CHAPTER II
YELLOW MAN'S LAND

YELLOW MAN'S LAND is the Far East. Here the group of kindred stocks usually termed Mongolian have dwelt for unnumbered ages. Down to the most recent times the yellows lived virtually a life apart. Sundered from the rest of mankind by stupendous mountains, burning deserts, and the illimitable ocean, the Far East constituted a world in itself, living its own life and developing its own peculiar civilization. Only the wild nomads of its northern marches-Huns, Mongols, Tartars, and the like-succeeded in gaining direct contact with the brown and white worlds to the West.

The ethnic focus of the yellow world has always been China. Since the dawn of history this immense human ganglion has been the centre from which civilization has radiated throughout the Far East. About this "Middle Kingdom," as it sapiently styled itself, the other yellow folk were disposed-Japanese and Koreans to the east; Siamese, Annamites, and Cambodians to the south; and to the north the nomad Mongols and Manchus. To all these peoples China was the august preceptor, sometimes chastising their presumption, yet always instilling the principles of its ordered civilization. However diverse may have been the individual developments of the various Far Eastern peoples, they spring from a common Chinese foundation. Despite modern Japan's meteoric rise to political mastery of the Far East, it must not be forgotten that China remains not only the cultural but also the territorial and racial centre of the yellow world. Four-fifths of the yellow race is concentrated in China, there being nearly 400,000,000 Chinese as against 60,000,000 Japanese, 16,000,000 Koreans, 26,000,000 Indo-Chinese, and perhaps 10,000,000 people of non-Chinese stocks included within China's political frontiers.

The age-long seclusion of the yellow world, first decreed by nature, was subsequently maintained by the voluntary decision of the yellow peoples themselves. The great expansive movement of the white race which began four centuries ago soon brought white men to the Far East, by sea in the persons of the Portuguese navigators and by land with the Cossack adventurers ranging through the empty spaces of Siberia. Yet after a brief acquaintance with the white strangers the yellow world decided that it wanted none of them, and they were rigidly excluded. This exclusion policy was not a Chinese peculiarity; it was common to all the yellow peoples and was adopted spontaneously at about the same time. In China, Japan, Korea, and Indo-China, the same reaction produced the same results. The yellow world instinctively felt the white man to be a destructive, dissolving influence on its highly specialized line of evolution, which it wished to maintain unaltered. For three centuries the yellow world succeeded in maintaining its isolation, then, in the middle of the last century, insistent white pressure broke down the barriers and forced the yellow races into full contact with the outer world.

At the moment, the "opening" of the Far East was hailed by white men with general approval, but of late years many white observers have regretted this forcible dragging of reluctant races into the full stream of world affairs. As an Australian writer, J. Liddell Kelly, remarks: "We have erred grievously by prematurely forcing ourselves upon Asiatic races. The instinct of the Asiatic in desiring isolation and separation from other forms of civilization was much more correct than our craze for imposing our forms of religion, morals, and industrialism upon them. It is not race-hatred, nor even race-antagonism, that is at the root of this attitude; it is an unerring intuition, which in years gone by has taught the Asiatic that his evolution in the scale of civilization could best be accomplished by his being allowed to develop on his own lines. Pernicious European compulsion has led him to abandon that attitude. Let us not be ashamed to confess that he was right and we were wrong." (J. Liddell Kelly, "What is the Matter with the Asiatic?" Westminister Review, September, 1910.)

However, rightly or wrongly, the deed was done, and the yellow races, forced into the world-arena, proceeded to adapt themselves to their new political environment and to learn the correct methods of survival under the strenuous conditions which there prevailed. In place of their traditional equilibrated, self-sufficient order, the yellow peoples now felt the ubiquitous impacts of the dynamic Western spirit, insistent upon rapid material progress and forceful, expansive evolution. Japan was the first yellow people to go methodically to the white man's school, and Japan's rapid acquirement of the white man's technology soon showed itself in dramatic demonstrations like her military triumphs over China in 1894, and over Russia a decade later.

Japan's easy victory over huge China astounded the whole world. That those "highly intelligent children," as one of the early British ministers to Japan had characterized them, should have so rapidly acquired the technique of Western methods was almost unbelievable. Indeed, the full significance of the lesson was not immediately grasped, and the power of New Japan was still underestimated. A good example of Europe's underestimation of Japanese strength was the proposal a Dutch writer made in 1896 to curb possible Japanese aggression on the Dutch Indies by taking from Japan the island of Formosa which Japan had acquired from China as one of the fruits of victory. "Holland," asserted this writer, "must take possession of Formosa." (Professor Schlegel in the Hague Dagblad. Quoted from The Literary Digest., November 7, 1896, p. 24.) The grotesqueness of this dictum as it appears to us in the light of subsequent history shows how the world has moved in twenty-five years.

But even at that time Japan's expansionist tendencies were well developed, and voices were warning against Japanese imperialism. In the very month when our Hollander was advocating a Dutch seizure of Formosa, an Australian wrote the following lines in a Melbourne newspaper concerning his recent travels in Japan: "While in a car with several Japanese officers, they were conversing about Australia, saying that it was a fine, large country, with great

16

forests and excellent soil for the cultivation of rice and other products. The whites settled in Australia, so thought these officers, are like the dog in the manger. Some one will have to take a good part of Australia to develop it, for it is a pity to see so fine a country lying waste. If any ill-feeling arose between the two countries, it would be a wise thing to send some battleships to Australia and annex part of it." (Audley Coote in the Melbourne Argus. Quoted from The Literary Digest, November 7, 1896, p. 24.)

Whatever may have been the world's misreading of the Chino-Japanese conflict, the same cannot be said of the Russo-Japanese War of 1904. The echoes of that yellow triumph over one of the great white Powers reverberated to the ends of the earth and started obscure trains of consequences even to-day not yet fully disclosed. The war's reactions in these remoter fields will be discussed in later chapters. Its effect upon the Far East is our present concern. And the well-nigh unanimous opinion of both natives and resident Europeans was that the war signified a body-blow to white ascendancy. So profound an English student of the Orient as Meredith Townsend wrote: "It may be taken as certain that the victory of Japan will be profoundly felt by the majority of European states. With the exception of Austria, all European countries have implicated themselves in the great effort to conquer Asia, which has now been going on for two centuries, but which, as this author thinks must now terminate.... The disposition, therefore, to edge out intrusive Europeans from their Asiatic possessions is certain to exist even if it is not manifested in Tokyo and it may be fostered by a movement of which, as yet, but little has been said. No one who has ever studied the question doubts that as there is a comity of Europe, so there is a comity of Asia, a disposition to believe that Asia belongs of right to Asiatics, and that any event which brings that right nearer to realization is to all Asiatics a pleasurable one. Japanese victories will give new heart and energy to all the Asiatic nations and tribes which now fret under European rule, will inspire in them a new confidence in their own power to resist, and will spread through them a strong impulse to avail themselves of Japanese instruction. It will take, of course, many years to bring this new force into play; but time matters nothing to Asiatics, and they all possess that capacity for complete secrecy which the Japanese displayed." (Meredith Townsend, "Asia and Europe" (fourth edition, 1911). From the preface to the fourth edition pages xvii-xix.)

That Meredith Townsend was reading the Asiatic mind aright seems clear from the pronouncements of Orientals themselves. For example, BUDDHISM, of Rangoon, Burma, a country of the Indo-Chinese borderland between the yellow and brown worlds, expressed hopes for an Oriental alliance against the whites. "It would, we think," said this paper, "be no great wonder if a few years after the conclusion of this war saw the completion of a defensive alliance between Japan, China, and not impossibly Siam-the formulation of a new Monroe Doctrine for the Far East, guaranteeing the integrity of existing states against further aggression from the West. The West has justified-perhaps with some reason - every aggression on weaker races by the doctrine of the Survival of the Fittest; on the ground that it is best for future humanity that the unfit should be eliminated and give place to the most able race. That doctrine applies equally well to any possible struggle between Aryan and Mongolian-whichever survives, should it ever come to a struggle between the two for world-mastery, will, on their own doctrine, be the one most fit to do so, and if the survivor be the Mongolian, then is the Mongolian no 'peril' to humanity, but the better part of it." (Quoted from The American Review of Reviews, February, 1905, p. 219.)

The decade which elapsed between the Russo-Japanese and European Wars saw in the Far East another event of the first magnitude: the Chinese Revolution of 1911. Toward the close of the nineteenth century the world had been earnestly discussing the " break-up " of China. The huge empire, with its 400,000,000 of people, one-fourth the entire human race, seemed at that time plunged in so hopeless a lethargy as to be foredoomed to speedy ruin. About the apparently moribund carcass the eagles of the earth were already gathered, planning a "partition of China" analogous to the recent partition of Africa. The partition of China, however, never came off. The prodigious moral shock of the Japanese War roused China's Èlite to the imminence of their country's peril. First attempts at reform wore blocked by the Dowager Empress, but her reactionary lurch ended in the Boxer nightmare and the frightful Occidental chastisement of 1900. This time the lesson was learned. China was at last shaken broad awake. The Bourbon Manchu court, it is true, wavered, but popular pressure forced it to keep the upward path. Every year after 1900 saw increasingly rapid reform - reform, be it noted, not imposed upon the country from above but forced upon the rulers from below. When the slow-footed Manchus showed themselves congenitally incapable of keeping step with the quickening national pace, the rising tide of national life overwhelmed them in the Republican Revolution of 1911, and they were no more.

Even with the Manchu handicap, the rate of progress during those years was such as to amaze the wisest foreign observers. "Could the sage, Confucius, have returned a decade ago," wrote that "old China hand," W. R. Manning, in 1910, "he would have felt almost as much at home as when he departed twenty-five centuries before. Should he return a decade hence he will feel almost as much out of place as Rip Van Winkle if the recent rate of progress continues." (W. R. Manning, "China and the Powers since the Boxer Movement, American Journal of International Law, October, 1910.) Toward the close of 1909 a close student of things Chinese, Harlan P. Beach, remarked: "Those who, like myself, can compare the China of twenty-five years ago with the China of this year, can hardly believe our senses." (Quoted by Manning, supra.) It was on top of all this that there came the revolution, a happening hailed by so sophisticated an observer as Doctor Dillon as "the most momentous event in a thousand years." (E. J. Dillon, "The Most Momentous Event in a Thousand Years," Contemporary Review, December, 1911.) Whatever may have been the political blunders of the revolutionists (and they were many), the revolution's moral results wore stupendous. The stream of Western innovation flowed at a vastly accelerated pace into every Chinese province. The popular masses wore for the first time awakened to genuine interest in

19

political, as distinguished from economic or personal, questions. Lastly, the semi-religlous feeling of family kinship, which in the past had been almost the sole recognized bond of Chinese race solidarity, was powerfully supplemented by those distinctively modern concepts, national self-consciousness and articulate patriotism.

Here was the Far Eastern situation at the outbreak of the Great War - a thoroughly modernized, powerful Japan, and a thoroughly aroused, but still disorganized, China. The Great War automatically made Japan supreme in the Far East by temporarily reducing all the European Powers to ciphers in Oriental affairs. How Japan proceeded to buttress this supremacy by getting a strangle-hold on China, every one knows. Japan's methods were brutal and cynical, though not a whit more so than the methods employed by white nations seeking to attain vital ends. And "vital" is precisely how Japan regards her hold over China. An essentially poor country with a teeming population, Japan feels that the exploitation of China's incalculable natural resources, a privileged position in the Chinese market, and guidance of Chinese national evolution in ways not inimical to Japan, can alone assure her future.

Japan's attitude toward her huge neighbor is one of mingled superiority and apprehension. She banks on China's traditional pacifism, yet she is too shrewd not to realize the explosive possibilities latent in the modern nationalist idea. As a Japanese publicist, Adachi Kinnosuke, remarks: "The Twentieth Century Jenghiz Khan threatening the Sun-Flag with a Mongol horde armed with Krupp guns may possibly strike the Western sense of humor. But it is not altogether pleasing to contemplate a neighbor of 400,000,000 population with modern armament and soldiers trained on the modern plan. The awakening of China means all this and a little more which we of the present are not sure of. Japan cannot forget that between this nightmare of armed China and herself there is only a very narrow sea." (Adachi Kinnosuke, "Does Japanese Trade Endanger the Peace of Asia? World's Work, April, 1909.) Certainly, "Young China" has already displayed much of that unpleasant ebullience which usually accompanies nationalist awakenings. A French observer, Jean Rodes, writes on this point: "One of the things that most disquiet thinking men is that this new generation, completely neglecting Chinese studies while knowing nothing of Western science, yet convinced that it knows everything, will no longer possess any standard of values, national culture, or foreign culture. We can only await with apprehension the results of such ignorance united with unbounded pride as characterize the Chinese youth of to-day." (Jean Rodes in L'Asie FranÁaise, June, 1911.)

And another French observer, RenÈ Pinon, as far back as 1905, found the primary school children of Kiang-Su province chanting the following lines: "I pray that the frontiers of my country become hard as bronze; that it surpass Europe and America; that it subjugate Japan; that its land and sea armies cover themselves with resplendent glory: that over the whole earth float the Dragon Standard; that the universal mastery of the empire extend and progress. May our empire, like a sleeping tiger suddenly awakened, spring roaring into the arena of combats." (RenÈ Pinon, "La Lutte pour le Pacifique," p. 152 (Paris, 1906).)

Japan's masterful policy in China is thus unquestionably hazardous. Chinese national feeling is today genuinely aroused against Japan, and resentment over Japanese encroachments is bitter and wide-spread. Nevertheless, Japan feels that the game is worth the risk and believes that both Chinese race-psychology and the general drift of world affairs combine to favor her ultimate success. She knows that China has in the past always acquiesced in foreign domination when resistance has proved patently impossible. She also feels that her aspirations for white expulsion from the Far East and for the winning of wider spheres for racial expansion should appeal strongly to yellow peoples generally and to the Chinese in particular. To turn China's nascent nationalism into purely anti-white channels and to transmute Chinese patriotism into a wider "Pan-Mongolism" would constitute a Japanese triumph of incalculable splendor. It would increase her effective force manyfold and would open up almost limitless vistas of power and glory.

Nor are the Chinese themselves blind to the advantages of Chino-Japanese co-operation. They have an instinctive assurance in their own capacities, they know how they have ultimately digested all their conquerors, and many Chinese to-day think that from a Chino-Japanese partnership, no matter how framed, the inscrutable "Sons of Han" would eventually get the lion's share. Certainly no one has ever denied the Chinaman's extraordinary economic efficiency. Winnowed by ages of grim elimination in a land populated to the uttermost limits of subsistence, the Chinese race is selected as no other for survival under the fiercest conditions of economic stress. At home the average Chinese lives his whole life literally within a hand's breadth of starvation. Accordingly, when removed to the easier environment of other lands, the Chinaman brings with him a working capacity which simply appalls his competitors. That urbane Celestial, Doctor Wu-Ting-Fang, well says of his own people: "Experience proves that the Chinese as all-round laborers can easily outdistance all competitors. They are industrious, intelligent, and orderly. They can work under conditions that would kill a man of less hardy race; in heat that would kill a salamander, or in cold that would please a polar bear, sustaining their energies, through long hours of unremitting toil with only a few bowls of rice." (Quoted by Alleyne Ireland, "Commercial Aspects of the Yellow Peril," North American Review, September, 1900.)

This Chinese estimate is echoed by the most competent foreign observers. The Australian thinker, Charles E. Pearson, wrote of the Chinese a generation ago in his epoch-making book, "National Life and Character": "Flexible as Jews, they can thrive on the mountain plateaux of Thibet and under the sun of Singapore; more versatile even than Jews, they are excellent laborers, and not without merit as soldiers and sailors; while they have a capacity for trade which no other nation of the East possesses. They do not need even the accident of a man of genius to develop their magnificent future." (Charles H. Pearson, "National Life and Character," p. 118 (2nd edition).)

And Lafcadio Hearn says: "A people of hundreds of millions

disciplined for thousands of years to the most untiring industry and the most self-denying thrift, under conditions which would mean worse than death for our working masses -- a people, in short, quite content to strive to the uttermost in exchange for the simple privilege of life." (Quoted by Ireland, supra.)

This economic superiority of the Chinaman shows not only with other races, but with his yellow kindred as well. As regards the Japanese, John Chinaman has proved it to the hilt. Wherever the two have met in economic competition, John has won hands down. Even in Japanese colonies like Korea and Formosa, the Japanese, with all the backing of their government behind them, have been worsted. In fact, Japan itself, so bitter at white refusals to receive her emigrants, has been obliged to enact drastic exclusion laws to protect her working classes from the influx of "Chinese cheap labor." It seems, therefore, a just calculation when Chinese estimate that Japanese triumphs against white adversaries would inure largely to China's benefit. After all, Chinese and Japanese are fundamentally of the same race and culture. They may have their very bitter family quarrels, but in the last analysis they understand each other and may arrive at surprisingly sudden agreements. One thing is certain: both these over-populated lands will feel increasingly the imperious need of racial expansion. For all these reasons, then, the present political tension between China and Japan cannot be reckoned as permanent, and we would do well to envisage the possibility of close Chinese co-operation in the ambitious programme of Japanese foreign policy.

This Japanese programme looks first to the prevention of all further white encroachment in the Far East by the establishment of a Far Eastern Monroe Doctrine based on Japanese predominance and backed if possible by the moral support of the other Far Eastern peoples. The next stage in Japanese foreign policy seems to be the systematic elimination of all existing white holdings in the Far East. Thus far practically all Japanese appear to be in substantial agreement. Beyond this point lies a wide realm of aspiration ranging from determination to secure complete racial equality and freedom of immigration into white lands to imperialistic dreams of wholesale conquests and "world-dominion." These last items do not represent the united aspiration of the Japanese nation, but they are cherished by powerful circles which, owing to Japan's oligarchical system of government, possess an influence over governmental action quite disproportionate to their numbers.

Although Japanese plans and aspirations have broadened notably since 1914, their outlines were well defined a decade earlier. Immediately after her victory over Russia, Japan set herself to strengthen her influence all over eastern Asia. Special efforts were made to establish intimate relations with the other Asiatic peoples. Asiatic students were invited to attend Japanese universities and as a matter of fact did attend by the thousand, while a whole series of societies was formed having for their object the knitting of close cultural and economic ties between Japan and specific regions like China, Siam, the Pacific, and even India. The capstone was a " Pan-Asiatic Association," founded by Count Okuma. Some of the facts regarding these societies, about which too little is known, make interesting reading. For instance, there was the "Pacific Ocean Society" ("Taheijoka"), whose preamble reads in part: "For a century the Pacific Ocean has been a battle-ground wherein the nations have straggled for supremacy. To-day the prosperity or decadence of a nation depends on its power in the Pacific: to possess the empire of the Pacific is to be the Master of the World. As Japan finds itself at the centre of that Ocean, whose waves bathe its shores, it must reflect carefully and have clear views on Pacific questions." (Quoted by Scie-Ton-Fa, "La Chine et le Japon," Revue Politique Internationale, September, 1915.)

Equally interesting is the "Indo-Japanese Association," whose activities appear somewhat peculiar in view of the political alliance between Japan and the British Empire. One of the first articles of its constitution (from Count Okuma's pen, by the way) reads: "All men wore born equal. The Asiatics have the same claim to be called men as the Europeans themselves. It is therefore quite unreasonable that the latter should have any right to predominate over the former."

24

(The Literary Digest, March 6, 1910, p. 429.) No mention is made anywhere in the document of India's political connection with England. In fact, Count Okuma, in the autumn of 1907, had this to say regarding India: "Being oppressed by the Europeans, the 300,000,000 people of India are looking for Japanese protection. They have commenced to boycott European merchandise. If, therefore, the Japanese let the chance slip by and do not go to India, the Indians will be disappointed. From old times, India has been a land of treasure. Alexander the Great obtained there treasure sufficient to load a hundred camels, and Mahmoud and Attila also obtained riches from India. Why should not the Japanese stretch out their hands toward that country, now that the people are looking to the Japanese? The Japanese ought to go to India, the South Ocean, and other parts of the world." (The Literary Digest, January 18, 1908, p. 81.)

In 1910, Putnam Weale, a competent English student of Oriental affairs asserted: "It can no longer be doubted that a very deliberate policy is certainly being quietly and cleverly pursued. Despite all denials, it is a fact that Japan has already a great hold in the schools and in the vernacular newspapers all over eastern Asia, and that the gospel of 'Asia for the Asiatics' is being steadily preached not only by her schoolmasters and her editors, but by her merchants and peddlers, and every other man who travels." (B. L. Putnam Weale, "The Conflict of Color," pp. 145-6 (New York, 1910).)

Exactly how much these Japanese propagandist efforts accomplished is impossible to say. Certain it is, however, that during the years just previous to the Great War the white colonies in the Far East were afflicted with considerable native unrest. In French Indo-China, for example, revolutionary movements during the year 1908 necessitated reinforcing the French garrison by nearly 10,000 men, and though the disturbances were sternly repressed, fresh conspiracies were discovered in 1911 and 1913. Much sedition and some sharp fighting also took place in the Dutch Indies, while in the Philippines the independence movement continued to gain ground.

What the growing self-consciousness of the Far East portended for the white man's ultimate status in those regions was indicated by an English publicist, J. D. Whelpley, who wrote, shortly after the outbreak of the European War: "With the aid of Western ideas the Far East is fast attaining a solidarity impossible under purely Oriental methods. The smug satisfaction expressed in the West at what is called the 'modernization' of the East shows lack of wisdom or an ineffective grasp of the meaning of comparatively recent events in Japan, China, eastern Siberia, and even in the Philippines. In years past the solidarity of the Far East was largely in point of view, while in other matters the powerful nations of the West played the game according to their own rules. To-day the solidarity of mental outlook still maintains, while in addition there is rapidly coming about a solidarity of political and material interests which in time will reduce Western participation in Far Eastern affairs to that of a comparatively unimportant factor. It might truly be said that this point is already reached, and that it only needs an application of the test to prove to the world that the Far East would resent Western interference as an intolerable impertinence." (J. D. Whelpley, "East and West: A New Line of Cleavage," Fortnightly Review, May, 1915.)

The scope of Japan's aspirations, together with differences of outlook between various sections of Japanese public opinion as to the rate of progress feasible for Japanese expansion, account for Japan's differing attitudes toward the white Powers. Officially, the keystone of Japan's foreign policy since the beginning of the present century has been the alliance with England, first negotiated in 1902 and renewed with extensive modifications in 1911. The 1902 alliance was universally popular in Japan. It was directed specifically against Russia and represented the common apprehensions of both the contracting parties. By 1911, however, the situation had radically altered. Japan's aspirations in the Far East, particularly as regards China, were arousing wide-spread uneasiness in many quarters, and the English communities in the Far East generally condemned the new alliance as a gross blunder of British diplomacy. In Japan also there was considerable protest. The official organs, to be sure, stressed the necessity of friendship with the Mistress of the Seas for an island empire like Japan, but opposition circles pointed to England's practical refusal to be drawn into a war with the United States under any circumstances which constituted the outstanding feature of the new treaty and declared that Japan was giving much and receiving nothing in return.

The growing divergence between Japanese and English views regarding China increased anti-English feeling, and in 1912 the semi-official Japan Magazine asserted roundly that the general feeling in Japan was that the alliance was a detriment rather than a benefit going on to forecast a possible alignment with Russia and Germany, and remarking of the latter: "Germany's healthy imperialism and scientific development would have a wholesome effect upon our nation and progress, while the German habit of perseverance and frugality is just what we need. German wealth and industry are gradually creeping upward to that of Great Britain and America, and the efficiency of the German army and navy is a model for the world. Her lease of the territory of Kiaochow Bay brings her into contact with us, and her ambition to exploit the coal-mines of Shantung lends her a community of interest with us. It is not too much to say that German interests in China are greater than those of any other European Power. If the alliance with England should ever be abrogated, we might be very glad to shake hands with Germany." (The Literary Digest, July 6, 1912, p. 9.)

The outbreak of the European War gave Japan a golden opportunity (of which she was not slow to take advantage) to eliminate one of the white Powers from the Far East. The German stronghold of Kiaochow was promptly reduced, while Germany's possessions in the Pacific Ocean north of the equator, the Caroline, Pelew, Marianne, and Marshall island-groups, wore likewise occupied by Japanese forces. Here Japan stopped and politely declined all proposals to send armies to Europe or western Asia. Her sphere was the Far East; her real objectives were the reduction of white influence there and the riveting of her control over China. Japanese comment was perfectly candid on these matters. As the semi-official

27

Japanese Colonial Journal put it in the autumn of 1914: "To protect Chinese territory, Japan is ready to fight no matter what nation. Not only will Japan try to erase the ambitions of Russia and Germany; it will also do its best to prevent England and the United States from touching the Chinese cake. The solution of the Chinese problem is of great importance for Japan, and Great Britain has little to do with it." (Quoted by Scie-Ton-Fa, supra.)

Equally frank were Japanese warnings to the English ally not to oppose Japan's progress in China. English criticism of the series of ultimatums by which Japan forced reluctant China to do her bidding roused angry admonitions like the following from the Tokio Universe in April, 1915: "Hostile English opinion seems to want to oppose Japanese demands in China. The English forget that Japan has, by her alliance, rendered them signal services against Russia in 1905 and in the present war by assuring security in their colonies of the Pacific and the Far East. If Japan allied herself with England, it was with the object of establishing Japanese preponderance in China and against the encroachments of Russia. To-day the English seem to be neglecting their obligations toward Japan by not supporting her cause. Let England beware! Japan will tolerate no wavering; she is quite ready to abandon the Anglo-Japanese alliance and turn to Russia-a Power with whom she can agree perfectly regarding Far Eastern interests. In the future, even, she is ready to draw closer to Germany. The English colonies will then be in great peril." (Quoted by Scie-Ton-Fa, supra.)

As to the imminence of a Russo-Japanese understanding, the journal just quoted proved a true prophet, for a year later, in July, 1916, the Japanese and Russian Governments signed a diplomatic instrument which amounted practically to an alliance. By this document Russia recognized Japan's paramountcy over the bulk of China, while Japan recognized Russia's special interests in China's Western dependencies, Mongolia and Turkestan. Japan had thus eliminated another of the white Powers from the Far East, since Russia renounced those ambitions to dominate China proper which had provoked the war of 1904.

28

Meanwhile the press campaign against England continued. A typical sample is this editorial from the Tokio Yamato: "Great Britain never wished at heart to become Japan's ally. She did not wish to enter into such intimate relations with us, for she privately regarded us as an upstart nation radically different from us in blood and religion. It was simply the force of circumstances which compelled her to enter into an alliance with us. It is the height of conceit on our part to think that England really cared for our friendship, for she never did. It was the Russian menace to India and Persia on the one hand, and the German ascendancy on the other, which compelled her to clasp our hands." (The Literary Digest, February 12, 1916, pp. 369-70.)

At the same time many good things were being said about Germany. At no time during the war was any real hostility to the Germans apparent in Japan. Germany was of course expelled from her Far Eastern footholds in smart, workmanlike fashion, but the fighting before Kiaochow was conducted without a trace of hatred, the German prisoners were treated as honored captives, and German civilians in Japan suffered no molestation. Japanese writers were very frank in stating that, once Germany resigned herself to exclusion from the Far East and acquiesced in Japanese predominance in China, no reason existed why Japan and Germany should not be good friends. Unofficial diplomatic exchanges certainly took place between the two governments during the war, and no rancor for the past appears to exist on either side to-day.

The year 1917 brought three momentous modifications into the world-situation: the entrance of the United States and China into the Great War and the Russian Revolution. The first two were intensely distasteful to Japan. The transformation of virtually unarmed America into a first-class fighting power reacted portentously upon the Far East, while China's adhesion to the Grand Alliance (bitterly opposed in Tokio) rescued her from diplomatic isolation and gave her potential friends. The Russian Revolution was also a source of perplexity to Tokio. In 1916, as we have seen, Japan had arrived at a thorough understanding with the Czarist rÈgime. The new Russian Government was an unknown quantity, acting quite differently from the old.

Russia's collapse into Bolshevist anarchy, however, presently opened up new vistas. Not merely northern Manchuria, but also the huge expanse of Siberia, an almost empty world of vast potential riches, lay temptingly exposed. At once the powerful imperialist elements m Japanese political life began clamoring for "forward" action. An opportunity far such action was soon vouchsafed by the Allied determination to send a composite force to Siberia to checkmate the machinations of the Russian Bolsheviki, now hostile to the Allies and playing into the hands of Germany. The imperialist party at Tokio took the bit in its teeth, and, in flagrant disregard of the inter-Allied agreement, poured a great army into Siberia, occupying the whole country as far west as Lake Baikal. This was in the spring of 1918. The Allies, then in their supreme death-grapple with the Germans, dared not even protest, but in the autumn, when the battle-tide had turned in Europe, Japan was called to account, the United States taking the lead in the matter. A furious debate ensued at Tokio between the imperialist and moderate parties, the hotter jingoes urging defiance of the United States even at the risk of war. Then, suddenly, came the news that Germany was cracking, and the moderates had their way. The Japanese armies in Siberia were reduced, albeit they still remained the most powerful military factor in the situation

Germany's sudden collapse and the unexpectedly quick ending of the war was a blow to Japanese hopes and plans in more ways than one. Despite official felicitations, the nation could hardly disguise its chagrin. For Japan the war had been an unmixed benefit. It had automatically made her mistress of the Far East and had amazingly enriched her economic life. Every succeeding month of hostilities had seen the white world grow weaker and had conversely increased Japanese power. Japan had counted on at least one more year of war. Small wonder that the sudden passing of this halcyon time provoked disappointment and regret.

The above outline of Japanese foreign policy reveals beneath all its surface mutations a fundamental continuity. Whatever may be its ultimate goals, Japanese foreign policy has one minimum objective:

Japan as hegemon of a Far East in which white influence shall have been reduced to a vanishing quantity. That is the bald truth of the matter - and no white man has any reason for getting indignant about it. Granted that Japanese aims endanger white vested interests in the Far East. Granted that this involves rivalry and perhaps war. That is no reason for striking a moral attitude and inveighing against Japanese "wickedness," as many people are to-day doing. These mighty racial tides flow from the most elemental of vital urges: self-expansion and self-preservation. Both outward thrust of expanding life and counter-thrust of threatened life are equally normal phenomena. To condemn the former as "criminal" and the latter as "selfish" is either silly or hypocritical and tends to envenom with unnecessary rancor what objective fairness might keep a candid struggle, inevitable yet alleviated by mutual comprehension and respect. This is no mere plea for "sportsmanship"; it is a very practical matter. There are critical times ahead; times in which intense race-pressures will engender high tensions and perhaps wars. If men will keep open minds and will eschew the temptation to regard those opposing their desires to defend or possess respectively as impious fiends, the struggles will lose half their bitterness, and the wars (if wars there must be) will be shorn of half their ferocity.

The unexpected ending of the European War was, as we have seen, a blow to Japanese calculations. Nevertheless, the skill of her diplomats at the ensuing Versailles Conference enabled Japan to harvest most of her war gains. Japan's territorial acquisitions in China were definitely written into the peace treaty, despite China's sullen veto, and Japan's preponderance in Chinese affairs was tacitly acknowledged. Japan also took advantage of the occasion to pose as the champion of the colored races by urging the formal promulgation of "racial equality" as part of the peace settlement, especially as regards immigration. Of course the Japanese diplomats had no serious expectation of their demands being acceded to; in fact, they might have been rather embarrassed if they had succeeded, in view of Japan's own stringent laws against immigration and alien landholding. Nevertheless, it was a politic move, useful for future propagandist purposes, and it advertised Japan broadcast as the standard-bearer of the colored cause.

The notable progress that Japan has made toward the mastery of the Far East is written plainly upon the map, which strikingly portrays the broadening territorial base of Japanese power effected in the past twenty-five years. Japan now owns the whole island chain masking the eastern sea frontage of Asia, from the tip of Kamchatka to the Philippines, while her acquisition of Germany's Oceanican islands north of the equator gives her important strategic outposts in mid-Pacific. Her bridge-heads on the Asiatic continent are also strong and well located. From the Korean peninsula (now an integral part of Japan) she firmly grasps the vast Chinese dependency of Manchuria, while just south of Manchuria across the narrow waters of the Pechili strait lies the rich Chinese province of Shantung, become a Japanese sphere of influence as a result of the late war. Thus Japan holds China's capital, Peking, as in the jaws of a vice and can apply military pressure whenever she so desires. In southern China lies another Japanese sphere of influence, the province of Fukien opposite the Japanese island of Formosa. Lastly, all over China runs a veritable network of Japanese concessions like the recently acquired control of the great iron deposits near Hankow, far up the Yangtse River in the heart of China.

Whether this Japanese imperium over China maintains itself or not, one thing seems certain: future white expansion in the Far East has become impossible. Any such attempt would instantly weld together Japanese imperialism and Chinese nationalism in a "sacred union" whose result would probably be at the very least the prompt expulsion of the white man from every foothold in eastern Asia.

That is what will probably come anyway as soon as Japan and China, impelled by overcrowding and conscious of their united potentialities, shall have arrived at a genuine understanding. Since population-pressure seems to be the basic factor in the future course of Far Eastern affairs, it would be well to survey possible outlets for surplus population within the Far East itself, in order to determine how much of this race expansion can be satisfied at home, thereby diminishing, or at least postponing, acute pressure upon the political and ethnic frontiers of the white world.

To begin with, the population of Japan (approximately 60,000,000) is increasing at the rate of about 800,000 per year. China has no modern vital statistics, but the annual increase of her 400,000,000 population, at the Japanese rate, would be 6,000,000. Now the settled parts of both Japan and China may be considered as fully populated so far as agriculture is concerned, further extensive increases of population being dependent upon the rise of machine industry. Both countries have, however, thinly settled areas within their present political frontiers. Japan's northern island of Hokkaido (Yezo) has a great amount of good agricultural land as yet almost unoccupied, some of her other island possessions offer minor outlets, while Korea and Manchuria afford extensive colonizing possibilities albeit Chinese and Korean competition preclude a Japanese colonization on the scale which the size and natural wealth of these regions would at first sight seem to indicate. China has even more extensive colonizable areas. Both Mongolia and Chinese Turkestan, though largely desert, contain within their vast areas enough fertile land to support many millions of Chinese peasants as soon as modern roads and railways are built. The Chinese colonization of Manchuria is also proceeding apace, and will continue despite anything Japan may do to keep it down. Lastly, the cold but enormous plateau of Tibet offers considerable possibilities.

Allowing for all this, however, it cannot be said that either China or Japan possess within their present political frontiers territories likely to absorb those prodigious accretions of population which seem destined to occur within the next couple of generations. From the resultant congestion two avenues of escape will naturally present themselves: settlement of other portions of the Far East to-day under white political control, but inhabited by colored populations; and pressure into accessible areas not merely under white political control, but also containing white populations. It is obvious that those are two radically distinct issues, for while a white nation might not unalterably oppose Mongolian immigration into its colored dependencies, it would almost certainly fight to the limit rather than witness the racial swamping of lands settled by its own flesh and blood.

Considering the former issue, then, it would appear that virtually all the peninsulas and archipelagoes lying between China and Australia offer attractive fields for yellow, particularly Chinese, race-expansion. Ethnically they are all colored men's lands; politically they are all, save Siam under white control; Britain, France, Holland, and the United States being the titular owners of these extensive territories. So far as the native races are concerned, none of them seem to possess the vitality and economic efficiency needed to maintain themselves against unrestricted Chinese immigration. Whether in the British Straits Settlements and North Borneo, French Indo-China, the Dutch Indies, the American Philippines, or independent Siam, the Chinaman, so far as he has been allowed, has displayed his practical superiority, and in places where, like the Straits Settlements, he has been allowed a free hand, he has virtually supplanted the native stock, reducing the latter to an impotent and vanishing minority. The chief barriers to Chinese race-expansion in these regions are legal hindrances or prohibitions of immigration, and of course such barriers are in their essence artificial and liable to removal under any shift of circumstances. Many observers predict that most of these lands will ultimately become Chinese. Says Alleyne Ireland, a recognized authority on these regions: "There is every reason to suppose that, throughout the tropics, possibly excepting India, the Chinaman, even though he should continue to emigrate in no greater force than hitherto, will gradually supersede all the native races." (Alleyne Ireland, "Commercial Aspects of the Yellow Peril," North American Review, September, 1900.) Certainly, if this be true, China has here a vast outlet for her surplus population. It has been estimated that the undeveloped portions of the Dutch Indies alone are capable of supporting 100,000,000 people living on the frugal Chinese plane. Their present population is 8,000,000 semi-savages.

China's possibilities of race-expansion in the colored regions of the Far East are thus excellent. The same cannot be said, however, for Japan. The Japanese, bred in a distinctively temperate, island environment, have not the Chinese adaptability to climatic variation. The Japanese, like the white man, does not thrive in tropic heat, nor does he possess the white man's ability to resist sub-Arctic cold. Formosa is not in the real tropics, yet Japanese colonists have not done well there. On the other hand, even the far-from-Arctic winters of Hokkaido (part of the Japanese archipelago) seem too chilly for the Japanese taste.

Japan thus does not have the same vital interest as China in the Asiatic tropics. Undoubtedly they would for Japan be valuable colonies of exploitation, just as they to-day are thus valuable for white nations. But they could never furnish outlets for Japan's excess population, and even commercially Japan would be exposed to increasing Chinese competition, since the Chinaman excels the Japanese in trade as well as in migrant colonization. Japanese lack of climatic adaptability is also the reason why Japan's present military excursion in eastern Siberia, even if it should develop into permanent occupation, would yield no adequate solution of Japan's population problem. For the Chinaman, Siberia would do very well. He would breed amusingly there and would fill up the whole country in a remarkably short space of time. But the Japanese peasant, so averse to the winters of Hokkaido, would find the sub-Arctic rigors of Siberia intolerable.

Thus, for Japanese migration, neither the empty spaces of northern or southern Asia will do. The natural outlets lie outside Asia in the United States, Australasia, and the temperate parts of Latin America. But all these outlets are rigorously barred by the white man, who has marked them for his own race-heritage, and nothing but force will break those barriers down.

There lies a danger, not merely to the peace of the Far Fast, but to the peace of the world. Fired by a fervent patriotism; resolved to make their country a leader among the nations; the Japanese writhe at the constriction of their present race-bounds. Placed on the flank of the Chinese giant whose portentous growth she can accurately forecast, Japan seas herself condemned to ultimate renunciation of her grandiose ambitions unless she can somehow broaden the racial as well as the political basis of her power. In short: Japan must find lands where Japanese can breed by the tens of millions if she is not to be automatically overshadowed in course of time, even assuming that she does not suffocate or blow up from congestion before that time arrives. This is the secret of her aggressive foreign policy, her chronic imperialism, her extravagant dreams of conquest and "world-dominion."

The longing to hack a path to greatness by the samurai sword lurks ever in the back of Japanese minds. The library of Nippon's chauvinist literature is large and increasing. A good example of the earlier productions is Satori Kato's brochure entitled "Mastery of the Pacific," published in 1909. Herein the author announces confidently: "In the event of war Japan could, as if aided by a magician's wand, overrun the Pacific with fleets manned by men who have made Nelson their model and transported to the armadas of the Far East the spirit that was victorious at Trafalgar. Whether Japan avows it or not, her persistent aim is to gain the mastery of the Pacific. Although peace seems to prevail over the world at present, no one can tell how soon the nations may be engaged in war. It does not need the English alliance to secure success for Japan. That alliance may be dissolved at any moment, but Japan will suffer no defeat. Her victory will be won by her men, not by armor-plates - things weak by comparison." (The Literary Digest, November 13, 1909.)

The late war has of course greatly stimulated these bellicose emotions. Viewing their own increased power and the debilitation of the white world, Japanese jingoes glimpse prospects of glorious fishing in troubled waters. The "world-dominion" note is stressed more often than of yore. For instance, in the summer of 1919 the Tokio Hochi, Count Okuma's organ, prophesied exultantly: "That age in which the Anglo-Japanese alliance was the pivot and

American-Japanese co-operation an essential factor of Japanese diplomacy is gone. In future we must not look eastward for friendship but westward. Let the Bolsheviki of Russia be put down and the more peaceful party established in power. In them Japan will find a strong ally. By marching then westward to the Balkans, to Germany, to France, and Italy, the greater part of the world may be brought under our sway. The tyranny of the Anglo-Saxons at the Peace Conference is such that it has angered both gods and men. Some may abjectly follow them in consideration of their petty interests, but things will ultimately settle down as has just been indicated." (The Literary Digest, July 5, 1919, p. 31.)

Still more striking are the following citations from a Japanese imperialist pronouncement written in the autumn of 1916:

"Fifty millions of our race wherewith to conquer and possess the earth! It is indeed a glorious problem! ...

"To begin with, we now have China; China is our steed! Far shall we ride upon her! Even as Rome rode Latium to conquer Italy, and Italy to conquer the Mediterranean; even as Napoleon rode Italy and the Rhenish States to conquer Germany, and Germany to conquer Europe; even as England to-day rides her colonies and her so-called 'allies' to conquer her robust rival, Germany - even so shall we ride China. So becomes our 50,000,000 race 500,000,000 strong; so grow our paltry hundreds of millions of gold into billions!

"How well have done our people! How well have our statesmen led them! No mistakes! There must be none now. In 1895 we conquered China - Russia, Germany, and France stole from us the booty. How has our strength grown since then - and still it grows! In ten years we punished and retook our own from Russia; in twenty years we squared and retook from Germany; with France there is no need for haste. She has already realized why we withheld the troops which alone might have driven the invader from her soil! Her fingers are clutching more tightly around her Oriental booty; yet she knows it is ours for the taking. But there is no need of haste: the world condemns the paltry thief; only the glorious conqueror wins the plaudits and approval of mankind.

"We are now well astride of our steed, China; but the steed has long roamed wild and is run down: it needs grooming, more grain, more training. Further, our saddle and bridle are as yet mere makeshifts: would steed and trappings stand the strain of war? And what would that strain be?

"As for America - that fatuous booby with much money and much sentiment, but no cohesion, no brains of government; stood she alone we should not need our China steed. Well did my friend speak the other day when he called her people a race of thieves with the hearts of rabbits. America, to any warrior race, is not as a foe, but as an immense melon, ripe for the cutting. But there are other warrior races - England, Germany - would they look on and let us slice and eat our fill? Would they?

"But, using China as our steed, should our first goal be the land? India? Or the Pacific, the sea that must be our very own, even as the Atlantic is now England's? The land is tempting and easy, but withal dangerous. Did we begin there, the coarse white races would too soon awaken, and combine, and forever immure us within our long since grown intolerable bounds. It must, therefore, be the sea; but the sea means the Western Americas and all the islands between; and with those must soon come Australia, India. And then the battling for the balance of world-power, for the rest of North America. Once that is ours, we own and control the whole - a dominion worthy of our race!

"North America alone will support a billion people; that billion shall be Japanese with their slaves. Not arid Asia, nor worn-out Europe (which, with its peculiar and quaint relics and customs should in the interests of history and culture, be in any case preserved), nor yet tropical Africa, is fit for our people. But North America, that continent so succulently green, fresh, and unsullied - except for the few chattering, mongrel Yankees - should have been ours by right of

discovery: it shall be ours by the higher, nobler right of conquest."
(The Military Historian and Economist, January, 1917, pp. 43-46.)

This apostle of Japanese world-dominion then goes on to discuss in detail how his programme can best be attained. It should be remembered that at the time he wrote America was still an unarmed nation, apparently ridden by pacifism. Such imperialist extravagances as the above do not represent the whole of Japan. But they do represent a powerful element in Japan, against which the white world should be forewarned.

CHAPTER III
BROWN MAN'S LAND

BROWN MAN'S LAND is the Near and Middle East. The brown world stretches in an immense belt clear across southern Asia and northern Africa, from the Pacífic to the Atlantic Oceans. The numbers of brown and yellow men are not markedly unequal (450,000,000 browns as against 500,000,000 yellows), but in most other respects the two worlds are sharply contrasted. In the first place, while the yellow world is a fairly compact geographical block, the brown world sprawls half-way round the globe, and is not only much greater in size, but also infinitely more varied in natural features.

This geographical diversity is reflected both in its history and in the character of its inhabitants. Unlike the secluded yellow world, the brown world is nearly everywhere exposed to foreign influences and has undergone an infinite series of evolutionary modifications. Racially it has been a vast melting-pot, or series of melting-pots, wherein conquest and migration have continually poured new heterogeneous elements, producing the most diverse racial amalgamations. In fact there is to-day no generalized brown type-norm as there are generalized yellow or white type-norms, but rather a series of types clearly distinguished from one another. Some of these types, like the Persians and Ottoman Turks, are largely white; others, like the southern Indians and Yemenite Arabs, are largely black; while still others, like the Himalayan and Central Asian peoples, have much yellow blood. Again, there is no generalized brown culture like those possessed by yellows and whites. The great spiritual bond is Islam, yet in India, the chief seat of brown population, Islam is professed by only one-fifth of the inhabitants.

Nevertheless, there is a fundamental comity between the brown peoples. This comity is subtle and intangible in character, yet it exists, and under certain circumstances it is capable of momentous manifestations. Its salient feature is the instinctive recognition by all Near and Middle Eastern peoples that they are fellow Asiatics, however bitter may be their internecine feuds. This instinctive Asiatic feeling has been noted by historians for more than two thousand years, and it is just as true to-day as in the past. Of course it comes out most strongly in face of the non-Asiatic - which in practice has always meant the white man. The action and reaction of the brown and white worlds has, indeed, been a constant, historic factor, the roles of hammer and anvil being continually reversed through the ages. For the last four centuries the white world has, in the main, been the dynamic factor. Certainly, during the last hundred years the white world has displayed an unprecedentedly aggressive vigor, the brown world playing an almost passive role.

Here again is seen a difference between browns and yellows. The yellow world did not feel the full tide of white aggression till the middle of the last century, while even then it never really lost its political independence and soon reacted so powerfully that its political freedom has to-day been substantially regained. The brown world, on the other hand, felt the impact of the white tide much earlier and was politically overwhelmed. The so-called "independence" of brown states has long been due more to white rivalries than to their own inherent strength. One by one they have been swallowed up by the white Powers. In 1914 only three (Turkey, Persia, and Afghanistan) survived, and the late war has sent them the way of the rest. Turkey and Persia have lost their independence, however they may still be painted on the map, while Afghanistan has been compelled to recognize white supremacy as never before. Thus the cycle is fulfilled, and white political mastery over the brown world is complete.

Political triumphs, however, of themselves guarantee nothing, and the permanence of the present order of things in the brown world appears more than doubtful when we glance beyond the map. The brown world, like the yellow world, is to-day in acute reaction against white supremacy. In fact, the brown reaction began a full century ago, and has been gathering headway ever since, moved thereto both by its own inherent vitality and by the external stimulus of white aggression. The great dynamic of this brown reaction is the Mohammedan Revival. But before analyzing that movement it would be well to glance at the human elements involved.

Four salient groupings stand out among the brown peoples: India, Iran, "Arabistán," and "Turkestán." The last two words are used in a special sense to denote ethnic and cultural aggregations for which no precise terms have hitherto been coined. India is the population-centre of the brown world. More than 300,000,000 souls live within its borders - two-thirds of all the brown men on earth. India has not, however, been the brown world's spiritual or cultural dynamic, those forces coming chiefly from the brown lands to the westward. Iran (the Persian plateau) is comparatively small in area and has less than 15,000,000 inhabitants, but its influence upon the brown world has been out of all proportion to its size and population. "Arabistán" denotes the group of peoples, Arab in blood or Arabized in language and culture, who inhabit the Arabian peninsula and its adjacent annexes, Syria and Mesopotamia, together with the vast band of North Africa lying between the Mediterranean and the Sahara Desert. The total number of these Arabic peoples is 40,000,000, three-fourths of them living in North Africa. The term "Turkestán" covers the group of kindred peoples, often called "Turanians," who stretch from Constantinople to Central Asia, including the Ottoman Turks of Asia Minor, the Tartars of South Russia and Transcaucasia, and the Central Asian Turkomans. They number in all about 25,000,000. Such are the four outstanding race-factors in the brown world. Let us now examine that spiritual factor, Islam, from which the brown renaissance originally proceeded, and on which most of its present manifestations are based.

Islam's warlike vigor has impressed men's minds ever since the far-

42

off days when its pristine fervor bore the Fiery Crescent from France to China. But with the passing cycles this fervor waned, and a century ago Islam seemed plunged in the stupor of senile decay. The life appeared to have gone out of it, leaving naught but the dry husks of empty formalism and soulless ritual. Yet at this darkest hour a voice came crying from out the vast Arabian desert, the cradle of Islam, calling the Faithful to better things. This puritan reformer was the famous Abd-el-Wahab, and his followers, known as Wahabees, soon spread over the length and breadth of the Mohammedan world, purging Islam of its sloth and rekindling the fervor of olden days. Thus began the great Mohammedan Revival.

That revival, like all truly regenerative movements, had its political as well as its spiritual side. One of the first things which struck the reformers was the political weakness of the Moslem world and its increasing subjection to the Christian West. It was during the early decades of the nineteenth century that the revival spread through Islam. But this was the very time when Europe, recovering from the losses of the Napoleonic Wars, began its unparalleled aggressions upon the Moslem East. The result in Islam was a fusing of religion and patriotism into a "sacred union" for the combined spiritual regeneration and political emancipation of the Moslem world.

Of course Europe's material and military superiority were then so great that speedy success was recognized to be a vain hope. Nevertheless, with true Oriental patience, the reformers were content to work for distant goals, and the results of their labors, though hidden from most Europeans, was soon discernible to a few keen-sighted white observers. Half a century ago the learned Orientalist Palgrave wrote these prophetic lines: "Islam is even now an enormous power, full of self-sustaining vitality, with a surplus for aggression; and a struggle with its combined energies would be deadly indeed.... The Mohammedan peoples of the East have awakened to the manifold strength and skill of their Western Christian rivals; and this awakening, at first productive of respect and fear, not unmixed with admiration, now wears the type of antagonistic dislike, and even of intelligent hate. No more zealous

Moslems are to be found in all the ranks of Islam than they who have sojourned longest in Europe and acquired the most intimate knowledge of its sciences and ways.... Mohammedans are keenly alive to the ever-shifting uncertainties and divisions that distract the Christianity of to-day, and to the woeful instability of modern European institutions. From their own point of view, Moslems are as men standing on a secure rock, and they contrast the quiet fixity of their own position with the unsettled and insecure restlessness of all else." (W. G. Palgrave, `'Essays on Eastern Questions," pp. 127-131 (London, 1872).)

This stability to which Palgrave alludes must not be confused with dead rigidity. Too many of us still think of the Moslem East as hopelessly petrified. But those Westerners best acquainted with the Islamic world assert that nothing could be farther from the truth; emphasizing, on the contrary, Islam's present plasticity and rapid assimilation of Western ideas and methods. "The alleged rigidity of Islam is a European myth," (Theodore Morison, "Can Islam Be Reformed?" Nineteenth Century, October, 1908.) says Theodore Morison, late principal of the Mohammedan Anglo-Oriental College at Aligarh, India; and another Orientalist, Marmaduke Pickthall writes: "There is nothing in Islam, any more than in Christianity, which should halt progress. The fact is that Christianity found, some time ago, a modus vivendi with modern life, while Islam has not yet arrived thither. But this process is even now being worked out." (Marmaduke Pickthall, "L'Angleterre et la Turquie," Revue Politique Internationale, January, 1914.)

The way in which the Mohammedan world has availed itself of white institutions such as the newspaper in forging its new solidarity is well portrayed by Bernard Temple. "It all comes to this, then," he writes. "World-politics, as viewed by Mohammedanism's political leaders, resolve themselves into a struggle - not necessarily a bloody struggle, but still an intense and vital struggle for place and power between the three great divisions of mankind. The Moslem mind is deeply stirred by the prospect. Every Moslem country is in communication with every other Moslem country: directly, by means of special emissaries, pilgrims, travellers, traders, and postal exchanges; indirectly, by means of Mohammedan newspapers, books, pamphlets, leaflets, and periodicals. I have met with Cairo newspapers in Bagdad, Teheran, and Peshawar; Constantinople newspapers in Basra and Bombay; Calcutta newspapers in Mohammerah, Kerbela, and Port Said." (Bernard Temple, "The Place of Persia in World-Politics," Proceedings of the Central Asian Society, May, 1910.)

These European judgments are confirmed by what Asiatics say themselves. For example, a Syrian Christian, Ameen Rihani, thus characterizes the present strength and vitality of the Moslem world: "A nation of 250,000,000 souls, more than one-half under Christian rule, struggling to shake off its fetters; to consolidate its opposing forces; replenishing itself in the south and in the east from the inexhaustible sources of the life primitive; assimilating in the north, but not without discrimination, the civilization of Europe; a nation with a glorious past, a living faith and language, an inspired Book, an undying hope, might be divided against itself by European diplomacy but can never be subjugated by European arms.... What Islam is losing on the borders of Europe it is gaining in Africa and Central Asia through its modern propaganda, which is conducted according to Christian methods. And this is one of the grand results of 'civilization by benevolent assimilation.' Europe drills the Moslem to be a soldier who will ultimately turn his weapons against her; and she sends her missionaries to awaken in the ulema the proselytizing evil." (Ameen Rihani, "The Crisis of Islam," Forum, May, 1912.)

Typical of Mohammedan literature on this subject are the following excerpts from a book published at Cairo in 1907 by an Egyptian, Yahya Siddyk, significantly entitled "The Awakening of the Islamic Peoples in the Fourteenth Century of the Hegira." (I.e., the twentieth century of the Christian era.) The book is doubly interesting because the author has a thorough Western education, holding a law degree from the French university of Toulouse, and is a judge on the Egyptian bench. Although writing as far back as 1907, Yahya Siddyk clearly foresaw the imminence of the European War.

45

"Behold," he writes, "these Great-Powers ruining themselves in terrifying armaments; measuring each other's strength with defiant glances; menacing each other; contracting alliances which continually break and which presage those terrible shocks which overturn the world and cover it with ruins, fire, and blood! The future is God's, and nothing is lasting save His Will!"

He considers the white world degenerate. "Does this mean," he asks, "that Europe, our 'enlightened guide,' has already reached the summit of its evolution? Has it already exhausted its vital force by two or three centuries of hyper-exertion? In other words: is it already stricken with senility, and will it see itself soon obliged to yield its civilizing role to other peoples less degenerate, less neurasthenic; that is to say, younger, more robust, more healthy, than itself? In my opinion, the present marks Europe's apogee, and its immoderate colonial expansion means, not strength, but weakness. Despite the aureole of so much grandeur, power, and glory, Europe is to-day more divided and more fragile than ever, and ill conceals its malaise, its sufferings, and its anguish. Its destiny is inexorably working out! . . .

"The contact of Europe on the East has caused us both much good and much evil: good, in the material and intellectual sense; evil, from the moral and political point of view. Exhausted by long struggles, enervated by a brilliant civilization, the Moslem peoples inevitably fell into a malaise, but they are not stricken, they are not dead! These peoples, conquered by the force of cannon, have not in the least lost their unity, even under the oppressive régimes to which the Europeans have long subjected them.... I have said that the European contact has been salutary to us from both the material and the intellectual point of view. What reforming Moslem Princes wished to impose by force on their Moslem subjects is to-day realized a hundredfold. So great has been our progress in the last twenty-five years in science, letters, and art that we may well hope to be in all those things the equals of Europeans in less than half a century....

" A new era opens for us with the fourteenth century of the Hegira,

46

and this happy century will mark our renaissance and our great future! A new breath animates the Mohammedan peoples of all races; all Moslems are penetrated with the necessity of work and instruction! We all wish to travel, do business, tempt fortune, brave dangers. There is in the East, among the Mohammedans, a surprising activity, an animation, unknown twenty-five years ago.... There is to-day a real public opinion throughout the East."

The author concludes: "Let us hold firm, each for all, and let us hope, hope, hope! We are fairly launched on the path of progress: let us profit by it! It is Europe's very tyranny which has wrought our transformation! It is our continued contact with Europe which favors our evolution and inevitably hastens our revival! It is simply History repeating itself; the Will of God fulfilling itself despite all opposition and all resistance.... Europe's tutelage over Asiatics is becoming more and more nominal-the gates of Asia are closing against the European! Surely we glimpse before us a revolution without parallel in the world's annals. A new age is at hand!" (Yahya Siddyk, "Le Réveil des Peuples Islamiques au Quatorzième Siècle de l'Hégire" (Cairo, 1907).)

If this be indeed the present spirit of Islam it is a portentous fact, for its numerical strength is very great. The total number of Mohammedans is estimated at from 200,000,000 to 250,000,000, and they not only predominate throughout the brown world with the exception of India, but they also count 10,000,000 adherents in China and are gaining prodigiously among the blacks of Africa.

The proselyting power of Islam is extraordinary, and its hold upon its votaries is even more remarkable. Throughout history there has been no single instance where a people, once become Moslem, has ever abandoned the faith. Extirpated they may have been, like the Moors of Spain, but extirpation is not apostasy. This extreme tenacity of Islam, this ability to keep its hold, once it has got a footing, under all circumstances short of downright extirpation, must be borne in mind when considering the future of regions where Islam is to-day advancing.

And, save in eastern Europe, it is to-day advancing along all its far-flung frontiers. Its most signal victories are being won among the negro races of central Africa, and this phase will be discussed in the next chapter, but elsewhere the same conditions, in lesser degree, prevail. Every Moslem is a born missionary and instinctively propagates his faith among his non-Moslem neighbors. The quality of this missionary temper has been well analyzed by Meredith Townsend. "All the emotions which impel a Christian to proselytize," he writes, "are in a Mussulman strengthened by all the motives which impel a political leader and all the motives which sway a recruiting sergeant, until proselytism has become a passion, which, whenever success seems practicable, and especially success on a large scale, develops in the quietest Mussulman a fury of ardor which induces him to break down every obstacle, his own strongest prejudices included, rather than stand for an instant in the neophyte's way. He welcomes him as a son, and whatever his own lineage, and whether the convert be negro, or Chinaman, or Indian, or even European, he will without hesitation or scruple give him his own child in marriage, and admit him fully, frankly, and finally into the most exclusive circle in the world." (Meredith Townsend, "Asia and Europe," pp. 46-47.)

Such is the vast and growing body of Islam, to-day seeking to weld its forces into a higher unity for the combined objectives of spiritual revival and political emancipation. This unitary movement is known as "Pan-Islamism." Most Western observers seem to think that Pan-Islamism centres in the "Caliphate," and European writers to-day hopefully discuss whether the Caliphate's retention by the discredited Turkish Sultans, its transferrence to the rulers of the new Arab Hedjaz Kingdom, or its total suppression, will best clip Islam's wings.

This, however, is a very short-sighted and partial view. The Khalifa or "Caliph" (to use the Europeanized form), the Prophet's representative on earth, has played an important historic role, and the institution is still venerated in Islam. But the Pan-Islamic leaders have long been working on a much broader basis. Pan-

Islamism's real driving power lies, not in the Caliphate, but in institutions like the "Hajj" or pilgrimage to Mecca, the propaganda of the "Hablul-Matin" or "Tie of True Believers," and the great religious fraternities. The Meccan Hajj, where tens of thousands of picked zealots gather every year from every quarter of the Moslem world, is really an annual Pan-Islamic congress, where all the interests of the faith are discussed at length, and where plans are elaborated for its defense and propagation. Similarly ubiquitous is the Pan-Islamic propaganda of the Habl-ul-Matin, which works tirelessly to compose sectarian differences and traditional feuds. Lastly, the religious brotherhoods cover the Islamic world with a network of far-flung associations, quickening the zeal of their myriad members and co-ordinating their energies for potential action.

The greatest of these brotherhoods (though there are others of importance) is the famous Senussiyah, and its history well illustrates Islam's evolution during the past hundred years. Its founder, Seyyid Mahommed ben Senussi, was born in Algeria about the beginning of the nineteenth century. He was of high Arab lineage, tracing his descent from Fatima, the daughter of the Prophet. In early youth he went to Arabia and there came under the influence of the Wahabee movement. In middle life he returned to Africa, settling in the Sahara Desert, and there built up the fraternity which bears his name. Before his death the order had spread to all parts of the Mohammedan world, but it is in northern Africa that it has attained its peculiar pro-eminence. The Senussi Order is divided into local "Zawias" or lodges, all absolutely dependent upon the Grand Lodge, headed by The Master, El Senussi. The Grand Mastership still remains in the family, a grandson of the founder being the order's present head. The Senussi stronghold is an oasis in the very heart of the Sahara. Only one European eye has ever seen this mysterious spot. Surrounded by absolute desert, with wells many leagues apart and the routes of approach known only to experienced Senussi guides, every one of whom would suffer a thousand deaths rather than betray him, El Senussi, The Master, sits serenely apart, sending his orders throughout North Africa.

The Sahara itself is absolutely under Senussi control, while "Zawias" abound in distant regions like Morocco, Lake Chad, and Somaliland. These local Zawias are more than mere "lodges." Their spiritual and secular heads, the "Mokaddem" or priest and the "Wekil" or civil governor, have discretionary authority not merely over the Zawia members, but also over the community at large - at least, so great is the awe inspired by the Senussi throughout North Africa that a word from Wekil or Mokaddem is always listened to and obeyed. Thus, beside the various European authorities, British, French or Italian as the case may be, there exists an occult government with which the colonial authorities are careful not to come into conflict.

On their part, the Senussi are equally careful to avoid a downright breach with the European Powers. Their long-headed, cautious policy is truly astonishing. For more than half a century the order has been a great force, yet it has never risked the supreme adventure. In all the numerous fanatic risings against Europeans which have occurred in various parts of Africa, local Senussi have undoubtedly taken part, but the order has never officially entered the lists.

These Fabian tactics as regards open warfare do not mean that the Senussi are idle. Far from it. On the contrary, they are ceaselessly at work with the spiritual arms of teaching, discipline, and conversion. The Senussi programme is the welding, first of Moslem Africa, and later of the whole Moslem world, into the revived "Imamat" of Islam's early days; into a great theocracy, embracing all true believers - in other words, Pan-Islamism. But they believe that the political liberation of Islam from Christian domination must be preceded by a profound spiritual regeneration, thereby engendering the moral forces necessary both for the war of liberation and for the fruitful reconstruction which should follow thereafter. This is the secret of the order's extraordinary self-restraint. This is the reason why, year after year, and decade after decade, the Senussi advance slowly, calmly, coldly, gathering great latent power but avoiding the temptation to expend it one instant before the proper tune.

Meanwhile they are covering Africa with their lodges and schools, disciplining the people to the voice of their Mokaddems and Wekils - and converting millions of pagan negroes to the faith of Islam.

And what is true of the Senussi holds equally for the other wise leaders who guide the Pan-Islamic movement. They know both Europe's strength and their own weakness. They know the peril of premature action. Feeling that time is on their side, they are content to await the hour when internal regeneration and external pressure shall have filled to overflowing the cup of wrath. This is why Islam has offered only local resistance to the unparalleled white aggressions of the last twenty years. This is the main reason why there was no real "Holy War" in 1914. But the materials for a Holy War have long been piling high, as a retrospective glance will show.

Europe's conquests of Africa and Central Asia toward the close of the last century, and the subsequent Anglo-French agreement mutually appropriating Egypt and Morocco, evoked murmurs of impotent fury from the Moslem world. Under such circumstances the Russo-Japanese War of 1904 sent a feverish tremor throughout Islam. The Japanese might be idolaters, but the traditional Moslem loathing of idolaters as beings much lower than Christians and Jews (recognized by Mohammed as "Peoples of The Book") was quite effaced by the burning sense of subjugation to the Christian yoke. Accordingly, the Japanese were hailed as heroes throughout Islam. Here we see again that tendency toward an understanding between Asiatic and African races and creeds (in other words, a "Pan-Colored" alliance against white domination) which has been so patent in recent years. The way in which Islamic peoples began looking to Japan is revealed by this editorial in a Persian newspaper, written in the year 1906: "Desirous of becoming as powerful as Japan and of safeguarding its national independence, Persia should make common cause with it. An alliance becomes necessary. There should be a Japanese ambassador at Teheran. Japanese instructors should be chosen to reorganize the army. Commercial relations should also be developed." (F. Farjanel, "Le Japon et l'Islam," Revue du Monde Musulman, November, 1906.)

Indeed, some pious Moslems hoped to bring this heroic people within the Islamic fold. Shortly after the Russo-Japanese War a Chinese Mohammedan sheikh wrote: "If Japan thinks of becoming some day a very great power and making Asia the dominator of the other continents, it will be only by adopting the blessed religion of Islam." (Farjanel, supra.) And Al Mowwayad, an Egyptian Nationalist journal, remarked: "England, with her 60,000,000 Indian Moslems, dreads this conversion. With a Mohammedan Japan, Mussulman policy would change entirely." (Ibid.) As a matter of fact, Mohammedan missionaries actually went to Japan, where they were smilingly received. Of course the Japanese had not the faintest intention of turning Moslems, but these spontaneous approaches from the brown world were quite in line with their ambitious plans, which, as the reader will remember, were just then taking concrete shape.

However, it soon became plain that Japan had no present intention of going so far afield as Western Asia, and Islam presently had to mourn fresh losses at Christian hands. In 1911 came Italy's barefaced raid on Turkey's African dependency of Tripoli. So bitter was the anger in all Mohammedan lands at this unprovoked aggression that many European observers became seriously alarmed. "Why has Italy found 'defenseless' Tripoli such a hornet's nest?" queried Gabriel Hanotaux, a former French minister of foreign affairs. "It is because she has to do, not merely with Turkey, but with Islam as well. Italy has set the ball rolling - so much the worse for her - and for us all." (Gabriel Hanotaux, "La Crise mÈditerranÈenne et l'Islam," Revue Hebdomadaire, April 13, 1912.) But the Tripoli expedition was only the beginning of the Christian assault, for next year came the Balkan War, which sheared away Turkey's European holdings to the walls of Constantinople and left her crippled and discredited. At those disasters a cry of wrathful anguish swept the world of Islam from end to end. Here is how a leading Indian Moslem interpreted the Balkan conflict:

"The King of Greece orders a new crusade. From the London Chancelleries rise calls to Christian fanaticism, and Saint Petersburg already speaks of the planting of the cross on the dome of Sant' Sophia. To-day they speak thus; to-morrow they will thus speak of Jerusalem and the Mosque of Omar. Brothers! Be ye of one mind, that it is the duty of every true beIiever to hasten beneath the Khalifa's banner and to sacrifice his life for the safety of the falth." (Arminius VambËry, "Die t,rkische Katastrophe und die Islamwelt," Deutsche Revue, July, 1913.) And another Indian Moslem leader thus adjured the British authorities: "I appeal to the present government to change its anti-Turkish attitude before the fury of millions of Moslem fellow subjects is kindled to a blaze and brings disaster." (Shab Mohammed Naimatullah, "Recent Turkish Events, and Moslem India," Asiatic Review, October, 1913.)

Still more significant were the appeals made by the Indian Moslems to their Brahman fellow countrymen, the traditionally despised "Idolaters." These appeals betokened a veritable revolution in outlook, as can be gauged from the text of one of them, significantly entitled "The Message of the East." "Spirit of the East," reads this noteworthy document, "arise and repel the swelling flood of Western aggression! Children of Hindustan, aid us with your wisdom, culture, and wealth; lend us your power, the birthright and heritage of the Hindu! Let the Spirit Powers hidden in the Himalayan mountain-peaks, arise. Let prayers to the god of battles float upward; prayers that right may triumph over might; and call to your myriad gods to annihilate the armies of the foe!" (VambËry, supra.) In China also the same fraternizing spirit was visible. During the Republican Revolution the Chinese Mohammedans, instead of holding jealously aloof, co-operated wholeheartedly with their Buddhist and Confucian fellow citizens, and Doctor Sun-Yat-Sen, the Republican leader, announced gratefully: "The Chinese will never forget the assistance which their Moslem compatriots have rendered in the interest of order and liberty." (Arminius VambËry, "An Approach Between Moslems and Buddhists," Nineteenth Century, April, 1912.) The Great War thus found Islam deeply stirred against European aggression, keenly conscious of its own solidarity, and frankly reaching out for colored allies in the projected struggle against white domination.

Under these circumstances it may at first sight appear strange that no general Islamic explosion occurred when Turkey entered the lists at the close of 1914 and the Sultan-Khalifa issued a formal summons to the Holy War. Of course this summons was not the flat failure which Allied reports led the West to believe at the time. As a matter of fact there was trouble in practically every Mohammedan land under Allied control. To name only a few of many instances: Egypt broke into a tumult smothered only by overwhelming British reinforcements, Tripoli burst into a flame of insurrection that drove the Italians headlong to the coast, Persia was prevented from joining Turkey only by prompt Russian intervention, and the Indian Northwest Frontier was the scene of fighting that required the presence of a quarter of a million Anglo-Indian troops. The British Government has officially admitted that during 1915 the Allies' Asiatic and African possessions stood within a hand's breadth of a cataclysmic insurrection.

That insurrection would certainly have taken place if Islam's leaders had everywhere spoken the fateful word. But the word was not spoken. Instead, influential Moslems outside of Turkey generally condemned the latter's action and did all in their power to calm the passions of the fanatic multitude. The attitude of these leaders does credit to their discernment.

They recognized that this was neither the time nor the occasion for a decisive struggle with the West. They were not yet materially prepared, and they had not perfected their understandings either among themselves or with their prospective non-Moslem allies. Above all, the moral urge was lacking. They knew that athwart the Khalifa's writ was stencilled "Made in Germany." They knew that the "Young Turk" clique which had engineered the coup was made up of Europeanized renegades, many of them not even nominal Moslems, but atheistic Jews. Far-sighted Moslems had no intention of pulling Germany's chestnuts out of the fire, nor did they wish to further Prussian schemes of world-dominion which for themselves would have meant a mere change of masters. Far better to let the white world fight out its desperate feud, weaken itself, and reveal fully its future intentions. Meanwhile Islam could bide its time, grow in strength, and await the morrow.

The Versailles Peace Conference was just such a revelation of European intentions as the Pan-Islamic leaders had been awaiting in order to perfect their programmes and enlist the moral solidarity of their peoples. At Versailles the European Powers showed unequivocally that they had no intention of relaxing their hold upon the Near and Middle East. By a number of secret treaties negotiated during the war the Ottoman Empire had been virtually partitioned between the victorious Allies, and these secret treaties formed the basis of the Versailles settlement. Further more, Egypt had been declared a British protectorate at the very beginning of the European struggle, while the Versailles Conference had scarcely adjourned before England announced an "agreement" with Persia which made that country another British protectorate, in fact, if not in name. The upshot was, as already stated, that the Near and Middle East were subjected to European political domination as never before.

But there was another side to the shield. During the war years the Allied statesmen had officially proclaimed times without number that the war was being fought to establish a new world-order based on such principles as the rights of small nations and the liberty of all peoples. These pronouncements had been treasured and memorized throughout the East. When, therefore, the East saw a peace settlement based, not upon these high professions, but upon the imperialistic secret treaties, it was fired with a moral indignation and sense of outraged justice never known before. A tide of impassioned determination began rising which has already set the entire East in tumultuous ferment, and which seems merely the premonitory ground-swell of a greater storm. Many European students of Eastern affairs are gravely alarmed at the prospect. Here, for example, is the judgment of Leone Caetani, Duke of Sermoneta, an Italian authority on Oriental and Mohammedan questions. Speaking in the spring of 1919 on the war's effect on the East, he said: "The convulsion has shaken Islamitic and Oriental civilization to its foundations. The entire Oriental world, from China to the Mediterranean, is in ferment. Everywhere the hidden fire of anti-European hatred is burning. Riots in Morocco, risings in Algiers, discontent in Tripoli, so-called Nationalist attempts in Egypt, Arabia, and Lybia, are all different manifestations of the same deep sentiment, and have as their object the rebellion of the Orienta1 world against European civilization." (Special cable to the New York Times, dated Rome, May 28, 1919.)

The state of affairs in Egypt is a typical illustration of what has been going on in the East ever since the close of the late war. Egypt was occupied by England in 1882, and British rule has conferred immense material benefits, raising the country from anarchic bankruptcy to ordered prosperity. Yet British rule was never really popular, and as the years passed a "Nationalist" movement steadily grew in strength, having for its slogan the phrase "Egypt for the Egyptians," and demanding Britain's complete evacuation of the country. This demand Great Britain refused even to consider. Practically all Englishmen are agreed that Egypt with the Suez Canal is the vital link between the eastern and western halves of the British Empire, and they therefore consider the permanent occupation of Egypt an absolute necessity. There is thus a clear deadlock between British imperial and Egyptian national convictions.

Some years before the war Egypt became so unruly that England was obliged to abandon all thoughts of conciliation and initiated a regime of frank repression enforced by Lord Kitchener's heavy hand. The European War and Turkey's adhesion to the Teutonic Powers caused fresh outbreaks in Egypt, but these were quickly repressed and England took advantage of Ottoman belligerency to abolish the fiction of Turkish overlordship and declare Egypt a protectorate of the British Empire.

During the war Egypt, flooded with British troops, remained quiet, but the end of the war gave the signal for an unparalleled outburst of Nationalist activity. Basing their claims on such doctrines as the "rights of small nations" and the "self-determination of peoples," the Nationalists demanded immediate independence and attempted to get Egypt's case before the Versailles Peace Conference. In defiance of English prohibitions, they even held a popular plebiscite which upheld their claims. When the British authorities answered this defiance by arresting Nationalist leaders, Egypt flamed into rebellion from end to end. Everywhere it was the same story. Railways and telegraph lines were systematically cut. Trains were stalled and looted. Isolated British officers and soldiers were murdered. In Cairo alone, thousands of houses were sacked by the mob. Soon the danger was rendered more acute by the irruption out of the desert of swarms of Bedouin Arabs bent on plunder. For a few days Egypt trembled on the verge of anarchy, and the British Government admitted in Parliament that all Egypt was in a state of insurrection.

The British authorities, however, met the crisis with vigor and determination. The number of British troops in Egypt was very large, trusty black regiments were hurried up from the Sudan, and the well-disciplined Egyptian native police generally obeyed orders. The result was that after several weeks of sharp fighting, lasting through the spring of 1919, Egypt was again gotten under control. The outlook for the future is, however, ominous in the extreme. Order is indeed restored, but only the presence of massed British and Sudanese black troops guarantees that order will be maintained. Even under the present rÈgime of stern martial law hardly a month passes without fresh rioting and heavy loss of life. Egypt appears Nationalist to the core, its spokesmen swear they will accept nothing short of independence, and in the long run Britain will realize the truth of that pithy saying: "You can do everything with bayonets except sit on them."

India is likewise in a state of profound unrest. The vast peninsula has been controlled by England for almost two centuries, yet here again the last two decades have witnessed a rapidly increasing movement against British rule. This movement was at first confined to the upper-class Hindus, the great Mohammedan element preserving its traditional loyalty to the British "Raj," which it considered a protection against the Brahmanistic Hindu majority. But, as already seen, the Pan-Islamic leaven presently reached the Indian Moslems, European aggressions on Islam stirred their resentment, and at length Moslem and Hindu adjourned their ancient feud in their new solidarity against European tutelage.

The Great War provoked relatively little sedition in India. Groups of Hindu extremists to be sure, hatched terroristic plots and welcomed German aid, but India as a whole backed England and helped win the war with both money and men. At the same time, Indians gave notice that they expected their loyalty to be rewarded, and at the close of the war various memorials were drawn up calling for drastic modifications of the existing governmental regime.

India is to-day governed by an English Civil Service whose fairness, honesty, and general efficiency no informed person can seriously impugn. But this no longer contents Indian aspirations. India desires not merely good government but self-governnent. The ultimate goal of all Indian reformers is emancipation from European tutelage, though they differ among themselves as to how and when this emancipation is to be attained. The most conservative would be content with self-government under British guidance, the middle group asks for the full status of a Dominion of the British Empire like Canada and Australia, while the radicals demand complete independence. Even the most conservative of these demands would, however, involve great changes of system and a diminution of British control. Such demands arouse in England mistrust and apprehension. Englishmen point out that India is not a nation but a congeries of diverse peoples spiritually sundered by barriers of blood, language, culture, and religion, and they conclude that, if England's control were really relaxed, India would get out of hand and drift toward anarchy. As for Indian independence, the average Englishman cannot abide the thought, holding it fatal both for the British Empire and for India itself. The result has been that England has failed to meet Indian demands, and this, in turn, has roused an acute recrudescence of dissatisfaction and unrest. The

British Government has countered with coercive legislation like the Rowlatt Acts and has sternly repressed rioting and terrorism. British authority is still supreme in India. But it is an authority resting more and more upon force. In fact, some Englishmen have long considered British rule in India, despite its imposing appearance, a decidedly fragile affair. Many years ago Meredith Townsend, who certainly knew India well, wrote:

"The English think they will rule India for many centuries or forever. I do not think so, holding rather the older belief that the empire which came in a day will disappear in a night.... Above all this inconceivable mass of humanity, governing all, protecting all, taxing all, rises what we call here 'the Empire,' a corporation of less than 1,500 men, partly chosen by examination, partly by co-optation, who are set to govern, and who protect themselves in governing by finding pay for a minute white garrison of 65,000 men, one-fifth of the Roman legions - though the masses to be controlled are double the subjects of Rome. That corporation and that garrison constitute the 'Indian Empire.' There is nothing else. Banish those 1,500 men in black, defeat that slender garrison in red, and the empire has ended, the structure disappears, and brown India emerges, unchanged and unchangeable. To support the official world and its garrison - both, recollect, smaller than those of Belgium - there is, except Indian opinion, absolutely nothing. Not only is there no white race in India, not only is there no white colony, but there is no white man who purposes to remain.... There are no white servants, not even grooms, no white policemen, no white postmen, no white anything. If the brown men struck for a week, the 'Empire' would collapse like a house of cards, and every ruling man would be a starving prisoner in his own house. He could not move or feed himself or get water." (Townsend, op. cit., pp. 82-87.)

These words aptly illustrate the truth stated at the beginning of this book that the basic factor in human affairs is not politics but race, and that the most imposing political phenomena, of themselves, mean nothing. And that is just the fatal weakness underlying the white man's present political domination over the brown world. Throughout that entire world there is no settled white population save in the French colonies of Algeria and Tunis along the Mediterranean seaboard, where whites form perhaps one-sixth of the total. Elsewhere, from Morocco to the Dutch Indies, there is in the racial sense, as Townsend well says, "no white anything," and if white rule vanished to-morrow it would not leave a human trace behind. White rule is therefore purely political, based on prescription, prestige, and lack of effective opposition. These are indeed fragile foundations. Let the brown world once make up its mind that the white man must go, and he will go, for his position will have become simply impossible. It is not solely a question of a "Holy War"; mere passive resistance, if genuine and general, would shake white rule to its foundations. And it is precisely the determination to get rid of white role which seems to be spreading like wild-fire over the brown world to-day. The unrest which I have described in Egypt and India merely typify what is going on in Morocco, Central Asia, the Dutch Indies, the Philippines, and every other portion of the brown world whose inhabitants are above the grade of savages.

Another factor favoring the prospects of brown emancipation is the lack of sustained resistance which the white world would probably offer. For the white world's interests in these regions, though great, are not fundamental; that is to say, racial. However grievously they might suffer politically and economically, racially the white peoples would lose almost nothing. Here again we see the basic importance of race in human affairs. Contrast, for example, England's attitude toward an insurgent India with France's attitude toward an insurgent North Africa. England, with nothing racial at stake, would hesitate before a reconquest of India involving millions of soldiers and billions of treasure. France, on the other hand, with nearly a million Europeans in her North African possessions, half of those full-blooded Frenchmen, might risk her last franc and her last poilu rather than see these blood-brothers slaughtered and enslaved.

Assuming, then, what to-day seems probable, that white political control over the brown world is destined to be sensibly curtailed if not generally eliminated, what are the larger racial implications? Above all: will the browns tend to impinge on white race-areas as the yellows show signs of doing? Probably, no; at least, not to any great extent. In the first place, the brown world has within its present confines plenty of room for potential race-expansion. Outside India, Egypt, Java, and a few lesser spots, there is scarcely a brown land where natural improvements such as irrigation would not open up extensive settlement areas. Mesopotamia alone, now almost uninhabited, might support a vast population, while Persia could nourish several times its present inhabitants.

India, to be sure, is almost as congested as China, and the spectre of the Indian coolie has lately alarmed white lands like Canada and South Africa almost as much as the Chinese coolie has done. But an independent India would fall under the same political blight as the rest of the brown world - the blight of internecine dissensions and wars. The brown world's present growing solidarity is not a positive but a negative phenomenon. It is an alliance, against a common foe, of traditional enemies who, once the bond was loosed in victory, would inevitably quarrel among themselves. Turk would fly at Arab and Turkoman at Persian, as of yore, while India would become a welter of contending Hindus, Moslems, Sikhs, Gurkhas, and heaven knows what, until perchance disciplined anew by the pressure of a Yellow Peril. In Western Asia it is possible that the spiritual and cultural bonds of Islam might temper these struggles, but Western Asia is precisely that part of the brown world where population - pressure is absent. India, the overpeopled brown land, would undergo such a cycle of strife as would devour its human surplus and render distant aggressions impossible.

A potential brown menace to white race-areas would, indeed, arise in case of a brown-yellow alliance against the white peoples. But such an alliance could occur only in the first stages of a pan-colored war of liberation while the pressure of white world-predominance was still keenly felt and before the divisive tendencies within the brown world had begun to take effect.

Short of such an alliance (wherein the browns would abet the yellows' aggressive, racial objectives in return for yellow support of their own essentially defensive, political ends), the brown world's emancipation from white domination would apparently not result in more than local pressures on white race areas. It would, however, affect another sphere of white political control - black Africa. The emancipation of brown, Islamic North Africa would inevitably send a sympathetic thrill through every portion of the Dark Continent and would stir both Mohammedan and pagan negroes against white rule. Islam is, in fact, the intimate link between the brown and black worlds. But this subject, with its momentous implications, will be discussed in the next chapter.

CHAPTER IV
BLACK MAN'S LAND

BLACK MAN'S LAND is primarily Africa south of the Sahara Desert. Here dwell the bulk of all the 150,000,000 black men on earth. The negro and negroid population of Africa is estimated at about 120,000,000 - four-fifths of the black race-total. Besides its African nucleus the black race has two distant outposts: the one in Australasia, the other in the Americas. The Eastern blacks are found mainly in the archipelagoes lying between the Asiatic land-mass and Australia. They are the Oriental survivors of the black belt which in very ancient times stretched uninterruptedly from Africa across southern Asia to the Pacific Ocean. The Asiatic blacks were overwhelmed by other races ages ago, and only a few wild tribes like the "Negritos" of the Philippines and the jungle-dwellers of Indo-China and southern India survive as genuine negroid stocks. All the peoples of southern Asia, however, are darkened by this ancient negroid strain. The peoples of south India are notably tinged with black blood. As for the pure blacks of the Australasian archipelagoes, they are so few in numbers (about 3,000,000) and so low in type that they are of negligible importance. Quite otherwise are the blacks of the Far West. In the western hemisphere there are some 25,000,000 persons of more or less mixed black blood, brought thither in modern times as slaves by the white conquerors of the New World. Still, whatever may be the destiny of these transplanted black folk, the black man's chief significance, from the world aspect, must remain bound up with the great nucleus of negro population in the African homeland.

Black Africa, as I have said, lies south of the Sahara Desert. Here the negro has dwelt for unnumbered ages. The key-note of black history, like yellow history, has been isolation. Cut off from the Mediterranean by the desert which he had no means of crossing, and bounded elsewhere by oceans which he had no skill in navigating, the black man vegetated in savage obscurity, his habitat being well named the "Dark Continent."

Until the white tide began breaking on its seafronts four centuries ago, the black world's only external stimuli had come from brown men landing on its eastern coasts or ascending the valley of the Nile. As time passed, both brown and white pressures became more intense, albeit the browns long led in the process of penetration. Advancing from the east and trickling across the desert from the north, Arab or Arabized adventurers conquered black Africa to the equator; and this political subjugation had also a racial side, for the conquerors sowed their blood freely and set a brownish stamp on many regions. As for the whites, they long remained mere birds of passage. Half a century ago they possessed little more than trading-posts along the littorals, their only real settle- ment lying in the extreme south.

Then, suddenly, all was changed. In the closing decades of the nineteenth century, Europe turned its gaze full upon the Dark Continent, and within a generation Africa was partitioned between the European Powers. Negro and Arab alike fell under European domination. Only minute Liberia and remote Abyssinia retained a qualified independence. Furthermore, white settlement also made distinct progress. The tropical bulk of Africa defied white colonization, but the continent's northern and southern extremities were climatically "white man's country." Accordingly, there are today nearly a million whites settled along the Algerian and Tunisian seaboard, while in South Africa, Dutch and British blood has built up a powerful commonwealth containing fully one and one-half million white souls. In Africa, unlike Asia, the European has taken root, and has thus gained at least local tenures of a fundamental nature.

The crux of the African problem therefore resolves itself into the question whether the white man, through consolidated racial holds north and south, will be able to perpetuate his present political control over the intermediate continental mass which climate debars him from populating. This is a matter of great importance, for Africa is a land of enormous potential wealth, the natural source of Europe's tropical raw materials and foodstuffs. Whether Europe is to retain possession depends, in the last analysis on the character of the inhabitants. It is, then, to the nature of the black man and his connection with the brown world that we must direct our attention.

From the first glance we see that, in the negro, we are in the presence of a being differing profoundly not merely from the white man but also from those human types which we discovered in our surveys of the brown and yellow worlds. The black man is, indeed, sharply differentiated from the other branches of mankind. His outstanding quality is superabundant animal vitality. In this he easily surpasses all other races. To it he owes his intense emotionalism. To it, again, is due his extreme fecundity, the negro being the quickest of breeders. This abounding vitality shows in many other ways, such as the negro's ability to survive harsh conditions of slavery under which other races have soon succumbed. Lastly, in ethnic crossings, the negro strikingly displays his prepotency, for black blood, once entering a human stock, seems never really bred out again.

Negro fecundity is a prime factor in Africa's future. In the savage state which until recently prevailed, black multiplication was kept down by a wide variety of checks. Both natural and social causes combined to maintain an extremely high death-rate. The negro's political ineptitude, never rising above the tribal concept, kept black Africa a mosaic of peoples, warring savagely among themselves and widely addicted to cannibalism. Then, too, the native religions were usually sanguinary, demanding a prodigality of human sacrifices. The killings ordained by negro wizards and witch-doctors sometimes attained unbelievable proportions. The combined result of all this was a wastage of life which in other races would have spelled a declining population. Since the establishment of white political control, however, these checks on black fecundity are no longer operative. The white rulers fight filth and disease, stop tribal wars, and stamp out superstitious abominations. In consequence, population increases by leaps and bounds, the latent possibilities being shown in the native reservations in South Africa, where tribes have increased as much as tenfold in fifty or sixty years. It is therefore practically certain that the African negroes will multiply prodigiously in the next few decades.

Now, what will be the attitude of these augmenting black masses toward white political dominion? To that momentous query no certain answer can be made. One thing, however, seems clear: the black world's reaction to white ascendancy will be markedly different from those of the brown and yellow worlds, because of the profound dissimilarities between negroes and men of other stocks. To begin with, the black peoples have no historic pasts. Never having evolved civilizations of their own, they are practically devoid of that accumulated mass of beliefs, thoughts, and experiences which render Asiatics so impenetrable and so hostile to white influences. Although the white race displays sustained constructive power to an unrivalled degree, particularly in its Nordic branches, the brown and yellow peoples have contributed greatly to the civilization of the world and have profoundly influenced human progress. The negro, on the contrary, has contributed virtually nothing. Left to himself, he remained a savage, and in the past his only quickening has been where brown men have imposed their ideas and altered his blood. The originating powers of the European and the Asiatic are not in him.

This lack of constructive originality, however, renders the negro extremely susceptible to external influences. The Asiatic, conscious of his past and his potentialities, is chary of foreign innovations and refuses to recognize alien superiority. The negro, having no past, welcomes novelty and tacitly admits that others are his masters. Both brown and white men have been so accepted in Africa. The relatively faint resistance offered by the naturally brave blacks to white and brown conquest, the ready reception of Christianity and Islam, and the extraordinary personal ascendancy acquired by individual Arabs and Europeans, all indicate a willingness to accept foreign tutelage which in the Asiatic is wholly absent.

The Arab and the European are, in fact, rivals for the mastership of black Africa. The Arab had a long start, but the European suddenly overtook him and brought not only the blacks but the African Arabs themselves under his sway. It remains to be seen whether the Arab, allying himself with the blacks, can oust his white rival. That some such move will be attempted, in view of the brown world's renaissance in general and the extraordinary activity of the Arab peoples in particular, seems a foregone conclusion. How the matter will work out depends on three things:

1. the brown man's inherent strength in Africa;
2. the possibilities of black disaffection against white tutelage;
3. the white man's strength and power of resistance.

The seat of brown power in Africa is of course the great belt of territory north of the Sahara. From Egypt to Morocco the inhabitants are Arabized in culture and Mohammedan in faith, while Arab blood has percolated ever since the Moslem conquest twelve centuries ago. In the eastern half of this zone Arabization has been complete, and Egypt, Tripoli, and the Sudan can be considered as unalterably wedded to the brown Islamic world. The zone's western half, however, is in different case. The majority of its inhabitants are Berbers, an ancient stock generally considered white, with close affinities to the Latin peoples across the Mediterranean. As usual, blood tells. The Berbers have been under Arab tutelage for over a thousand years, yet their whole manner of life remains distinct, they have largely kept their language, and there has been comparatively little intermarriage. Pure-blooded Arabs abound, but they are still, in a way, foreigners. To-day the entire region is under white, French, rule. Algeria, in particular, has been politically French for almost a hundred years. Europeans have come in and number nearly a million souls. The Arab element shows itself sullen and refractory, but the Berbers display much less aversion to French rule, which, as usual, is considerate of native susceptibilities. The French colonial authorities are alive to the Berber's ethnic affinities and tactfully seek to stimulate his dormant white consciousness. In Algeria intermarriage between Europeans and Berbers has actually begun. Of course the process is merely in its first stages. Still, the blood is there, the leaven is working, and in time Northwest Africa may return to the white world, where it was in Roman days and where it racially belongs. In the anti-European disturbances now taking place in Algeria and Tunis it is safe to say that the Arab element is making most of the trouble.

It is Northeast Africa, then, which is the real nucleus of Arabism. Here Arabism and Islam rule unchecked, and in the preceding chapter we saw how the Senussi Order was marshalling the fierce nomads of the desert. These tribesmen are relatively few in numbers, but more splendid fighting material does not exist in the wide world. Furthermore, the Arab-negroid peoples which have developed along the southern edge of the desert so blend the martial qualities of both strains that they frequently display an almost demoniacal fighting-power. It is Pan-Islamism's hope to use these Arab or Arabized fanatics as an officers' corps for the black millions whom it is converting to the faith.

Concerning Islam's steady progress in black Africa there can be no shadow of a doubt. Every candid European observer tells the same story. "Mohammedanism," says Sir Charles Elliott, " can still give the natives a motive for animosity against Europeans and a unity of which they are otherwise incapable." (A. R. Colquhoun, "Pan-Islam," North American Review, June, 1906.) Twenty years ago another English observer, T. R. Threlfall, wrote: "Mohammedanism is making marvellous progress in the interior of Africa. It is crushing paganism out. Against it the Christian propaganda is a myth.... The rapid spread of militant Mohammedanism among the savage tribes to the north of the equator is a serious factor in the fight for racial supremacy in Africa. With very few exceptions the colored races of Africa are preeminently fighters. To them the law of the stronger is supreme; they have been conquered, and in turn they conquered. To them the fierce, warlike spirit inherent in Mohammedanism is infinitely more attractive than is the gentle, peace-loving, high moral standard of Christianity: hence, the rapid headway the former is making in central Africa, and the certainty that it will soon spread to the south of the Zambezi." (T. R. Threlfall, "Senussi and His Threatened Holy War," Nineteenth Century, March, 1900.)

The way in which Islam is marching southward is dramatically shown by a recent incident. A few years ago the British authorities suddenly discovered that Mohammedanism was pervading Nyassaland. An investigation brought out the fact that it was the work of Zanzibar Arabs. They began their propaganda about 1900. Ten years later almost every village in southern Nyassaland had its Moslem teacher and its mosque-hut. Although the movement was frankly anti-European, the British authorities did not dare to check it for fear of repercussions elsewhere. Another interesting fact, probably not unconnected, is that Nyassaland has lately been the theatre of an anti-white "Christian" propaganda - the so-called "Ethiopian Church," of which I shall presently speak.

Islam has thus two avenues of approach to the African negro - his natural preference for a militant faith and his resentment at white tutelage. It is the disinclination of the more martial African peoples for a pacific creed which perhaps accounts for Christianity's slow progress among the very warlike tribes of South Africa, such as the Zulus and the Matabele. Islam is as yet unknown south of the Zambezi, but white men universally dread the possibility of its appearance, fearing its effect upon the natives. Of course Christianity has made distinct progress in the Dark Continent. The natives of the South African Union are predominantly Christianized. In east-central Africa Christianity has also gained many converts, particularly in Uganda, while on the West African Guinea coast Christian missions have long been established and have generally succeeded in keeping Islam away from the seaboard. Certainly, all white men, whether professing Christians or not, should welcome the success of missionary efforts in Africa. The degrading fetishism and demonology which sum up the native pagan cults cannot stand, and all negroes will some day be either Christians or Moslems. In so far as he is Christianized, the negro's savage instincts will be restrained and he will be disposed to acquiesce in white tutelage. In so far as he is Islamized, the negro's warlike propensities will be inflamed, and he will be used as the tool of Arab Pan-Islamism seeking to drive the white man from Africa and make the continent its very own.

As to specific anti-white sentiments among negroes untouched by Moslem propaganda, such sentiments undoubtedly exist in many quarters. The strongest manifestations are in South Africa, where interracial relations are bad and becoming worse, but there is much diffused, half-articulate dislike of white men throughout central Africa as well. Devoid though the African savage is of either national or cultural consciousness, he could not be expected to welcome a tutelage which imposed many irksome restrictions upon him. Furthermore, the African negro does seem to possess a certain rudimentary sense of race-solidarity. The existence of both these sentiments is proved by the way in which the news of white military reverses have at once been known and rejoiced in all over black Africa; spread, it would seem, by those mysterious methods of communication employed by negroes everywhere and called in our Southern States "grape-vine telegraph." The Russo-Japanese War, for example, produced all over the Dark Continent intensely exciting effects.

This generalized anti-white feeling has, during the past decade, taken tangible form in South Africa.

The white population of the Union, though numbering 1,500,000, is surrounded by a black population four times as great and increasing more rapidly, while in many sections the whites are outnumbered ten to one. The result is a state of affairs exactly paralleling conditions in our own South, the South African whites feeling obliged to protect their ascendancy by elaborate legal regulations and social taboos. The negroes have been rapidly growing more restive under these discriminations, and unpleasant episodes like race-riots, rapings, and lynchings are increasing in South Africa from year to year.

One of the most significant, not to say ominous, signs of the times is the "Ethiopian Church" movement. The movement began about fifteen years ago, some of its founders being Afro-American Methodist preachers - a fact which throws a curious light on possible American negro reflexes upon their ancestral homeland. The movement spread rapidly, many native mission congregations cutting loose from white ecclesiastical control and joining the negro organization. It also soon displayed frankly anti-white tendencies, and the government became seriously alarmed at its unsettling influence upon the native mind. It was suspected of having had a hand in the Zulu rising which broke out in Natal in 1907 and which was put down only after many whites and thousands of natives had lost their lives. Shortly afterward the authorities outlawed the Ethiopian Church and forbade Afro-American preachers to enter South Africa, but the movement, though legally suppressed, lived surreptitiously on and appeared in new quarters.

In 1915 a peculiarly fanatical form of Ethiopianism broke out in Nyassaland. Its leader was a certain John Chilembwe, an Ethiopian preacher who had been educated in the United States. His propaganda was bitterly anti-white, asserting that Africa belonged to the black man, that the white man was an intruder, and that he ought to be killed off until he grew discouraged and abandoned the country. Chilembwe plotted a rising all over Nyassaland, the killing of the white men, and the carrying off of the white women. In January, 1915, the rising took place. Some plantations were sacked and several whites killed, their heads being carried to Chilembwe's "church," where a thanksgiving service for victory was held. The whites, however, acted with great vigor, the poorly armed insurgents were quickly scattered, and John Chilembwe himself was soon hunted down and killed. In itself, the incident was of slight importance, but, taken in connection with much else, it does not augur well for the future. (For details, see The Annual Register for 1915 and 1916.)

An interesting indication of the growing sense of negro race-solidarity was the "Pan-African Congress" held at Paris early in 1919. Here delegates from black communities throughout the world gathered to discuss matters of common interest. Most of the delegates were from Africa and the Americas, but one delegate from New Guinea was also present, thus representing the Australasian branch of the black race. The Congress was not largely attended and was of a some what provisional character but arrangements for the holding of subsequent congresses were made.

Here, then, is the African problem's present status: To begin with, we have a rapidly growing black population, increasingly restive under white tutelage and continually excited by Pan-Islamic propaganda with the further complication of another anti-white propaganda spread by negro radicals from America.

The African situation is thus somewhat analogous to conditions in Asia. But the analogy must not be pressed too far. In Asia white hegemony rests solely on political bases, while the Asiatics themselves, browns and yellows alike, display constructive power and possess civilizations built up by their own efforts from the remote past. The Asiatics are to-day once more displaying their innate capacity by not merely adopting, but adapting, white ideas and methods. We behold an Asiatic renaissance, whose genuineness is best attested by the fact that there have been similar movements in past times.

None of this applies to Africa. The black race has never shown real constructive power. It has never built up a native civilization. Such progress as certain negro groups have made has been due to external pressure and has never long outlived that pressure's removal, for the negro, when left to himself, as in Haiti and Liberia, rapidly reverts to his ancestral ways. The negro is a facile, even eager, imitator; but there he stops. He adopts; but he does not adapt, assimilate, and give forth creatively again.

The whole of history testifies to this truth. As the Englishman Meredith Townsend says: "None of the black races, whether negro or Australian, have shown within the historic time the capacity to develop civilization. They have never passed the boundaries of their

72

own habitats as conquerors, and never exercised the smallest influence over peoples not black. They have never founded a stone city, have never built a ship, have never produced a literature, have never suggested a creed.... There seams to be no reason for this except race. It is said that the negro has been buried in the most 'massive' of the four continents, and has been, so to speak, lost to humanity; but he was always on the Nile, the immediate road to the Mediterranean, and in West and East Africa he was on the sea. Africa is probably more fertile, and almost certainly richer than Asia, and is pierced by rivers as mighty, and some of them at least as navigable. What could a singularly healthy race, armed with a constitution which resists the sun and defies malaria, wish for better than to be seated on the Nile, or the Congo, or the Niger, in numbers amply sufficient to execute any needed work, from the cutting of forests and the making of roads up to the building of cities? How was the negro more secluded than the Peruvian; or why was he 'shut up' worse than the Tartar of Samarcand, who one day shook himself, gave up all tribal feuds, and, from the Sea of Okhotsk to the Baltic and southward to the Nerbudda, mastered the world? . . . The negro went by himself far beyond the Australian savage. He learned the use of fire, the fact that sown grain will grow, the value of shelter, the use of the bow and the canoe, and the good of clothes; but there to all appearances he stopped, unable, until stimulated by another race like the Arab, to advance another step." (Townsend, op. cit. pp. 92, 356-8.)

Unless, then, every lesson of history is to be disregarded, we must conclude that black Africa is unable to stand alone. The black man's numbers may increase prodigiously and acquire alien veneers, but the black man's nature will not change. Black unrest may grow and cause much trouble. Nevertheless, the white man must stand fast in Africa. No black "renaissance " impends, and Africa, if abandoned by the whites, would merely fall beneath the onset of the browns. And that would be a great calamity. As stated in the preceding chapter, the brown peoples, of themselves, do not directly menace white race-areas, while Pan-Islamism is at present an essentially defensive movement. But Islam is militant by nature, and the Arab is a restless and warlike breed. Pan-Islamism once possessed of the Dark Continent and fired by militant zealots, might forge black Africa into a sword of wrath, the executor of sinister adventures.

Fortunately the white man has every reason for keeping a firm hold on Africa. Not only are its central tropics prime sources of raw materials and foodstuffs which white direction can alone develop, but to north and south the white man has struck deep roots into the soil. Both extremities of the continent are "white man's country," where strong white peoples should ultimately arise. Two of the chief white Powers, Britain and France, are pledged to the hilt in this racial task and will spare no effort to safeguard the heritage of their pioneering children. Brown influence in Africa is strong, but it is supreme only in the northeast and its line of communication with the Asiatic homeland runs over the narrow neck of Suez. Should stern necessity arise, the white world could hold Suez against Asiatic assault and crush brown resistance in Africa.

In short, the real danger to white control of Africa lies, not in brown attack or black revolt, but in possible white weakness through chronic discord within the white world itself. And that subject must be reserved for later chapters.

CHAPTER V
RED MAN'S LAND

RED MAN'S LAND is the Americas between the Rio Grande and the tropic of Capricorn. Here dwells the "Amerindian" race. At the time of Columbus the whole western hemisphere was theirs, but the white man has extirpated or absorbed them to north and south, so that to-day the United States and Canada in North America and the southern portions of South America are genuine "white man's country." In the intermediate zone above mentioned, however, the Amerindian has survived and forms the majority of the population, albeit considerably mixed with white and to a lesser degree with negro blood. The total number of "Indians," including both full-bloods and mixed types, is about 40,000,000 - more than two-thirds of the whole population. In addition, there are several million negroes and mulattoes, mostly in Brazil. The white population of the intermediate zone, even if we include "near-whites," does not average more than 10 per cent, though it varies greatly with different regions. The reader should remember that neither the West India Islands nor the southern portion of the South American continent are included in this gener- alization. In the West Indies the Amerindian has com- pletely died out and has been replaced by the negro, while southern South America, especially Argentina and Uruguay, are genuine white man's country in which there is little Indian and no negro blood. Despite these exceptions, however, the fact remains that, taken as a whole, "Latin America," the vast land-block from the Rio Grande to Cape Horn, is racially not "Latin" but Amerindian or negroid, with a thin Spanish or Portuguese veneer. In other words, though commonly considered part of the white world, most of Latin America is ethnically colored man's land, which has been growing more colored for the past hundred years.

Latin America's evolution was predetermined by the Spanish

Conquest. That very word "conquest" tells the story. The United States was settled by colonists planning homes and bringing their women. It was thus a genuine migration, and resulted in a full transplanting of white stock to new soil. The Indians encountered were wild nomads, fierce of temper and few in number. After sharp conflicts they were extirpated, leaving virtually no ethnic traces behind. The colonization of Latin America was the exact antithesis. The Spanish Conquistadores were bold warriors descending upon vast regions inhabited by relatively dense populations, some of which, as in Mexico and Peru, had attained a certain degree of civilization. The Spaniards, invincible in their shining armor, paralyzed with terror the people still dwelling in the age of bronze and polished stone. With ridiculous ease mere handfuls of whites overthrew empires and forded it like gods over servile and adoring multitudes. Cortez marched on Mexico with less than 600 followers, while Pizarro had but 310 companions when he started his conquest of Peru. Of course the fabulous treasures amassed in these exploits drew swarms of bold adventurers from Spain. Nevertheless, their numbers were always infinitesimal compared with the vastness of the quarry, while the proportion of women immigrants continued to lag far behind that of the men. The breeding of pure whites in Latin America was thus both scanty and slow.

On the other hand, the breeding of mixed-bloods began at once and attained notable proportions. Having slaughtered the Indian males or brigaded them in slave-gangs, the Conquistadores took the Indian women to themselves. The humblest man-at-arms had several female attendants, while the leaders became veritable pashas with great harems of concubines. The result was a prodigious output of half breed children, known as "mestizos" or "cholos."

And soon a new ethnic complication was added. The Indians having developed a melancholy trick of dying off under slavery, the Spaniards imported African negroes to fill the servile ranks, and since they took negresses as well as Indian women for concubines, other half-breeds - mulattoes - appeared. Here and there Indians

76

and negroes mated on their own account, the offspring being known as "zambos." In time these various hybrids bred among themselves, producing the most extraordinary ethnic combinations. As Garcia-Calderon well puts it: "Grotesque generations with every shade of complexion and every conformation of skull were born in America - a crucible continually agitated by unheard-of fusions of races.... But there was little Latin blood to be found in the homes formed by the sensuality of the first conquerors of a desolated America." (F. Garcia-Calderon, "Latin America: Its Rise and Progress," p. 49 (English translation, London, 1913).)

To be sure, this mongrel population long remained politically negligible. The Spaniards regarded themselves as a master-caste, and excluded all save pure whites from civic rights and social privileges. In fact, the European-born Spaniards refused to recognize even their colonial-born kinsmen as their equals, and "Creoles" (Although loose usage has since obscured its true meaning, the term "Creole" has to do, not with race, but with birthplace. "Creole" originally meant "one born in the colonies." Down to the nineteenth century, this was perfectly clear. Whites were "Creole" or "European"; negroes were "Creole" or "African.") could not aspire to the higher distinctions or offices. This attitude was largely inspired by the desire to maintain a lucrative monopoly. Yet the European's sense of superiority had some valid grounds. There can be no doubt that the Creole whites, as a class, showed increasing signs of degeneracy. Climate was a prime cause in the hotter regions, but there were many plateau areas, as in Colombia, Mexico, and Peru, which though geographically in the tropics had a temperate climate from their elevation.

Even more than by climate the Creole was injured by contact with the colored races. Pampered and corrupted from birth by obsequious slaves, the Creole usually led an idle and vapid existence, disdaining work as servile and debarred from higher callings by his European-born superiors. As time passed, the degeneracy due to climate and custom was intensified by degeneracy of blood. Despite legal enactment and social taboo, colored strains percolated insidiously into the creole stock. The leading families, by elaborate precautions, might succeed in keeping their escutcheons clean, but humbler circles darkened significantly despite fervid protestations of "pure-white" blood. Still, so long as Spain kept her hold on Latin America, the process of miscegenation, socially considered, was a slow one. The whole social system was based on the idea of white superiority, and the colors were carefully graded. "In America," wrote Humboldt toward the close of Spanish rule, " the more or less white skin determines the position which a man holds in society."

The revolution against Spain had momentous consequences for the racial future of Latin America. In the beginning, to be sure, it was a white civil war - a revolt of the Creoles against European oppression and discrimination. The heroes of the revolution - Bolivar, Miranda, San Martin, and the rest - were aristocrats of pure-white blood. But the revolution presently developed new features. To begin with, the struggle was very long. Commencing in 1809, it lasted almost twenty years. The whites were decimated by fratricidal fury and when the Spanish cause was finally lost, multitudes of loyalists mainly of the superior social classes left the country. Meanwhile, the half-castes, who had rallied wholesale to the revolutionary banner, were demanding their reward. The Creoles wished to close the revolutionary cycle and establish a new society based, like the old, upon white supremacy, with themselves substituted for the Spaniards. Bolivar planned a limited monarchy and a white electoral oligarchy. But this was far from suiting the half-castes. For them the revolution had just begun. Raising the cry of "democracy," then become fashionable through the North American and French revolutions, they proclaimed the doctrine of "equality" regardless of skin. Disillusioned and full of foreboding, Bolivar, the master-spirit of the revolution, disappeared from the scene, and his lieutenants, like the generals of Alexander, quarrelled among themselves, split Latin America into jarring fragments, and waged a long series of internecine wars. The flood-gates of anarchy were opened, the result being a steady weakening of the whites and a corresponding rise of the half-castes in the political and social scale. Everywhere ambitious soldiers led the mongrel mob against the white aristocracy, breaking its power and making themselves dictators. These "caudillos" were apostles of equality and miscegenation. Says Garcia-Calderon: "Tyrants found democracies; they lean on the support of the people, the half-breeds and negroes, against the oligarchies; they dominate the colonial nobility, favor the crossing of races, and free the slaves." (Garcia-Calderon, p. 50.)

The consequences of all this were lamentable in the extreme. Latin America's level of civilization fell far below that of colonial days. Spanish rule, though narrow and tyrannical, had maintained peace and social stability. Now all was a hideous chaos wherein frenzied castes and colors grappled to the death. Ignorant mestizos and brutal negroes trampled the fine flowers of culture under foot, while as by a malignant inverse selection the most intelligent and the most cultivated perished.

These deplorable conditions prevailed in Latin America until well past the middle of the nineteenth century. Of course, here as elsewhere, anarchy engendered tyranny, and strong caudillos sometimes perpetuated their dictatorship for decades, as in Paraguay under Doctor Francia and in Mexico under Porfirio Diaz. However, these were mere interludes, of no constructive import. Always the aging lion lost his grip, the lurking hyenas of anarchy downed him at Iast, and the land sank once more into revolutionary chaos. Some parts of Latin America did, indeed, definitely emerge into the light of stable progress. But those favored regions owed their deliverance, not to dictatorship, but to race. One of two factors always operated: either (1) an efficient white oligarchy; or (2) Aryanization through wholesale European immigration.

Stabilization through oligarchy is best illustrated by Chile. Chilean history differs widely from that of the rest of Latin America. A land of cool climate, no gold, and warlike Araucanian Indians, Chile attracted the pioneering settler rather than the swashbuckling seeker of treasure-trove. Now the pioneering types in Spain come mainly from those northern provinces which have retained considerable Nordic blood. The Chilean colonists were thus largely blond Asturians or austere, reasonable Basques, seeking homes and bringing their women. Of course there was crossing with the natives, but the fierce Araucanian aborigines clung to their wild freedom and kept up an interminable frontier warfare in which the occasions for race-mixture were relatively few. The country was thus settled by a resident squirearchy of an almost English type. This ruling gentry jealously guarded its racial integrity. In fact, it possessed not merely a white but a Nordic race-consciousness. The Chilean gentry called themselves sons of the Visigoths, scions of Euric and Pelayo, who had found in remote Araucania a chance to slake their racial thirst for fighting and freedom.

In Chile, as elsewhere, the revolution provoked a cycle of disorder. But the cycle was short, and was more a political struggle between white factions than a social welter of caste and race. Furthermore, Chile was receiving fresh accessions of Nordic blood. Many English, Scotch, and Irish gentleman-adventurers, taking part in the War of Independence, settled down in a land so reminiscent of their own. Germans also came in considerable numbers, settling especially in the colder south. Thus the Chilean upper classes, always pure white, became steadily more Nordic in ethnic character. The political and social results were unmistakable. Chile rapidly evolved a stable society, essentially oligarchic and consciously patterned on aristocratic England. Efficient, practical, and extremely patriotic, the Chilean oligarchs made their country at once the most stable and the most dynamic factor in Latin America.

The distinctly "Northern" character of Chile and the Chileans strike foreign observers. Here, for example, are the impressions of a recent visitor, the North American sociologist, Professor E. A. Ross. Landing at the port of Valparaiso, he is "struck by signs of English influence. On the commercial streets every third man suggests the Briton, while a large proportion of the business people look as if they have their daily tub. The cleanliness of the streets, the freshness of the parks and squares, the dressing of the shop-windows, and the style of the mounted police remind one of

England." (Edward Alsworth Rose, "South of Panama," pp. 97-98 (New York, 1914) 'Ross, p. 109.) As to the Nordic affinities of the upper classes: "One sees it in stature, eye color, and ruddy complexion.... Among the pupils of Santiago College there are as many blonds as brunets."2 Even among the peon or "roto" class, despite considerable Indian crossing, Professor Ross noted the strong Nordic strain, for he met Chilean peasants "whose stature, broad shoulders, big faces, and tawny mustaches pro-claimed them as genuine Norsemen as the Icelanders in our Red River Valley." (Ross, p. 109.)

Chile is thus the prime example of social stability and progress attained through white oligarchic rule. Other, though less successful, instances are to be noted in Peru, Colombia, and Costa Rica. Peru and Colombia, though geographically within the tropics, have extensive temperate plateaux. Here numerous whites settled during the colonial period, forming an upper caste over a large Indian population. Unlike Chile, few Nordics came to leaven society with those qualities of constructive genius and racial self-respect which are the special birthright of Nordic man. Unlike Chile again, not only were there dense Indian masses, but there was also an appreciable negro element. Lastly, the number of mixed-bloods was very Large. It is thus not surprising that for both Peru and Colombia the revolution ushered in a period of turmoil from which neither have even yet emerged. The whites have consistently fought among themselves, invoking the half-castes as auxiliaries and using Indians and negroes as their pawns. The whites are still the dominant element, but only the first families retain their pure blood, and miscegenation creeps upward with every successive generation. As for Costa Rica, it is a tiny bit of cool hill-country, settled by whites in colonial times, and to-day rises an oasis of civilization, above the tropic jungle of degenerate, mongrel Central America.

The second method of social stabilization in Latin America - Aryanization through wholesale European immigration - is exemplified by Argentina and Uruguay. Neither of these lands had very promising beginnings. Their populations, at the revolution, contained strong Indian infusions and traces of negro blood, while after the revolution both fell under the sway of tyrannical dictators who persecuted the white aristocrats and favored miscegenation. However, Argentina and Uruguay possessed two notable advantages: they were climatically white man's country, and they at first contained a very small population. Since they produced neither gold nor tropical luxuries, Spain had neglected them, so that at the revolution they consisted of little more than the port-towns of Buenos Aires and Montevideo with a few dependent river-settlements. Their vast hinterlands of fertile prairie then harbored only wandering tribes of nomad savages.

During the last half of the nineteenth century, however, the development of ocean transport gave these antipodean prairies value as stock-raising and grain-growing sources for congested Europe, and Europe promptly sent immigrants to supply her needs. This immigrant stream gradually swelled to a veritable deluge. The human tide was, on the whole, of sound stock, mostly Spaniards and north Italians, with some Nordic elements from northern Europe in the upper strata. Thus Europe locked antipodean America securely to the white world. As for the colonial stock, it merged easily into the newer, kindred flood. Here and there signs of former miscegenation still show, the Argentino being sometimes, as Madison Grant well puts it, "suspiciously swarthy." (Madison Grant, "The Passing of the Great Race," p. 78. (2d edition, New York, 1918.)) Nevertheless, these are but vestigial traces which the ceaseless European inflow will ultimately eradicate. The large impending German immigration to Argentina and Uruguay should bring valuable Nordic elements.

This same tide of European immigration has likewise pretty well Aryanized the southern provinces of Brazil, adjacent to the Uruguayan border. Those provinces were neglected by Portugal as Argentina and Uruguay were by Spain, and half a century ago they had a very sparse population. To-day they support millions of European immigrants, mostly Italians and European Portuguese, but with the further addition of nearly half a million Germans.

Brazil is, in fact, evolving into two racially distinct communities. The southern provinces are white man's country, with little Indian or negro blood, and with a distinct "color line." The tropical north is saturated with Indian and negro strains, and the whites are rapidly disappearing in a universal mongrelization. Ultimately this must produce momentous political consequences.

Bearing in mind the exceptions above noted, let us now observe the vast tropical and semi-tropical bulk of Latin America. Here we find notable changes since colonial days. White predominance is substantially a thing of the past. Persons of unmixed Spanish or Portuguese descent are relatively few, most of the so-called "whites" being really near-whites, more or less deeply tinged with colored bloods. It is a striking token of white race-prestige that these near-whites, despite their degeneracy and inefficiency, are yet the dominant element; occupying, in fact, much the same status as the aristocratic Creoles immediately after the War of Independence. Nevertheless, the near-whites' supremacy is now threatened. Every decade of chronic anarchy favors the darker halfbreeds, while below these, in turn, the Indian and negro full-bloods are beginning to stir, as in Mexico to-day.

Most informed observers agree that the mixed-bloods of Latin America are distinctly inferior to the whites. This applies to both mestizos and mulattoes, albeit the mestizo (the cross between white and Indian) seems less inferior than the mulatto-the cross between white and black. As for the zambo, the Indian-negro cross, everybody is agreed that it is a very bad one. Analyses of these hybrid stocks show remarkable similarities to the mongrel chaos of the declining Roman Empire. Here is the judgment of Garcia-Calderon, a Peruvian scholar and generally considered the most authoritative writer on Latin America. "The racial question," he writes, "is a very serious problem in American history. It explains the progress of certain peoples and the decadence of others, and it is the key to the incurable disorder which divides America. Upon it depend a great number of secondary phenomena; the public wealth, the industrial system, the stability of governments, the solidity of patriotism.... This complication of castes, this admixture of diverse bloods, has created many problems. For example, is the formation of a national consciousness possible with such disparate elements? Would such heterogeneous democracies be able to resist the invasion of superior races? Finally, is the South American half-caste absolutely incapable of organization and culture?" (Garcia-Calderon, pp. 351-2.)

While qualifying his answers to these queries, Garcia-Calderon yet deplores the half-caste's "decadence." (Ibid., p. 287.) "In the Iberian democracies," he says, "an inferior Latinity, a Latinity of the decadence, prevails; verbal abundance, inflated rhetoric, oratorical exaggeration, just as in Roman Spain.... The half-caste loves grace, verbal elegance, quibbles even, and artistic form; great passions and desires do not move him. In religion he is sceptical, indifferent, and in politics he disputes in the Byzantine manner. No one could discover in him a trace of his Spanish forefather, stoical and adventurous." (Ibid., p. 360.)

Garcia-Calderon therefore concludes: "The mixture of rival castes, Iberians, Indians, and negroes, has generally had disastrous consequences.... None of the conditions established by the French psychologists are realized by the Latin American democracies, and their populations are therefore degenerate. The lower castes struggle successfully against the traditional rules: the order which formerly existed is followed by moral anarchy; solid conviction by a superficial scepticism; and the Castilian tenacity by indecision. The black race is doing its work, and the continent is returning to its primitive barbarism." (Garcia-Calderon, pp. 361-2.) This melancholy fate can, according to Garcia-Calderon, be averted only by wholesale white immigration: "In South America civilization is dependent upon the numerical predominance of the victorious Spaniard, on the triumph of the white man over the mulatto, the negro, and the Indian. Only a plentiful European immigration can re-establish the shattered equilibrium of the American races." (Ibid., p. 362.)

Garcia-Calderon's pronouncements are echoed by foreign observers.

During his South American travels Professor Ross noted the same melancholy symptoms and pointed out the same unique remedy. Speaking of Ecuador, he says: "I found no foreigners who have faith in the future of this people. They point out that while this was a Spanish colony there was a continual flow of immigrants from Spain, many of whom, no doubt, were men of force. Political separation interrupted this current, and since then the country has really gone back. Spain had provided a ruling, organizing element, and, with the cessation of the flow of Spaniards, the mixed-bloods took charge of things, for the pure-white element is so small as to be negligible. No one suggests that the mestizos equal the white stock either in intellect or in character.... Among the rougher foreigners and Peruvians the pet name for these people is 'monkeys.' The thoughtful often liken them to Eurasians, clever enough, but lacking in solidity of character. Natives and foreigners alike declare that a large white immigration is the only hope for Ecuador." (Ross, "South of Panama," pp. 29-30.)

Concerning Bolivia, Professor Ross writes: "The wisest sociologist in Bolivia told me that the zambo, resulting from the union of Indian with negro, is inferior to both the parent races, and that likewise the mestizo is inferior to both white and Indian in physical strength, resistance to disease, longevity, and brains. The failure of the South American republics has been due, he declares, to mestizo domination. Through the colonial period there was a flow of Spaniards to the colonies, and all the offices down to corregidor and cura were filled by white men. With independence, the whites ceased coming, and the lower offices of state and church were filled with mestizos. Then, too, the first crossing of white with Indian gave a better result than the union between mestizos, so that the stock has undergone progressive degeneration. The only thing, then, that can make these countries progress is a large white immigration, something much talked about by statesmen in all these countries, but which has never materialized." (Ross, p. 41.)

These judgments refer particularly to Spanish America. Regarding Portuguese Brazil, however, the verdict seems to be the same. Many years ago Professor Agassiz wrote: "Let any one who doubts the evil of this mixture of races, and is inclined from mistaken philanthropy to break down all barriers between them, come to Brazil. He cannot deny the deterioration consequent upon the amalgamation of races, more widespread here than in any country in the world, and which is rapidly effacing the best qualities of the white man, the negro, and the Indian, leaving a mongrel, nondescript type, deficient in physical and mental energy." (A. P. Schultz, Race or Mongrel," p. 155 (Boston, 1908).)

The mongrel's political ascendancy produces precisely the results which might have been expected. These unhappy beings, every cell of whose bodies is a battle-ground of jarring heredities, express their souls in acts of hectic violence and aimless instability. The normal state of tropical America is anarchy, restrained only by domestic tyrants or foreign masters. Garcia-Calderon exactly describes its psychology when he writes: "Precocious, sensual, impressionable, the Americans of these vast territories devote their energies to local politics. Industry, commerce, and agriculture are in a state of decay, and the unruly imagination of the Creole expends itself in constitutions, programmes, and lyrical disoourses; in these regions anarchy is sovereign mistress." (Garcia-Calderon, p. 222.) The tropical republics display, indeed, a tendency toward "atomic disintegration.... Given to dreaming, they are led by presidents suffering from neurosis." (Ibid., p. 336.)

The stock feature of the mongrel tropics is, of course, the "revolution." These senseless and perennial outbursts are often ridiculed in the United States as comic opera, but the grim truth of the matter is that few Latin American revolutions are laughing matters. The numbers of men engaged may not be very large according to our standards, but measured by the scanty populations of the countries concerned, they lay a heavy blood-tax on the suffering peoples. The tatter-demalion "armies" may excite our mirth, but the battles are real enough, often fought out to the death with razor-edged machetes and rusty bayonets, and there is no more ghastly sight than a Latin American battle-field. The commandeerings, burnings, rapings, and assassinations inflicted upon the hapless civilian population cry to heaven. There is always wholesale destruction of property, frequently appalling loss of life, and a general paralysis of economic and social activity. These wretched lands have now been scourged by the revolutionary plague for a hundred years, and W. B. Hale does not overstate the consequences when he says: "Most of the countries clustering about the Caribbean have sunk into deeper and deeper mires of misrule, unmatched for profligacy and violence anywhere on earth. Revolution follows revolution; one band of brigands succeeds another; atrocities revenge atrocities; the plundered people grow more and more abject in poverty and slavishness; vast natural resources lie neglected, while populations decrease, civilization recedes, and the jungle advances." (W. B. Hale, "Our Danger in Central America," World's Work, August, 1912.) Of course, under these frightful circumstances, the national character, weak enough at best, degenerates at an ever-quickening pace. Peaceful effort of any sort appears vain and ridiculous, and men are taught that wealth is procurable only by violence and extortion.

Another important point should be noted. I have said that Latin American anarchy was restrained by dictatorship. But the reader must not infer that dictatorships are halcyon times for the dictated. On the contrary, they are usually only a trifle less wretched and demoralizing than times of revolution. The "caudillos" are nearly always very sinister figures. Often they are ignorant brutes; oftener they are bloodthirsty, lecherous monsters; oftenest they are human spiders who suck the land dry of all fluid wealth, banking it abroad against the day when they shall fly before the revolutionary blast to the safe haven of Paris and the congenial debaucheries of Montmartre. The millions amassed by tyrants like Castro of Venezuela and Zelaya of Nicaragua are almost beyond belief, considering the backward, bankrupt lands they have "administered."

Yet how can it be otherwise? Consider Critchfield's incisive account of a caudillo's accession to power: "When an ignorant and brutal

87

man, whose entire knowledge of the world is confined to a few Indian villages, and whose total experience has been gained in the raising of cattle, doffs his alpagartes, and, machete in hand, cuts his way to power in a few weeks, with a savage horde at his back who know nothing of the amenities of civilization and care less than they know - when such a man comes to power, evil and evil only can result. Even if the new dictator were well-intentioned, his entire ignorance of law and constitutional forms, of commercial processes and manufacturing arts, and of the fundamental and necessary principles underlying all stable and free governments, would render a successful administration by him extremely difficult, if not impossible. But he is surrounded by all the elements of vice and flattery, and he is imbued with that vain and absurd egotism which makes men of small caliber imagine themselves to be Napoleons or Caesars. Thus do petty despotisms, unrestrained by constitutional provisions or by anything like a virile public opinion, lead from absurdity to outrage and crime." (G. W. Critchfield, "American Supremacy," vol. 1, p. 277 (New York, 1908).)

Such is the situation in mongrel-ruled America: revolution breeding revolution, tyranny breeding tyranny, and the twain combining to ruin their victims and force them ever deeper into the slough of degenerate barbarism. The whites have lost their grip and are rapidly disappearing. The mixed-breeds have had their chance and have grotesquely failed. The oft quoted panacea - white immigration - is under present conditions a vain dream, for white immigrants will not expose themselves (and still less their women) to the horrors of mongrel rule. So far, then, as internal factors are concerned, anarchy seems destined to continue unchecked.

In fact, new conflicts loom on the horizon. The lndian masses, so docile to the genuine white man, begin to stir. The aureole of white prestige has been besmirched by the near-whites and half-castes who have traded so recklessly upon its sanctions. Strong in the poise of normal heredity, the Indian full-blood commences to despise these chaotic masters who turn his homelands into bear-gardens and witches' sabbaths. An "Indianista" movement is to-day on foot throughout mongrel-ruled America. It is most pronounced in Mexico, whose interminable agony becomes more and more a war of Indian resurgence, but it is also starting along the west coast of South America. Long ago, wise old Professor Pearson saw how the wind was blowing. Noting how whites and near-whites were "everywhere fighting and intriguing for the spoils of office," he also noted that the Indian masses, though relatively passive and "seemingly unobservant," were yet "conquering a place for themselves in other ways than by increasing and multiplying," and he concluded: "the general level of the autochthonous race is being raised; it is acquiring riches and self-respect, and must sooner or later get the country back into its hands." (Pearson, op. cit., p. 60.)

Recent visitors to the South American west coast note the signs of Indian unrest. Some years ago Lord Bryce remarked of Bolivia: "There have been Indian risings, and firearms are more largely in their hands than formerly. They so preponderate in numbers that any movement which united them against the upper class might, could they find a leader, have serious conse- quences." (James Bryce, "South America," p. 181 (London, 1912).) Still more recently Professor Ross wrote concerning Peru: "In Cuzco I met a gentleman of education and travel who is said to be the only living lineal descendant of the Incas. He has great influence with the native element and voices their bitterness and their aspirations. He declares that the politics of Peru is a struggle between the Spanish mestizos of Lima and the coast and the natives of Cuzco and the interior, and predicts an uprising unless Cuzco is made the capital of the nation. He even dreams of a Kechua republic, with Cuzco as its capital and the United States its guarantor, as she is guarantor of the Cuban republic." (Ross, op. cit., p. 74.) And of Bolivia, Professor Ross writes: "Lately there has been a general movement of the Bolivian Indians for the recovery of the lands of which they have been robbed piecemeal. Conflicts have broken out and, although the government has punished the ringleaders, there is a feeling that, so long as the exploiting of the Indian goes on, Bolivians are living 'in the crater of a slumbering volcano.'" (Ross , p. 89.)

Since the white man has gone and the Indian is preparing to wrest the sceptre of authority from the mongrel's worthless hands, let us examine this Indian race, to see what potentiality it possesses of restoring order and initiating progress.

To begin with, there can be no doubt that the Indian is superior to the negro. The negro, even when quickened by foreign influences, never built up anything approaching a real civilization; whereas the Indian, though entirely sundered from the rest of mankind, evolved genuine polities and cultures like the Aztec of Mexico, the Inca of Peru, and the Maya of Yucatan. The Indian thus possesses creative capacity to an appreciable degree. However, that degree seems strictly limited. The researches of archaeologists have sadly discounted the glowing tales of the Conquistadores, and the "Empires" of Mexico and Peru, though far from contemptible, certainly rank well below the achievements of European and Asiatic races in mediaeval and even in classic times.

The Indian possesses notable stability and poise, but the very intensity of these qualities fetters his progress and renders questionable his ability to rise to the modern plane. His conservatism is immense. With incredible tenacity he clings to his ancestral ways and exhibits a dull indifference to alien innovation. Of course the Indian sub-races differ considerably among themselves, but the same fundamental tendencies are visible in all of them. Says Professor Ellsworth Huntington: "The Indians are very backward. They are dull of mind and slow to adopt new ideas. Perhaps in the future they will change, but the fact that they have been influenced so little by four hundred years of contact with the white man does not afford much ground for hope. Judging from the past, there is no reason to think that their character is likely to change for many generations. . .

Those who dwell permanently in the white man's cities are influenced somewhat, but here as in other cases the general tendency seems to be to revert to the original condition as soon as the special impetus of immediate contact with the white man is removed." (Ellsworth Huntington, "The Adaptability of the White

Man to Tropical America," Journal of Race Development, October, 1914.) And Lord Bryce writes in similar vein: " With plenty of stability, they lack initiative. They make steady soldiers, and fight well under white or mestizo leaders, but one seldom hears of a pure Indian accomplishing anything or rising either through war or politics, or in any profession, above the level of his class...." (Bryce, op. cit., p. 184.)

The truth about the Indian seems to be substantially this: Left alone, he would probably have continued to progress, albeit much more slowly than either white or Asiatic peoples. But the Indian was not left alone. On the contrary, he was suddenly felled by brutal and fanatical conquerors, who uprooted his native culture and plunged him into abject servitude. The Indian's spiritual past was shorn away and his evolution was perverted. Prevented from developing along his own lines, and constitutionally incapable of adapting himself to the ways of his Spanish conquerors, the Indian vegetated, learning nothing and forgetting much that he knew. This has continued for four hundred years. Is it not likely that his ancestral aptitudes have atrophied or decayed? Slavery and mental sloth have indeed scarred him with their fell stigmata. Says Garcia-Calderon: "Without sufficient food, without hygiene, a distracted and laborious beast, he decays and perishes; to forget the misery of his daily lot he drinks, becomes an alcoholic, and his numerous progeny present the characteristics of degeneracy." (Garcia-Calderon, p. 354.)

Furthermore, the Indian degenerates from another cause - mongrelization. Miscegenation is a dual process. It works upward and downward at one and the same time. In Latin America hybridization has been prodigious, the hybrids to-day numbering millions. In some regions, as in Venezuela and parts of Central America, there are very few full-blooded Indians left, hybrids forming practically the entire population. Now, on the whole, the white or "mestizo" crossing seems hurtful to the Indian, for what he gains in intelligence he more than loses in character. But the mestizo crossing is not the worst. There is another, much graver, racial danger. The hot coastlands swarm with negroes, and the zambo or negro-Indian is universally adjudged the worst of matings. Thus, for the Indian, white blood appears harmful, while black blood is absolutely fatal. Yet the mongrelizing tide sweeps steadily on. The Indian draws no "color Iine," and continually impairs the purity of his blood and the poise of his heredity.

Bearing all the above facts in mind, can we believe the Indian capable of drawing mongrel-ruled America from its slough of despond ? Can he set it on the path of orderly progress? It does not seem possible. Assuming for the sake of argument complete freedom from foreign intervention, the Indian might in time displace his mongrel rulers - provided he himself were not also mongrelized. But the present "Indianista" movement is not a sign of Indian political efficiency; not the harbinger of an Indian "renaissance." It is the instinctive fuming of the harried beast on his tormentor. Maddened by the cruel vagaries of mongrel rule and increasingly conscious of the mongrel's innate worthlessness, the Indian at last bares his teeth. Under civilized white tutelage the "Indianista" movement would have been practically inconceivable.

However, guesses as to the final outcome of an Indian-mongrel conflict are academic speculation, because mongrel America will not be left to itself. Mongrel America cannot stand alone. Indeed, it never has stood alone, for it has always been bolstered up by the Monroe Doctrine. But for our protection, outside forces would have long since rushed into this political and economic vacuum, and every omen to-day denotes that this vacuum, like all others, will presently be filled. A world close packed as never before will not tolerate countries that are a torment to themselves and a dangerous nuisance to their neighbors. A world half bankrupt will not allow vast sources of potential wealth to lie in hands which idle or misuse. Thus it is practically certain that mongrel America will presently pass under foreign tutelage. Exactly how, is not yet clear. It may be done by the United States alone, or, what is more probable, in "Pan-American" cooperation with the Iusty young white nations of the antipodean south. It may be done by an even larger combination, including some European states. After all, the details of such action do not lie within the scope of this book, since they fall exclusively within the white man's sphere of activity.

There is, however, another dynamic which might transform mongrel America. This dynamic is yellow Asia. The Far East teems with virile and laborious life. It thrills to novel ambitions and desires. Avid with the urge of swarming myriads, it hungrily seeks outlets for its superabundant vitality. We have already seen how the Mongolian has earmarked the whole Far East for his own, and in subsequent pages we shall see how he also beats restlessly against the white world's race-frontiers. But mongrel America! What other field offers such tempting possibilities for Mongolian race-expansion? Vast regions of incalculable, unexploited wealth, sparsely inhabited by stagnant populations cursed with anarchy and feeble from miscegenation - how could such lands resist the onslaught of tenacious and indomitable millions? The answer is self-evident. They could not resist; and such an invasion, once begun, would be consummated with a celerity and thoroughness perhaps unexampled in human history.

Now the yellow world is alive to this momentous possibility. Japan, in particular, has glimpsed in Latin America precious avenues to that racial expansion which is the key-note of Japanese foreign policy. For years Japanese statesmen and publicists have busied themselves with the problem. The Chinese had, in fact, already pointed the way, for during the later decades of the nineteenth century Chinamen frequented Latin America's Pacific coast, economically vanquishing the natives with ease, and settling in Peru in such numbers that the alarmed Peruvians hastily stopped the inflow by drastic exclusion acts. The successes of these Chinese pioneers, humble coolies entirely without official backing, have fired the Japanese imagination. The Japanese press has long discussed Latin America in optimistic vein. Count Okuma is a good exemplar of these Japanese aspirations. Some years ago he told the American sociologist Professor Ross: "South America, especially the northern part, will furnish ample room for our surplus." (Ross, p. 90.) To his fellow countrymen Count Okuma was still more specific. In 1907 he stated in the Tokio Economist that the Japanese were to overspread the earth like a cloud of locusts, alighting on the North American coasts, and swarming into Central and South America. Count Okuma expressed a strong preference for Latin American countries as fields for Japanese immigration, because most of them were "much easier to include within the sphere of influence of Japan in the future." (The American Review of Reviews, November, 1907, p. 622.)

And the Japanese have supplemented words with deeds. Especially since 1914, Japanese activity in Latin America has been ubiquitous and striking. The west coast of South America, in particular, is to-day flooded with Japanese goods, merchants, commercial missions, and financial agents seeking concessions of every kind. Our State Department has had to exercise special vigilance concerning Japanese concession-hunting in Mexico.

Japan's present activity is of course mere reconnoitering - testings and mappings of terrain for possible later action on a more extensive scale. One thing alone gives Japan pause - our veto. Japan knows that real aggression against our southern neighbors would spell war with the United States. Japan does not contemplate war with us at present. She has many fish to fry in the Far East. So in Latin America she plays safe. But she bides her time. In Latin America itself she has friends - even partisans. Japan seeks to mobilize to her profit that distrust of the "Yanqui" which permeates Latin America. The half-castes, in particular, rage at our "color line" and see in the United States the Nemesis of their anarchic misrule. They flout the Monroe Doctrine, caress dreams of Japanese aid, and welcome Nippon's pose as the champion of color throughout the world.

Japanese activities in Mexico are of especial interest. Here Japan has three strong strings to her bow:

1. patriotic dislike of the United States;

2. mestizo hatred of the white "gringo";

3. the Indianista movement.

In Mexico the past decade of revolutionary turmoil has developed into a complicated race-war of the mestizos against the white or near-white upper class and of the Indian full-bloods against both whites and mestizos. The one bond of union is dislike of the gringo, which often rises to fanatical hatred. Our war against Mexico in 1847 has never been forgotten, and many Mexicans cherish hopes of revenge and even aspire to recover the territories then ceded to us. During the early stages of the European War our military unpreparedness and apparent pacifism actually emboldened some Mexican hotheads to concoct the notorious "Plan of San Diego." The conspirators plotted to rouse the Mexican population of our southern border, sow disaffection among our Southern negroes, and explode the mine at the psychological moment by means of a "Reconquering Equitable Army" invading Texas. Our whole Southwest was to be rejoined to Mexico, while our Southern States were to form a black republic. The projected war was conceived strictly in terms of race, the reconquering equitable army to be composed solely of "Latins," negroes, and Japanese. The racial results were to be decisive, for the entire white population of both our South and Southwest was to be pitilessly massacred. Of course the plot completely miscarried, and sporadic attempts to invade Texas during 1915 were easily repulsed.

Nevertheless, this incident reveals the trend of many Mexican minds. The framers of the "Plan of San Diego" were not ignorant peons, but persons of some standing. The outrages and tortures inflicted upon numerous Americans in Mexico during recent years are further indications of that wide-spread hatred which expresses itself in vitriolic outbursts like the following editorial of a Mexican provincial paper, written during our chase after the bandit Villa in 1916: "Above all, do not forget that at a time of national need, humanity is a crime and frightfulness is a virtue. Pull out eyes, snatch out hearts, tear open breasts, drink - if you can - the blood in the skulls of the invaders from the cities of Yankeeland. In defense of liberty be a Nero, be a Caligula - that is to be a good patriot. Peace between Mexico and the United States will be closed in throes of terror and barbarism." (The newspaper was La Reforma of Saltillo. The editorial was quoted in an Associated Press despatch dated El Paso, Texas, June 26, 1916. The despatch mentions La Reforma as "a semi-official paper.")

All this is naturally grist for the Japanese mill. Especially interesting are Japanese attempts to play upon Mexican Indianista sentiment. Japanese writers point out physical and cultural similarities between the Mexican native races and themselves, deducing therefrom innate racial affinities springing from the remote and forgotten past. All possible sympathetic changes were rung during the diplomatic mission of Senor de la Barra to Japan at the beginning of 1914. His reception in Tokio was a memorable event. Senor de la Barra was greeted by cheering multitudes, and on every occasion the manifold bonds between the two peoples were emphasized. This of course occurred before the European War. During the war Japanese-Mexican relations remained amicable. So far as official evidence goes, the Japanese Government has never entered into any understandings with the Mexican Government, though some Mexicans have hinted at a secret agreement, and one Mexican writer, Gutierrez de Lara, asserts that in 1912 Francisco Madero, then President, "threw himself into the arms of Japan," and goes on: "We are well aware of the importance of this statement and of its tremendous international significance, but we make it deliberately with full confidence in our authority. Not only did Madero enlist the ardent support of the South American republics in the cause of Mexico's inviolability, but he entered into negotiations with the Japanese minister in Mexico City for a close offensive and defensive alliance with Japan to checkmate United States aggression. When during the fateful twelve days' battle in Mexico City a rumor of American intervention, more alarming than usual, was communicated to Madero, he remarked coldly that he was thoroughly anxious for that intervention, for he was confident of the surprise the American Government would receive in discovering that they had to deal with Japan." (Gutierrez de Lara,

"The Mexican People: Their Struggle for Freedom" (New York, 1914).)

But, after all, an official Japanese-Mexican understanding is not the fundamental issue. The really significant thing is Mexican popular antagonism to the United States, which is so wide-spread that Japan could in a crisis probably count on Mexican benevolent neutrality if not on Mexican support. The present Carranza government of Mexico is of course notoriously anti-American. Its consistent policy, notably revealed in its complaisance toward Germany and its intrigues with other anti-American regimes like those of Colombia and Venezuela, makes Mexico the centre of anti-Americanism in Latin America. As for the numerous Japanese residents in Mexico, they have lost no opportunity to abet this attitude. Here, for instance, is the text of a manifesto signed by prominent members of the Japanese colony during the American-Mexican crisis of 1916: "Japanese: Mexico is a friendly nation. Our commercial bonds with her are great. She is, like us, a nation of heroes who will never consent to the world-domination of a hard and brutal race, as are the Yankees. We cannot abandon Mexico in her struggle against a nation supposedly stronger. The Mexicans know how to defend themselves, but there is lacking aid which we can furnish. If the Yankees invade Mexico, if they seize the California coasts, Japanese commerce and the Japanese navy will face a grave peril. The Yankees believe us impotent because of the European War, and we will be expelled from American soil and our children from American schools. We will aid the Mexicans. We will aid Mexico against Yankee rapacity. This great and beautiful country is a victim of Yankee hatred toward Japan. Our indifference would be a lack of patriotism, since the Yankees already are against us and our divine Emperor. They have seized Hawaii, they have seized the Philippine Islands, near our coasts, and are now about to crush under foot our friend and possible ally, and injure our commerce and imperil our naval power." (The Literary Digest, September 16, 1916, p. 662.)

The fact is that Latin America's attitude toward the yellow world tends everywhere to crystallize along race lines. The half-castes, naturally hostile to the United States, see in Japan a welcome offset to the "Colossus of the North." The self-conscious Indianista elements likewise heed Japanese suggestions of ethnic affinity. On the other hand, the whites and near-whites instinctively react against Japanese advances. Even those who have no love for the Yankee see in the Mongolian the greatest of perils. Garcia-Calderon typifies this point of view. He dreads our imperialistic tendencies, yet he reproves those Latin Americans who, in a Japanese-American clash, would favor Japan. "Victorious," he writes, "the Japanese would invade Western America and convert the Pacific into a vast closed sea, closed to foreign ambitions, mare nostrum, peopled with Japanese colonies. The Japanese hegemony would not be a mere change of tutelage for the nations of America. In spite of essential differences, the Latins oversea have certain common ties with the people of the (United) States: a long-established religion, Christianity, and a coherent, European, Occidental civilization. Perhaps there is some obscure fraternity between the Japanese and the American Indians, between the yellow men of Nippon and the copper-colored Quechuas, a disciplined and sober people. But the ruling race, the dominant type of Spanish origin, which imposes the civilization of the white man upon America, is hostile to the entire invading East." (Garcia-Calderon, pp. 329-330.)

White men throughout Latin America generally echo these sentiments. Chile and Argentina repulse Oriental immigration, and the white oligarchs of Peru dread keenly Japanese designs directed so specifically against their country. Very recently a Peruvian, Doctor Jorge M. Corbacho, (Despatch to La Prensa (New York), December 13, 1919.) wrote most bitterly about the Japanese infiltration into Peru and adjacent Bolivia, while some years ago Senor Augustin Edwards, owner of the leading Chilean periodical, El Mercurio, denounced Count Okuma's menaces and called for a Pan-American rampart against Asia from Behring Strait to Cape Horn. "Japanese immigration," asserted Senor Edwards, "must be firmly opposed, not only in South America, but in the whole American continent. The same remark applies to Chinese immigration.... In short, these threats of Okuma should induce the nations of South America to adopt the Monroe Doctrine - an invincible weapon against the plans and intentions of that 'Empire of the Orient,' which has so lately risen up to new life, and already manifests so dire a greed of conquest." (The American Review of Reviews, November, 1907, p. 623.) From Central America similar voices arise. A Salvadorean writer urges political federation with the United States as the sole refuge against the "Yellow Peril," to avoid becoming "slaves and utterly insignificant";(The Literary Digest, December 30, 1911, p. 1222.) and a well-known Nicaraguan politician, Senor Moncada, (J. M. Moncada, "Social and Political Influences of the United States in Central America" (New York, 1911).) writes in similar vein.

The momentous implications of Mongolian pressure upon Latin America are admirably described by Professor Ross. "Provided that no barrier be interposed to the inflow from man-stifled Asia," he says, "it is well within the bounds of probability that by the close of this century South America will be the home of twenty or thirty millions of Orientals and descendants of Orientals.... But Asiatic immigration of such volume would change profoundly the destiny of South America. For one thing, it would forestall and frustrate that great immigration of Europeans which South American statesmen are counting on to relieve their countries from mestizo unprogressiveness and misgovernment. The white race would withhold its increase or look elsewhere for outlets; for those with the higher standard of comfort always shun competition with those of a lower standard. Again, large areas of South America might cease to be parts of Christendom. Some of the republics there might come to be as dependent upon Asiatic Powers as the Cuban republic is dependent upon the United States." (Ross, pp. 91-92.)

Very pertinent is Professor Ross's warning as to the fate of the Indian population - a warning which Indianista believers in Japanese "affinity" should seriously take to heart. Whatever might be the lot of the Latin American whites, Professor Ross points out that "an Asiatic influx would seal the doom of the Indian element in these countries.... The Indians could make no effective economic stand against the wide-awake, resourceful, and aggressive Japanese or Chinese. The Oriental immigrants could beat the Indians at every point, block every path upward, and even turn them out of most of their present employments. In great part the Indians would become a cringing sudra caste, tilling the poorer lands and confined to the menial or repulsive occupations. Filled with despair, and abandoning themselves even more than they do now to pisco and coca, they would shrivel into a numerically ncgligible element in the population." (Ross, PP. 92-93.)

Such are the underlying factors in the Latin American situation. Once more we see the essential instability of mere political phenomena. Once more we see the supreme importance of race. No conquest could have been completer than that of the Spaniards four centuries ago. The Indians were helpless as sheep before the mail-clad Conquistadores. And military conquest was succeeded by complete political domination. The Indian even lost his cultural heritage, and became a passive tool in the hands of his white masters.

But the Spaniard did not seal his title-deed with the indelible signet of race. Indian blood remained numerically predominant, and the conqueror further weakened his tenure by bringing in black blood - the most irreducible of ethnic factors. The inflow of white blood was small, and much of what did come lost itself in the dismal swamp of miscegenation. Lastly, the whites quarrelled among themselves.

The result was inevitable. The colonial whites triumphed only by aid of the half-castes, who promptly claimed their reward. A fresh struggle ensued, ending (save in the antipodean regions) in the triumph of the half-castes. But these, in turn, had called in the Indians and negroes. Furthermore, the half-castes recklessly squandered the white political heritage. So the colored full-bloods stirred in their turn, and a new movement began which, if allowed to run its natural course, might result in complete de-Aryanization. In other words, the white race has been going back, and Latin

America has been getting more Indian and negro for the past hundred years.

This cycle, however, now nears its end. Latin America will be neither red nor black. It will ultimately be either white or yellow. The Indian is patently unable to construct a progressive civilization. As for the negro, he has proved as incapable in the New World as in the Old. Everywhere his presence has spelled regression, and his one New World field of triumph-- Haiti - has resulted in an abysmal plunge to the jungle-level of Guinea and the Congo. Thus is created a political vacuum. And this vacuum unerring nature makes ready to fill.

The Latin American situation is, indeed, akin to that of Africa. Latin America, like Africa, cannot stand alone. An inexorable dilemma impends: white or yellow. The white man has been first in the field and holds the central colored zone between two strong bases, north and south, where his tenure is the unimpeachable title of race. The yellow man has to conquer every step, though he has already acquired footholds and has behind him the welling reservoirs of Asia. Nevertheless, white victory in Latin America is sure - if internecine discord does not rob the white world of its strength. In Latin America, as in Africa, therefore, the whites must stand fast - and stand together.

PART II

The Ebbing Tide of White

CHAPTER VI
THE WHITE FLOOD

The world-wide expansion of the white race during the four centuries between 1500 and 1900 is the most prodigious phenomenon in all recorded history. In my opening pages I sketched both the magnitude of this expansion and its ethnic and political implications. I there showed that the white stocks together constitute the most numerous single branch of the human species, nearly one-third of all the human souls on earth to-day being whites. I also showed that white men racially occupy four-tenths of the entire habitable land-area of the globe, while nearly nine-tenths of this area is under white political control. Such a situation is unprecedented. Never before has a race acquired such combined preponderance of numbers and dominion.

This white expansion becomes doubly interesting when we realize how sudden was its inception and how rapid its evolution. A single decade before the voyage of Columbus, he would have been a bold prophet who should have predicted this high destiny. At the close of the fifteenth century the white race was confined to western and central Europe, together with Scandinavia and the northwestern parts of European Russia. The total white race-area was then not much aver 2,000,000 square miles - barely one-tenth its area today. And in numbers the proportion was almost as unfavorable. At that moment (say, A. D. 1480) England could muster only about 2,000,000 inhabitants, the entire population of the British Isles not much exceeding 3,000,000 souls. To be sure, the continent was relatively better peopled. Still, the population of Europe in 1480 was probably not one-sixth that of 1914.

Furthermore, population had dwindled notably in the preceding one hundred and fifty years. During the fourteenth century Europe had been hideously scourged by the "Black Death" (bubonic plague), which carried off fully one-half of its inhabitants, while thereafter a series of great wars had destroyed immense numbers of people. These losses had not been repaired. Mediaeval society was a static, equilibrated affair, which did not favor rapid human multiplication. In fact, European life had been intensive and recessive ever since the fall of the Roman Empire a thousand years before. Europe's one mediaeval attempt at expansion (the Crusades) had utterly failed. In fact, far from expanding, white Europe had been continuously assailed by brown and yellow Asia. Beginning with the Huns in the last days of Rome, continuing with the Arabs, and ending with the Mongols and Ottoman Turks, Europe had undergone a millennium of Asiatic aggression; and though Europe had substantially maintained its freedom, many of its outlying marches had fallen under Asiatic domination. In 1480, for example, the Turk was marching triumphantly across southeastern Europe, embryonic Russia was a Tartar dependency, while the Moor still clung to southern Spain.

The outlook for the white race at the cIose of the fifteenth century thus seemed gloomy rather than bright. With a stationary or declining population, exposed to the assaults of powerful external foes, and racked by internal pains betokening the demise of the mediaeval order, white Europe's future appeared a far from happy one.

Suddenly, in two short years, all was changed. In 1492 Columbus discovered America, and in 1494 Vasco da Gama, doubling Africa, found the way to India. The effect of these discoveries cannot be overestimated. We can hardly conceive how our mediaeval forefathers viewed the ocean. To them the ocean was a numbing, constricting presence; the abode of darkness and horror. No wonder mediaeval Europe was static, since it faced on ruthless, aggressive Asia, and backed on nowhere. Then, in the twinkling of an eye, dead-end Europe became mistress of the ocean - and thereby mistress of the world.

No such strategical opportunity had, in fact, ever been vouchsafed. From classic times down to the end of the fifteenth century, white Europe had confronted only the most martial and enterprising of Asiatics. With such peoples war and trade had alike to be conducted on practically equal terms, and by frontal assault no decisive victory could be won. But, after the great discoveries, the white man could flank his old opponents. Whole new worlds peopled by primitive races were unmasked, where the white man's weapons made victory certain, and whence he could draw stores of wealth to quicken his home life and initiate a progress that would soon place him immeasurably above his once-dreaded assailants.

And the white man proved worthy of his opportunity. His inherent racial aptitudes had been stimulated by his past. The hard conditions of mediaeval life had disciplined him to adversity and had weeded him by natural selection. The hammer of Asiatic invasion, clanging for a thousand years on the brown-yellow anvil, had tempered the iron of Europe into the finest steel. The white man could think, could create, could fight superlatively well. No wonder that redskins and negroes feared and adored him as a god, while the somnolent races of the Farther East, stunned by this strange apparition rising from the pathless ocean, offered no effective opposition.

Thus began the swarming of the whites, like bees from the hive, to the uttermost ends of the earth. And, in return, Europe was quickened to intenser vitality. Goods, tools, ideas, men: all were produced at an unprecedented rate. So, by action and reaction, white progress grew by 1eaps and bounds. The Spanish and Portuguese pioneers presently showed signs of lassitude, but the northern nations - even more vigorous and audacious - instantly sprang to the front and carried forward the proud oriflamme of white expansion and world-dominion. For four hundred years the pace never slackened, and at the close of the nineteenth century the white man stood the indubitable master of the world.

Now four hundred years of unbroken triumph naturally bred in the white race an instinctive belief that its expansion would continue indefinitely, leading automatically to ever higher and more splendid destinies. Before the Russo-Japanese War of 1904 the thought that white expansion could be stayed, much less reversed, never entered the head of one white man in a thousand. Why should it, since centuries of experience had taught the exact contrary? The settlement of America, Australasia, and Siberia, where the few colored aborigines vanished like smoke before the white advance; the conquest of brown Asia and the partition of Africa, where colored millions bowed with only sporadic resistance to mere handfuls of whites; both sets of phenomena combined to persuade the white man that he was invincible, and that the colored types would everywhere give way before him and his civilization. The continued existence of dense colored populations in the tropics was ascribed to climate; and even in the tropics it was assumed that whites would universally form a governing caste, directing by virtue of higher intelligence and more resolute will, and exploiting natural resources to the incalculable profit of the whole white race. Indeed, some persons believed that the tropics would become available for white settlement as soon as science had mastered tropical diseases and had prescribed an adequate hygiene.

This uncritical optimism, suggested by experience, was fortified by ill-assimilated knowledge. During the closing decades of the past century, not only were biology and economics less advanced than to-day, but they were also infinitely less widely understood, exact knowledge being confined to academic circles. The general public had only a vulgarized smattering, mostly crystallizing about catchwords into which men read their prepossessions and their prejudices. For instance: biologists had recently formulated the law of the "Survival of the Fittest." This sounded very well. Accordingly, the public, in conformity with the prevailing optimism, promptly interpreted "fittest" as synonymous with "best," in utter disregard of the grim truth that by "fittest" nature denotes only the type best adapted to existing conditions of environment, and that if the environment favors a low type, this low type (unless humanly prevented) will win, regardless of all other considerations. So again with economics. A generation ago relatively few persons realized that low-standard men would drive out high standard men as inevitably as bad money drives out good, no matter what the results to society and the future of mankind. These are but two instances of that shallow, cock-sure nineteenth-century optimism, based upon ignorance and destined to be so swiftly and tragically disillusioned.

However, for the moment, ignorance was bliss. Accordingly, the fin de siecle white world, having partitioned Africa and fairly well dominated brown Asia, prepared to extend its sway over the one portion of the colored world which had hitherto escaped subjection - the yellow Far East. Men began speaking glibly of "manifest destiny" or piously of "the white man's burden." European publicists wrote didactically on "the break-up of China," while Russia, bestriding Siberia, dipped behemoth paws in Pacific waters and eyed Japan.

Such was the white world's confident, aggressive temper at the close of the last century. To be sure, voices were occasionally raised warning that all was not well. Such were the writings of Professor Pearson and Meredith Townsend. But the white world gave these Cassandras the reception always accorded prophets of evil in joyous times - it ignored them or laughed them to scorn. In fact, few of the prophets displayed Pearson's immediate certainty. Most of them qualified their prophecies with the comforting assurance that the ills predicted were relatively remote.

Meredith Townsend is a good case in point. The reader may recall his prophecy of white expulsion from Asia, quoted in my second chapter. (p. 22.) That prophecy occurs in the preface to the fourth edition, published in 1911, and written in the light of the Russo-Japanese War. Now, of course, Mr. Townsend's main thesis - Europe's inability permanently to master and assimilate Asia - had been elaborated by him long before the close of the nineteenth century. Nevertheless, the preface to the fourth edition speaks of Europe's failure to conquer Asia as absolute and eviction from present holdings as probable within a relatively short time; whereas, in his original introduction, written in 1899, he foresaw a great European assault upon Asia, which would probably succeed and from which Asia would shake itself free only after the lapse of more than a century.

In fact, Mr. Townsend's words of 1899 so exactly portray white confidence at that moment that I cannot do better than quote him. His object in publishing his book is, he says, "to make Asia stand out clearer in English eyes, because it is evident to me that the white races under the pressure of an entirely new impulse are about to renew their periodic attempt to conquer or at least to dominate that vast continent.... So grand is the prize that failures will not daunt the Europeans, still less alter their conviction. If these movements follow historic lines they will recur for a time upon a constantly ascending scale, each repulse eliciting a greater effort, until at last Asia like Africa is 'partitioned,' that is, each section is left at the disposal of some white people. If Europe can avoid internal war, or war with a much-aggrandized America, she will by A. D. 2000 be mistress in Asia, and at liberty, as her people think, to enjoy." (Townsend ("Asia and Europe "), pp. 1-4) If the reader will compare these lines with Mr. Townsend's 1911 judgment, he will get a good idea of the momentous change wrought in white minds by Asia's awakening during the first decade of the twentieth century as typified by the Russo-Japanese War.

1900 was, indeed, the high-water mark of the white tide which had been flooding for four hundred years. At that moment the white man stood on the pinnacle of his prestige and power. Pass four short years, and the flash of the Japanese guns across the murky waters of Port Arthur harbor revealed to a startled world - the beginning of the ebb.

CHAPTER VII
THE BEGINNING OF THE EBB

THE Russo-Japanese War is one of those landmarks in human history whose significance increases with the lapse of time. That war was momentous, not only for what it did, but even more for what it revealed. The legend of white invincibility was shattered, the veil of prestige that draped white civilization was torn aside, and the white world's manifold ills were laid bare for candid examination.

Of course previous blindness to the trend of things had not been universal. The white world had had its Cassandras, while keen-sighted Asiatics had discerned symptoms of white weakness. Nevertheless, so imposing was the white world's aspect and so unbroken its triumphant progress that these seers had been a small and discredited minority. The mass of mankind, white and non-white alike, remained oblivious to signs of change.

This, after all, was but natural. Not only had the white advance been continuous, but its tempo had been ever increasing. The nineteenth century, in particular, witnessed an unprecedented outburst of white activity. We have already surveyed white territorial gains, both as to area of settlement and sphere of political control. But along many other lines white expansion was equally remarkable. White race-increase - the basis of all else - was truly phenomenal. In the year 1500 the white race (then confined to Europe) could not have numbered more than 70,000,000. In 1800 the population of Europe was 150,000,000, while the whites living outside Europe numbered over 10,000,000. The white race had thus a trifle more than doubled its numbers in three centuries. But in the year 1900 the population of Europe was nearly 450,000,000, while the extra European whites numbered fully 100,000,000. Thus the whites had increased threefold in the European homeland, while in the new areas of settlement outside Europe they had increased tenfold. The total number of whites at the end of the nineteenth century was thus nearly 550,000,000 - a gain in numbers of almost 400,000,000, or over 400 per cent. This spelled an increase six times as great as that of the preceding three centuries.

White race-growth is most strikingly exemplified by the increase of its most expansive and successful branch - the Anglo-Saxons. In 1480, as already seen, the population of England proper was not much over 2,000,000. Of course this figure was abnormally low even for mediaeval times, it being due to the terrible vital losses of the Wars of the Roses, then drawing to a close. A century later, under Elizabeth, the population of England had risen to 4,000,000. In 1900 the population of England was 31,000,000, and in 1910 it was 35,000,000, the population of the British Isles at the latter date being 45,500,000. But in the intervening centuries British blood had migrated to the ends of the earth, so that the total number of Anglo-Saxons in the world to-day cannot be much less than 100,000,000. This figure includes Scotch and Scotch Irish strains (which are of course identical with English in the Anglo-Saxon sense), and adopts the current estimate that some 50,000,000 of people in the United States are predominantly of Anglo-Saxon origin. Thus, in four centuries, the Anglo-Saxons multiplied between forty and fifty fold.

The prodigious increase of the white race during the nineteenth century was due not only to territorial expansion but even more to those astounding triumphs of science and invention which gave the race unprecedented mastery over the resources of nature. This material advance is usually known as the "industrial revolution." The industrial revolution began in the later decades of the eighteenth century, but it matured during the first half of the nineteenth century, when it swiftly and utterly transformed the face of things.

This transformation was, indeed, absolutely unprecedented in the world's history. Hitherto man's material progress had been a gradual evolution. With the exception of gunpowder, he had tapped no new sources of material energy since very ancient times. The horse-drawn mail-coach of our great-grandfathers was merely a logical elaboration of the horse-drawn Egyptian chariot; the wind-driven clipper-ship traced its line unbroken to Ulysses's lateen bark before Troy; while industry still relied on the brawn of man and beast or upon the simple action of wind and waterfall. Suddenly all was changed. Steam, electricity, petrol, the Hertzian wave, harnessed nature's hidden powers, conquered distance, and shrunk the terrestrial globe to the measure of human hands. Man entered a new material world, differing not merely in degree but in kind from that of previous generations.

When I say "Man," I mean, so far as the nineteenth century was concerned, the white man. It was the white man's brain which had conceived all this, and it was the white man alone who at first reaped the benefits. The two outstanding features of the new order were the rise of machine industry with its incalculable acceleration of mass-production, and the correlative development of cheap and rapid transportation. Both these factors favored a prodigious increase in population, particularly in Europe, since Europe became the workshop of the world. In fact, during the nineteenth century, Europe was transformed from a semi-rural continent into a swarming hive of industry, gorged with goods, capital, and men, pouring forth its wares to the remotest corners of the earth, and drawing thence fresh stores of raw material for new fabrication and exchange. The amount of wealth amassed by the white world in general and by Europe in particular since the beginning of the nineteenth century is simply incalculable. Some faint conception of it can be gathered from the growth of world-trade. In the year 1818 the entire volume of international commerce was valued at only $2,000,000,000. In other words, after countless millenniums of human life upon our globe, man had been able to produce only that relatively modest volume of world-exchange. In 1850 the volume of world-trade had grown to $4,000,000,000. In 1900 it had increased to $20,000,000,000, and in 1913 it swelled to the inconceivable total of $40,000,000,000-a twentyfold increase in a short hundred years.

Such were the splendid achievements of nineteenth century civilization. But there was a seamy side to this cloth of gold. The vices of our age have been portrayed by a thousand censorious pens, and there is no need here to recapitulate them. They can mostly be summed up by the word "Materialism." That absorption in material questions and neglect of idealistic values which characterized the nineteenth century has been variously accounted for. But, after all, was it not primarily due to the profound disturbance caused by drastic environmental change? Civilized man had just entered a new material world, differing not merely in degree but in kind from that of his ancestors. It is a scientific truism that every living organism, in order to survive, must adapt itself to its environment. Therefore any change of environment must evoke an immediate readjustment on the part of the organism, and the more pronounced the environmental change, the more rapid and thoroughgoing the organic readjustment must be. Above all, speed is essential. Nature brooks no delay, and the disharmonic organism must attune itself or perish.

Now, is not readaptation precisely the problem with which civilized man has been increasingly confronted for the past hundred years? No one surely can deny that our present environment differs vastly from that of our ancestors. But if this be so, the necessity for profound and rapid adaptation becomes equally true. In fact, the race has instinctively sensed this necessity, and has bent its best energies to the task, particularly on the materialistic side. That was only natural. The pioneer's preoccupation with material matters in opening up new country is self-evident, but what is not so generally recognized is the fact that nineteenth-century Europe and the eastern United States are in many respects environmentally "newer" than remote backwoods settlements.

Of course the changed character of our civilization called for idealistic adaptations no less sweeping. These were neglected, because their necessity was not so compellingly patent. Indeed, man was distinctly attached to his existing idealistic outfit, to the elaboration of which he had so assiduously devoted himself in former days, and which had fairly served the requirements of his simpler past. Therefore nineteenth century man concentrated intensively, exclusively upon materialistic problems, feeling that he could thus concentrate because he believed that the idealistic conquests of preceding epochs had given him sound moral bases upon which to build the new material edifice.

Unfortunately, that which had at first been merely a means to an end presently became an end in itself.

Losing sight of his idealisms, nineteenth-century man evolved a thoroughly materialistic philosophy. The upshot was a warped, one-sided development which quickly revealed its unsoundness. The fact that man was much less culpable for his errors than many moralists aver is quite beside the point, so far as consequences are concerned. Nature takes no excuses. She demands results, and when these are not forthcoming she inexorably inflicts her penalties.

As the nineteenth century drew toward its close the symptoms of a profound malaise appeared on every side. Even those most fundamental of all factors, the vitality and quality of the race, were not immune. Vital statistics began to display features highly disquieting to thoughtful minds. The most striking of these phenomena was the declining birth-rate which affected nearly all the white nations toward the close of the nineteenth century and which in France resulted in a virtually stationary population.

Of course the mere fact of a lessened birth-rate, taken by itself, is not the unmixed evil which many persons assume. Man's potential reproductive capacity, like that of all other species, is very great. In fact, the whole course of biological progress has been marked by a steady checking of that reproductive exuberance which ran riot at the beginning of life on earth. As Havelock Ellis well says: "Of one minute organism it is estimated that, if its reproduction were not checked by death or destruction, in thirty days it would form a mass a million times larger than the sun.

The conger-eel lays 15,000,000 eggs, and if they all grew up, and reproduced themselves on the same scale, in two years the whole sea would become a wriggling mass of fish. As we approach the higher forms of life reproduction gradually dies down. The animals nearest to man produce few offspring, but they surround them with parental care, until they are able to lead independent lives with a fair chance of surviving. The whole process may be regarded as a mechanism for slowly subordinating quantity to quality, and so promoting the evolution of life to ever higher stages."[1]

While man's reproductive power is slight from the standpoint of bacteria and conger-eels, it is yet far from negligible, as is shown by the birth-rate of the less-advanced human types at all times, and by the birth-rate of the higher types under exceptionally favorable circumstances. The nineteenth century was one of these favorable occasions. In the new areas of settlement outside Europe, vast regions practically untenanted by colored competitors invited the white colonists to increase and multiply; while Europe itself, though historically "old country," was so transformed environmentally by the industrial revolution that it suddenly became capable of supporting a much larger population than heretofore. By the close of the century, however, the most pressing economic stimuli to rapid multiplication had waned in Europe and in many of the race dependencies.

[1] Havelock Ellis, "Essays in War-Time," p. 198 (American Edition, Boston, 1917).

Therefore the rate of increase, even under the most favorable biological circumstances, should have shown a decline.

The trouble was that this diminishing human output was of less and less biological value. Wherever one looked in the white world, it was precisely those peoples of highest genetic worth whose birth-rate fell off most sharply, while within the ranks of the several peoples it was those social classes containing the highest proportion of able strains which were contributing the smallest quotas to the population. Everywhere the better types (on which the future of the race depends) were numerically stationary or dwindling, while conversely, the lower types were gaining ground, their birth-rate showing relatively slight diminution.

This "disgenic" trend, so ominous for the future of the race, is a melancholy commonplace of our time, and many efforts have been made to measure its progress in economic or social terms. One of the most striking and easily measured examples, however, is furnished by the category of race. As explained in the Introduction, the white race divides into three main sub-species - the Nordics, the Alpines, and the Mediterraneans. All three are good stocks, ranking in genetic worth well above the various colored races. However, there seems to be no question that the Nordic is far and away the most valuable type; standing, indeed, at the head of the whole human genus. As Madison Grant well expresses it, the Nordic is "The Great Race."

Now it is the Nordics who are most affected by the disgenic aspects of our civilization. In the newer areas of white settlement like our Pacific coast or the Canadian Northwest, to be sure, the Nordics even now thrive and multiply. But in all those regions which typify the transformation of the industrial revolution, the Nordics do not fit into the altered environment as well as either Alpines or Mediterraneans, and hence tend to disappear. Before the industrial revolution the Nordic's chief eliminator was war. His pre-eminent fighting ability, together with the position of leadership which he had generally acquired, threw on his shoulders the brunt of battle and exposed him to the greatest losses, whereas the more stolid Alpine and the less robust Mediterranean stayed at home and reproduced their kind. The chronic turmoil of both the mediaeval and modern periods imposed a perpetual drain on the Nordic stock, while the era of discovery and colonization which began with the sixteenth century further depleted the Nordic ranks in Europe, since it was adventurous Nordics who formed the overwhelming majority of explorers and pioneers to new lands. Thus, even at the end of the eighteenth century, Europe was much less Nordic than it had been a thousand years before.

Nevertheless, down to the close of the eighteenth century, the Nordics suffered from no other notable handicaps than war and migration, and even enjoyed some marked advantages. Being a high type, the Nordic is naturally a "high standard" man. He requires healthful living conditions, and quickly pines when deprived of good food, fresh air, and exercise. Down to the close of the eighteenth century, Europe was predominantly agricultural. In cool northern and central Europe, therefore, environment actually favored the big, blond Nordics, especially as against the slighter, less muscular Mediterranean; while in the hotter south the Nordic upper class, being the rulers, were protected from field labor, and thus survived as an aristocracy. In peaceful times, therefore, the Nordics multiplied and repaired the gaps wrought by proscription and war.

The industrial revolution, however, profoundly modified this state of things. Europe was transformed from an agricultural to an urbanized, industrial area. Numberless cities and manufacturing centres grew up, where men were close packed and were subjected to all the evils of congested living. Of course such conditions are not ideal for any stock. Nevertheless, the Nordic suffered more than any one else. The cramped factory and the crowded city weeded out the big, blond Nordic with portentous rapidity, whereas the little brunet Mediterranean, in particular, adapted himself to the operative's bench or the clerk's stool, prospered - and reproduced his kind.

The result of these new handicaps, combined with the continuance of the traditional handicaps (war and migration), has been a startling decrease of Nordics all over Europe throughout the nineteenth century, with a corresponding resurgence of the Alpine, and still more of the Mediterranean, elements. In the United States it has been the same story. Our country, originally settled almost exclusively by Nordics, was toward the close of the nineteenth century invaded by hordes of immigrant Alpines and Mediterraneans, not to mention Asiatic elements like Levantines and Jews. As a result, the Nordic native American has been crowded out with amazing rapidity by these swarming, prolific aliens, and after two short generations he has in many of our urban areas become almost extinct.

The racial displacements induced by a changed economic or social environment are, indeed, almost incalculable. Contrary to the popular belief, nothing is more unstable than the ethnic make-up of a people. Above all, there is no more absurd fallacy than the shibboleth of the "melting-pot." As a matter of fact, the melting-pot may mix but does not melt. Each race-type, formed ages ago, and "set" by millenniums of isolation and inbreeding, is a stubbornly persistent entity. Each type possesses a special set of characters: not merely the physical characters visible to the naked eye, but moral, intellectual, and spiritual characters as well. All these characters are transmitted substantially unchanged from generation to generation. To be sure, where members of the same race-stock intermarry (as English and Swedish Nordics, or French and British Mediterraneans), there seems to be genuine amalgamation. In most other cases, however, the result is not a blend but a mechanical mixture. Where the parent stocks are very diverse, as in matings between whites, negroes, and Amerindians, the offspring is a mongreI - a walking chaos, so consumed by his jarring heredities that he is quite worthless. We have already viewed the mongrel and his works in Latin America.

Such are the two extremes. Where intermarriage takes place between stocks relatively near together, as in crossings between the main divisions of the white species, the result may not be bad, and is sometimes distinctly good. Nevertheless, there is no true amalgamation. The different race-characters remain distinct in the mixed offspring. If the race-types have generally intermarried, the country is really occupied by two or more races, the races always tending to sort themselves out again as pure types by Mendelian inheritance. Now one of these race-types will be favored by the environment, and it will accordingly tend to gain at the other's expense, while conversely the other types will tend to be bred out and to disappear. Sometimes a modification of the environment through social changes will suddenly reverse this process and will penalize a hitherto favored type. We then witness a "resurgence," or increase, of the previously submerged element.

A striking instance of this is going on in England. England is inhabited by two race-stocks - Nordics and Mediterraneans. Down to the eighteenth century, England, being an agricultural country with a cool climate, favored the Nordics, and but for the Nordic handicaps of war and migration the Mediterraneans might have been entirely eliminated. Two hundred years ago the Mediterranean element in England was probably very small. The industrial revolution, however, reversed the selective process, and today the small, dark types in England increase noticeably with every generation. The swart "cockney" is a resurgence of the primitive Mediterranean stock, and is probably a faithful replica of his ancestors of Neolithic times.

Such was the ominous "seamy side" of nineteenth-century civilization. The regressive trend was, in fact, a vicious circle. An ill-balanced, faulty environment penalized the superior strains and favored the inferior types; while, conversely, the impoverishing race-stocks, drained of their geniuses and overloading with dullards and degenerates, were increasingly unable to evolve environmental remedies.

Thus, by action and reaction, the situation grew steadily worse, disclosing its parlous state by numberless symptoms of social ill-health. All the unlovely fin de siecle phenomena, such as the decay of ideals, rampant materialism, political disruption, social unrest, and the "decadence" of art and literature, were merely manifestations of the same basic ills.

Of course a thoughtful minority, undazzled by the prevalent optimism, pointed out evils and suggested remedies. Unfortunately these "remedies" were superficial, because the reformers confused manifestations with causes and combated symptoms instead of fighting the disease. For example: the white world's troubles were widely ascribed to the loss of its traditional ideals, especially the decay of religious faith. But, as the Belgian sociologist Rene Gerard acutely remarks, "to reason in this manner is, we think, to mistake the effect for the cause. To believe that philosophic and religious doctrines create morals and civilizations is a seductive error, but a fatal one. To transplant the beliefs and the institutions of a people to new regions in the hope of transplanting thither their virtues and their civilization as well is the vainest of follies.... The greater or less degree of vigor in a people depends on the power of its vital instinct, of its greater or less faculty for adapting itself to and dominating the conditions of the moment. When the vital instinct of a people is healthy, it readily suggests to the people the religious and moral doctrines which assure its survival. It is not, therefore, because a people possesses a definite belief that it is healthy and vigorous, but rather because the people is healthy and vigorous that it adopts or invents the belief which is useful to itself. In this way, it is not because it ceases to believe that it falls into decay, it is because it is in decay that it abandons the fertile dream of its ancestors without replacing this by a new dream, equally fortifying and creative of energy." (Rene Gerard, "Civilization in Danger," The Hibbert Journal, January, 1912.)

Thus we return once more to the basic principle of race. For what is "vital instinct" but the imperious urge of superior heredity? As Madison Grant well says: " The lesson is always the same, namely, that race is everything. Without race there can be nothing except the slave wearing his master's clothes, stealing his master's proud name, adopting his master's tongue, and living in the crumbling ruins of his master's palace." (Grant, op. cit., p. 100.)

The disastrous consequences of failure to realize this basic truth is nowhere more strikingly exemplified than in the field of white world-politics during the half-century preceding the Great War. That period was dominated by two antithetical schools of political thinking: national-imperialism and internationalism. Swayed by the ill-balanced spirit of the times, both schools developed extremist tendencies; the former producing such monstrous aberrations as Pan-Germanism and Pan-Slavism, the latter evolving almost equally vicious concepts like cosmopolitanism and proletarianism. The adherents of these rival schools combated one another and wrangled among themselves. They both disregarded the basic significance of race, together with its immediate corollary, the essential solidarity of the white world.

As a matter of fact, white solidarity has been one of the great constants of history. For ages the white peoples have possessed a true "symbiosis" or common life, ceaselessly mingling their bloods and exchanging their ideas. Accordingly, the various white nations which are the race's political expression may be regarded as so many planets gravitating about the sun of a common civilization. No such sustained and intimate race-solidarity has ever before been recorded in human annals. Not even the solidarity of the yellow peoples is comparable in scope.

Of course the white world's internal frictions have been legion, and at certain times these frictions have become so acute that white men have been led to disregard or even to deny their fundamental unity. This is perhaps also because white solidarity is so pervasive that we live in it, and thus ordinarily do not perceive it any more than we do the air we breathe. Should white men ever really lose their instinct of race-solidarity, they would asphyxiate racially as swiftly and surely as they would asphyxiate physically if the atmospheric oxygen should suddenly be withdrawn. However, down to 1914 at least, the white world never came within measurable distance of this fatal possibility. On the contrary, the white peoples were continually expressing their fundamental solidarity by various unifying concepts like the "Pax Romana" of antiquity, the "Civitas Dei" or Christian commonwealth of the Middle Ages, and the "European Concert" of nineteenth-century diplomacy.

It was typical of the malaise which was overtaking the white world that the close of the nineteenth century should have witnessed an ominous ignoring of white solidarity; that national-imperialists should have breathed mutual slaughter while internationalists caressed visions of " human solidarity " culminating in universal race-amalgamation; lastly, that Asia's incipient revolt against white supremacy, typified by the Russo-Japanese War, should have found zealous white sponsors and abetters.

Nothing, indeed, better illustrates the white world's unsoundness at the beginning of the present century than its reaction to the Russo-

Japanese conflict. The tremendous significance of that event was no more lost upon the whites than it was upon the colored peoples. Most far-seeing white men recognized it as an omen of evil import for their race-future. And yet, even in the first access of apprehension, these same persons generally admitted that they saw no prospect of healing, constructive action to remedy the ills which were driving the white world along the downward path. Analyzing the possibility of Europe's presenting a common front to the perils disclosed by the Japanese victories, the French publicist Rene Pinon sadly concluded in the negative, believing that political passions, social hates, and national rivalries would speak louder than the general interest. "Contemporary Europe," he wrote, in 1905, "is probably not ready to receive and understand the lesson of the war. What are the examples of history to those gigantic commercial houses, uneasy for their New Year's balances, which are our modern nations? It is in the nature of States founded on mercantilism to content themselves with a hand-to-mouth policy, without general views or idealism, satisfied with immediate gains and unable to prepare against a distant future.

"Whence, in the Europe of to-day, could come the principle of an entente, and on what could it be based? Too many divergent interests, too many rival ambitions, too many festering hates, too many 'dead who speak,' are present to stifle the voice of Europe's conscience.

"However menacing the external danger, we fear that political rancors would not down; that the enemy from without would find accomplices, or at least unconscious auxiliaries, within. Far more than in its regiments and battleships, the power of Japan lies in our discords, in the absence of an ideal capable of lifting the European peoples above the daily pursuit of immediate interests, capable of stirring their hearts with the thrill of a common emotion. The true 'Yellow Peril' lies within us." (Rene Pinon, "La Lutte pour le Pacifique," pp. 184-185.)

Rene Pinon was a true prophet. Not only was the "writing on the wall" not taken to heart, the decade following the Russo-Japanese conflict witnessed a prodigious aggravation of all the ills which had afflicted white civilization during the nineteenth century. As if scourged by a tragic fate, the white world hurtled along the downward path, until it entered the fell shadow of - the modern Peloponnesian War.

CHAPTER VIII
THE MODERN PELOPONNESIAN WAR

The Peloponnesian War was the suicide of Greek civilization. It is the saddest page of history. In the brief Periclean epoch preceding the catastrophe Hellas had shone forth with unparalleled splendor, and even those wonderful achievements seemed but the prelude to still loftier heights of glory. On the eve of its self-immolation the Greek race, far from being exhausted, was bubbling over with exuberant vitality and creative genius.

But the half-blown rose was nipped by the canker of discord. Jealous rivalries and mad ambitions smouldered till they burst into a consuming flame. For a generation Hellas tore itself to pieces in a delirium of fratricidal strife. And even this was not the worst. The "peace" which closed the Peloponnesian War was no peace. It was a mere truce, dictated by the victors of the moment to sullen and vengeful enemies. Imposed by the sword and infused with no healing or constructive virtue, the Peloponnesian War was but the first of a war cycle which completed Hellas's ruin.

The irreparable disaster had, indeed, occurred: the gulfs of sundering hatred had become fixed, and the sentiment of Greek race-unity was destroyed. Having lost its soul, the Greek race soon lost its body as well.

Drained of its best strains, the diminished remnant bowed to foreign masters and bastardized its blood with the hordes of inferior aliens who swarmed into the land. By the time of the Roman conquest the Greeks were degenerate, and the Roman epithet "Graeculus" was a term of deserved contempt.

Thus perished the Greeks - the fairest slip that ever budded on the tree of life. They perished by their own hands, in the flower of their youth, carrying with them to the grave, unborn, potencies which might have blessed and brightened the world for ages. Nature is inexorable. No living being stands above her law; and protozoön or demigod, if they transgress, alike must die.

The Greek tragedy should be a warning to our own day. Despite many unlikenesses, the nineteenth century was strangely reminiscent of the Periclean age. In creative energy and fecund achievement, surely, its like had not been seen since "the glory that was Greece," and the way seemed opening to yet higher destinies.

But the brilliant sunrise was presently dimmed by gathering clouds. The birth of the twentieth century was attended with disquieting omens. The ills which had afflicted the preceding epoch grew more acute, synchronizing into an all-pervading, militant unrest. The spirit of change was in the air. Ancient ideals and shibboleths withered before the fiery breath of a destructive criticism, while the solid crust of tradition cracked and heaved under the premonitory tremors of volcanic forces working far below. Everywhere were seen bursting forth increasingly acute eruptions of human energy: a triumph of the dynamic over the static elements of life; a growing preference for violent and revolutionary, as contrasted with peaceful and evolutionary, solutions, running the whole politico-social gamut from "Imperialism" to "Syndicalism." Everywhere could be discerned the spirit of unrest setting the stage for the great catastrophe.

Grave disorders were simply inevitable. They might perhaps have been localized. They might even have taken other forms. But the ills of our civilization were too deep-seated to have avoided grave disturbances. The Prussian plotters of "Weltmacht" did, indeed, precipitate the impending crisis in its most virulent and concentrated form, yet after all they were but sublimations of the abnormal trend of the times.

The best proof of this is the white world's acutely pathological condition during the entire decade previous to the Great War. That fierce quest after alliances and mad piling-up of armaments; those paroxysmal "crises" which racked diplomacy's feverish frame; those ferocious struggles which desolated the Balkans: what were all these but symptoms denoting a consuming disease? To-day, by contrast, we think of the Great War as having smitten a world basking in profound peace. What a delusion! Cast back the mind's eye, and recall how hectic was the eve of the Great War, not merely in politics but in most other fields as well. Those opening months of 1914! Why, Europe seethed from end to end! When the Great War began, England was on the verge of civil strife, Russia was in the throes of an acute social revolt, Italy had just passed through a "red week" threatening anarchy, and every European country was suffering from grave internal disorders. It was a strange, nightmarish time, that early summer of 1914, to-day quite overshadowed by subsequent events, but which later generations will assign a proper place in the chain of world-history.

Well, Armageddon began and ran its horrid course. With the grim chronology of those dreary years this book is not concerned. It is with the aftermath that we here deal. And that is a sufficiently gloomy theme. The material losses are prodigious, the vital losses appalling, while the spiritual losses have well-nigh bankrupted the human soul.

Turning first to the material losses, they are of course in the broadest sense incalculable, but approximate estimates have been made. Perhaps the best of them is the analysis made by Professor Ernest L. Bogert, who places the direct costs of the war at $186,000,000,000 and the indirect costs at $151,000,000,000, thus arriving at the stupendous total of $337,000,000,000. These well-nigh inconceivable estimates still do not adequately represent the total losses, figured even in monetary terms, for, as Professor Bogert remarks:

"The figures presented in this summary are both incomprehensible and appalling, yet even these do not take into account the effect of the war on life, human vitality, economic well-being, ethics, morality, or other phases of human relationships and activities which have been disorganized and injured. It is evident from the present disturbances in Europe that the real costs of the war cannot be measured by the direct money outlays of the belligerents during the five years of its duration, but that the very breakdown of modern economic society might be the price exacted."

Yet prodigious as has been the destruction of wealth, the destruction of life is even more serious. Wealth can sooner or later be replaced, while vital losses are, by their very nature, irreparable. Never before were such masses of men arrayed for mutual slaughter. During the late war nearly 60,000,000 soldiers were mobilized, and the combatants suffered 33,000,000 casualties, of whom nearly 8,000,000 were killed or died of disease, nearly 19,000,000 were wounded, and 7,000,000 taken prisoners. The greatest sufferer was Russia, which had over 9,000,000 casualties, while next in order came Germany with 6,000,000 and France with 4,500,000 casualties. The British Empire had 3,000,000 casualties. America's losses were relatively slight, our total casualties being a trifle under 300,000.

And this is only the beginning of the story. The figures just quoted refer only to fighting men. They take no account of the civilian population. But the civilian losses were simply incalculable, especially in eastern Europe and the Ottoman Empire. It is estimated that for every soldier killed, five civilians perished by hunger, exposure, disease, massacre, or heightened infant mortality. The civilian deaths in Poland and Russia are placed at many millions, while other millions died in Turkey and Serbia through massacre and starvation. One item alone will give some idea of the wastage of human life during the war. The deaths beyond the normal mortality due to influenza and pneumonia induced by the war are estimated at 4,000,000. The total loss of life directly attributable to the war is probably fully 40,000,000, while if decreased birth-rates be added the total would rise to nearly 50,000,000. Furthermore, so far as civilian deaths are concerned, the terrible conditions prevailing over a great part of Europe since the close of 1918 have caused additional losses relatively as severe as those during the war years.

The way in which Europe's population has been literally decimated by the late war is shown by the example of France. In 1914 the population of France was 39,700,000. From this relatively moderate population nearly 8,000,000 men were mobilized during the war. Of these, nearly 1,400,000 were killed, 3,000,000 were wounded, and more than 400,000 were made prisoners. Of the wounded, between 800,000 and 900,000 were left permanent physical wrecks. Thus fully 2,000,000 men - mostly drawn from the flower of French manhood - were dead or hopelessly incapacitated.

Meanwhile, the civilian population was also shrinking. Omitting the civilian deaths in the northern departments under German occupation, the excess of deaths over births was more than 50,000 for 1914, and averaged nearly 300,000 for the four succeeding war years. And the most alarming feature was that these losses were mainly due, not to deaths of adults, but to a slump in the birth-rate. French births, which had been 600,000 in 1913, dropped to 315,000 in 1916 and 343,000 in 1917. All told, it seems probable that between 1913 and 1919 the population of France diminished by almost 3,000,000-nearly one-tenth of the entire population.

France's vital losses are only typical of what has to a greater or less extent occurred all over Europe. The disgenic effect of the Great War is simply appalling. The war was nothing short of a headlong plunge into white race-suicide. It was essentially a civil war between closely related white stocks; a war wherein every physical and mental effective was gathered up and hurled into a hell of lethal machinery which killed out unerringly the youngest, the bravest, and the best.

Even in the first frenzied hours of August, 1914, wise men realized the horror that stood upon the threshold. The crowd might cheer, but the reflective already mourned in prospect the losses which were in store. As the English writer Harold Begbie then said: "Remember this. Among the young conscript soldiers of Europe who will die in thousands, and perhaps millions, are the very flower of civilization; we shall destroy brains which might have discovered for us in ten or twenty years easements for the worst of human pains and solutions for the worst of social dangers. We shall blot those souls out of our common existence. We shall destroy utterly those splendid burning spirits reaching out to enlighten our darkness. Our fathers destroyed those strange and valuable creatures whom they called 'witches.' We are destroying the brightest of our angels." (The Literary Digest, August 29, 1914, p. 346.)

But it is doubtful if any of these seers realized the full price which the race was destined to pay during more than four long, agonizing years. Never before had war shown itself such an unerring gleaner of the best racial values. As early as the summer of 1915 Mr. Will Irwin, an American war correspondent, remarked the growing convictions among all classes, soldiers as well as civilians, that the war was fatally impoverishing the race. "I have talked," he wrote," with British officers and British Tommies, with English ladies of fashion and English housewives, with French deputies and French cabmen, and in all minds alike I find the same idea fixed - what is to become of the French race and the British race, yes, and the German race, if this thing keeps up?"

Mr. Irwin then goes on to describe the cumulative process by which the fittest were selected - for death.

"I take it for granted," he says, "that, in a general way, the bravest are the best, physically and spiritually. Now, in this war of machinery, this meat-mill, it is the bravest who lead the charges and attempt the daring feats, and, correspondingly, the loss is greatest among those bravest.

"So much when the army gets into line. But in the conscript countries, like France and Germany, there is a process of selection

128

in picking the army by which the best - speaking in general terms - go out to die, while the weakest remain. The undersized, the undermuscled, the underbrained, the men twisted by hereditary deformity or devitalized by hereditary disease - they remain at home to propagate the breed. The rest - all the rest - go out to take chances.

"Furthermore, as modern conscript armies are organized, it is the youngest men who sustain the heaviest losses - the men who are not yet fathers. And from the point of view of the race, that is, perhaps, the most melancholy fact of all.

"All the able-bodied men between the ages of nineteen and forty-five are in the ranks. But the older men do not take many chances with death.... These European conscript armies are arranged in classes according to age, and the younger classes are the men who do most of the actual fighting. The men in their late thirties or their forties, the 'territorials,' guard the lines, garrison the towns, generally attend to the business of running up the supplies. When we come to gather the statistics of this war we shall find that an overwhelming majority of the dead were less than thirty years old, and probably that the majority were under twenty-five. Now, the territorial of forty or forty-five has usually given to the state as many children as he is going to give, while the man of twenty-five or under has usually given the state no children at all." (The Literary Digest, August 7, 1915.)

Mr. Irwin was gauging the racial cost by the criterion of youth. A leading English scholar, Mr. H. A. L. Fisher, obtained equally alarming results by applying the test of genius. He analyzed the casualty lists "filled with names which, but for the fatal accidents of war, would certainly have been made illustrious for splendid service to the great cause of life.... A government actuated by a cold calculus of economic efficiency would have made some provision for sheltering from the hazards of war young men on whose exceptional intellectual powers our future progress might be thought to depend. But this has not been done, and it is impossible to estimate the extent to which the world will be impoverished in quality by the disappearance of so much youthful genius and talent.... The spiritual loss to the universe cannot be computed, and probably will exceed the injury inflicted on the world by the wide and protracted prevalence of the celibate orders in the Middle Ages." (Ibid., August 11, 1917.)

The American biologist S. K. Humphrey did not underestimate the extent of the slaughter of genius-bearing strains when he wrote: "It is safe to say that among the millions killed will be a million who are carrying superlatively effective inheritances - the dependence of the race's future. Nothing is more absurd than the notion that these inheritances can be replaced in a few generations by encouraging the fecundity of the survivors. They are gone forever. The survivors are going to reproduce their own less-valuable kind. Words fail to convey the appalling nature of the loss." (S. K. Humphrey, "Mankind: Racial Values and the Racial Prospect," p. 132 (New York, 1917).)

It is the same melancholy tale when we apply the test of race. Of course the war bore heavily on all the white race-stocks, but it was the Nordics - the best of all human breeds - who suffered far and away the greatest losses. War, as we have seen, was always the Nordic's deadliest scourge, and never was this truer than in the late struggle. From the racial standpoint, indeed, Armageddon was a Nordic civil war, most of the officers and a large proportion of the men on both sides belonging to the Nordic race. Everywhere it was the same story: the Nordic went forth eagerly to battle, while the more stolid Alpine and, above all, the little brunet Mediterranean either stayed at home or even when at the front showed less fighting spirit, took fewer chances, and oftener saved their skins.

The Great War has thus unquestionably left Europe much poorer in Nordic blood, while conversely it has relatively favored the Mediterraneans. Madison Grant well says: "As in all wars since Roman times, from the breeding point of view the little dark man is the final winner." (Grant, p. 74.)

Furthermore, it must be remembered that those disgenic effects which I have been discussing refer solely to losses inflicted upon the actual combatants. But we have already seen that for every soldier killed the war took five civilian lives. In fact, the war's profoundly devitalizing effects upon the general population can hardly be overestimated. Those effects include not merely such obvious matters as privation and disease, but also obscurer yet highly destructive factors like nervous shock and prolonged overstrain. To take merely one instance, consider Havelock Ellis's remarks concerning "the ever-widening circles of anguish and misery and destitution which every fatal bullet imposes on humanity." He concludes: "It is probable that for every 10,000,000 soldiers who fall on the field, 50,000,000 other persons at home are plunged into grief, or poverty, or some form of life-diminishing trouble." (Ellis, p. 32.)

Most serious has been the war's effect upon the children. At home, as at the front, it is the young who have been sacrificed. The heaviest civilian losses have come through increased infant mortality and decreased birth-rates. The "slaughter of the innocents" has thus been twofold: it has slain millions of those already alive, and it has prevented millions more from being born or conceived. The decreased fecundity of women during the war even under good material conditions apparently shows that war's psychological reflexes tend to induce sterility.

An Italian savant, Professor Sergi, has elaborated this hypothesis in considerable detail. He contends that "war continued for a long time is the origin of this phenomenon (relative sterility), not only in the absolute sense of the loss of men in battle, but also through a series of special conditions which arise simultaneously with an unbalancing of vital processes and which create in the latter a complex phenomenon difficult to examine in every one of its elements.

"The biological disturbance does not derive solely from the destruction of young lives, the ones best adapted to fecundity, but also from the unfavorable conditions into which a nation is unexpectedly thrown; from these come disorders of a mental and sentimental nature, nervousness, anxiety, grief, and pain of all kinds, to which the serious economic conditions of wartime also contribute; all these things have a harmful effect on the general organic economy of nations." (New York Times Current History, vol. IX, p. 272; October-December, 1916.)

>From the combination of these losses on the battlefield and in the cradle arises what the biologist Doctor Saleeby terms "the menace of the dearth of youth." The European populations to-day contain an undue proportion of adults and the aged, while "the younger generation is no longer knocking at the door. We senescents may grow old in peace; but the facts bode ill for our national future." (Current Opinion, April, 1919, p. 237.)

Furthermore, this "dearth of youth" will not be easily repaired. The war may be over, but its aftermath is only a degree less unfavorable to human multiplication, especially of the better kinds. Bad industrial conditions and the fearfully high cost of living continue to depress the birth-rate of all save the most reckless and improvident elements, whose increase is a curse rather than a blessing.

To show only one of the many causes that to-day keep down the birth-rate, take the crushing burden of taxation, which hits especially the increase of the upper classes. The London Saturday Review recently explained this very clearly when it wrote: "From a man with Pound2,000 a year the tax-gatherer takes Pound600. The remaining Pound1,400, owing to the decreased value of money, has a purchasing power about equal to Pound700 a year before the war. No young man will therefore think of marrying on less than Pound2,000 a year. We are thinking of the young man in the upper and middle classes. The man who starts with nothing does not, as a rule, arrive at Pound2,000 a year until he is past the marrying age. So the continuance of the species will be carried on almost exclusively by the class of manual workers of a low average caliber of brain. The matter is very serious. Reading the letters and memoirs of a hundred years ago, one is struck by the size of the families of the aristocracy. One smiles at reading of the overflowing nurseries of Edens, and Cokes, and Fitzgeralds. Fourteen or fifteen children were not at all unusual amongst the county families." (Saturday Review, November 1, 1919, p. 407.)

Europe's convalescence must, at the very best, be a slow and difficult one. Both materially and spiritually the situation is the reverse of blight. To begin with, the political situation is highly unsatisfactory. The diplomatic arrangements made by the Versailles Peace Conference offer neither stability nor permanence. In the next chapter I shall have more to say about the Versailles Conference. For the moment, let me quote the observations of the well-known British publicist J. L. Garvin, who adequately summarizes the situation when he says: "As matters stand, no great war ever was followed by a more disquieting and limited peace. Everywhere the democratic atmosphere is charged with agitation. There is still war or anarchy, or both, between the Baltic and the Pacific across a sixth part of the whole earth. Without a restored Russia no outlook can be confident. Either a Bolshevist or reactionary or even a patriotic junction between Germany and Russia might disrupt civilization as violently as before or to even worse effect." (. L. Garvin, "The Economic Foundations of Peace," page xiv (London, 1919).)

Political uncertainty is a poor basis on which to rebuild Europe's shattered economic life. And this economic reconstruction would, under the most favorable circumstances, be very difficult. We have already seen how, owing to the industrial revolution, Europe became the world's chief workshop, exporting manufactured products in return for foodstuffs to feed its workers and raw materials to feed its machines, these imports being drawn from the four quarters of the globe. In other words, Europe had ceased to be self-sufficing, the very life of its industries and its urban populations being dependent upon foreign importations from the most distant regions. Europe's prosperity before the war was due to the development of a marvellous system of world-trade; intricate, nicely adjusted, functioning with great efficiency, and running at high speed.

Then down upon this delicately organized mechanism crashed the trip-hammer of the Great War, literally smashing it to pieces. To reconstruct so intricate a fabric takes time. Meanwhile, how are the huge urban masses to live, unfitted and unable as they are to draw their sustenance from their native soil? If their sufferings become too great there is a real danger that all Europe may collapse into hopeless chaos. Mr. Frank A. Vanderlip did not overstate the danger when he wrote: "I believe it is possible that there may be let loose in Europe forces that will be more terribly destructive than have been the forces of the Great War." (Frank A. Vanderlip, "Political and Economic Conditions in Europe," The American Review of Reviews, July, 1919, p. 42.)

The best description of Europe's economic situation is undoubtedly that of Mr. Herbert Hoover, who, from his experience as inter-Allied food controller, is peculiarly qualified to pass authoritative judgment. Says Mr. Hoover:

"The economic difficulties of Europe as a whole at the signature of peace may be almost summarized in the phrase 'demoralized productivity.' The production of necessaries for this 450,000,000 population (including Russia) has never been at so low an ebb as at this day.

"A summary of the unemployment bureaus in Europe will show that 15,000,000 families are receiving unemployment allowances in one form or another, and are, in the main, being paid by constant inflation of currency. A rough estimate would indicate that the population of Europe is at least 100,000,000 greater than can be supported without imports, and must live by the production and distribution of exports; and their situation is aggravated not only by lack of raw materials, and imports, but also by low production of European raw materials. Due to the same low production, Europe is to-day importing vast quantities of certain commodities which she formerly produced for herself and can again produce. Generally, in production, she is not only far below even the level of the time of the signing of the armistice, but far below the maintenance of life and health without an unparalleled rate of import....

"From all these causes, accumulated to different intensity in different localities, there is the essential fact that, unless productivity can be rapidly increased, there can be nothing but political, moral, and economic chaos, finally interpreting itself in loss of life on a scale hitherto undreamed of." (Herbert Hoover, "The Economic Situation in Europe," World's Work, November, 1919, pp. 98-99.)

Such are the material and vital losses inflicted by the Great War. They are prodigious, and they will not easily be repaired. Europe starts its reconstruction under heavy handicaps, not the least of these being the drain upon its superior stocks, which has deprived it of much of the creative energy that it so desperately needs. Those 16,000,000 or more dead or incapacitated soldiers represented the flower of Europe's young manhood - the very men who are especially needed to-day. It is young men who normally alone possess both maximum driving power and maximum plasticity of mind. All the European belligerents are dangerously impoverished in their stock of youth. The resultant handicap both to Europe's working ability and Europe's brain-activity is only too plain.

Moreover, material and even vital losses do not tell the whole story. The moral and spiritual losses, though not easily measured, are perhaps even more appalling. In fact, the darkest cloud on the horizon is possibly the danger that reconstruction will be primarily material at the expense of moral and spiritual values, thus leading to a warped development even more pronounced than that of the nineteenth century and leading inevitably to yet more disastrous consequences.

The danger of purely material reconstruction is of course the peril which lurks behind every great war, and which in the past has wrought such tragic havoc. At the beginning of the late war we heard much talk of its morally "regenerative" effects, but as the grim holocaust went on year after year, far-sighted moralists warned against a fatal drain of Europe's idealistic forces which might break the thin crust of European civilization so painfully wrought since the Dark Ages.

That these warning voices were not without reason is proved by the chaos of spiritual, moral, and even intellectual values which exists in Europe to-day, giving play to such monstrous insanities as Bolshevism. The danger is that this chaos may be prolonged and deepened by the complex of two concurrent factors: spiritual drain during the war, and spiritual neglect in the immediate future due to overconcentration upon material reconstruction.

Many of the world's best minds are seriously concerned at the outlook. For example, Doctor Gore, the Bishop of Oxford, writes: "There is the usual depression and lowering of moral aims which always follows times of war. For the real terror of the time of war is not during the war; then war has certain very ennobling powers. It is after-war periods which are the curse of the world, and it looks as if the same severe going to prove true of this war. I own that I never felt anxiety such as I do now. I think the aspect of things has never been so dark as at this moment. I think the temper of the nations has degraded since the declaration of the armistice to a degree that is almost terrifying." (The Literary Digest, May 3, 1919, pp. 39-40.)

The intellectual impoverishment wrought by the war is well summarized by Professor C. G. Shawl " We did more before the war than we shall do after it," he writes. "War will have so exhausted man's powers of action and thought that he will have little wit or will left for the promotion of anything over and above necessary repair." (Current Opinion, April, 1919, p. 248.)

Europe's general impoverishment in all respects was vividly portrayed by a leading article of the London Saturday Review entitled "The True Destructiveness of War." Pointing to the devastated areas of northern France as merely symptomatic of the devastation wrought in spiritual as well as material fields, it said:

"Reflection only adds to the effect upon us of these miles of wasted country and ruined towns. All this represents not a thousandth part of the desolation which the war has brought upon our civilization. These devastated areas scarring the face of Europe are but a symbol of the desolation which will shadow the life of the world for at least a generation. The coming years will be bleak, in respect of all the generous and gracious things which are the products of leisure and of minds not wholly taken up by the necessity to live by bread alone. For a generation the world will have to concentrate upon material problems.

"The tragedy of the Great War - a tragedy which enhances the desolation of Rheims - is that it should have killed almost everything which the best of our soldiers died to preserve, and that it should have raised more problems than it has solved.

"We would sacrifice a dozen cathedrals to preserve what the war has destroyed in England .... We would readily surrender our ten best cathedrals to be battered by the artillery of Hindenburg as a ransom. Surely it would be better to lose Westminster Abbey than never again to have anybody worthy to be buried there." (Quoted from The Living Age, June 21, 1919, pp. 722-4.)

Europe is, indeed, passing through the most critical spiritual phase of the war's aftertnath - what I may term the zero hour of the spirit. When the trenches used to fill with infantry waiting in the first cold flicker of the dawn for the signal to go "over the top," they called it the "zero hour." Well, Europe now faces the zero hour of peace. It is neither a pleasant nor a stimulating moment. The "tumult and the shouting" have died. The captains, kings - and presidents - have departed. War's hectic urge wanes, losses are counted, the heroic pose is dropped. Such is the moment when the peoples are bidden to go "over the top" once more, this time toward peace objectives no less difficult than those of the battle-field. Weakened,, tired Europe knows this, feels this - and dreads the plunge into the unknown. Hence the malaise of the zero hour.

The extraordinary turmoil of the European soul is strikingly set forth by the French thinker Paul Valery.

"We civilizations," he writes, "now know that we are mortal. We had heard tell of whole worlds vanished, of empires gone to the bottom with all their engines; sunk to the inexplorable bottom of the centuries with their gods and their laws, their academies, their science, pure and applied; their grammars, their dictionaries, their classics, their romantics and their symbolists, their critics and their critics' critics. We knew well that all the apparent earth is made of ashes, and that ashes have a meaning. We perceived, through the mists of history, phantoms and huge ships laden with riches and spiritual things. We could not count them. But these wrecks, after all, were no concern of ours.

"Elam, Nineveh, Babylon were vague and lovely names, and the total ruin of these worlds meant as little to us as their very existence. But France, England, Russia - these would also be lovely names. Lusitania also is a lovely name. And now we see that the abyss of history is large enough for every one. We feel that a civilization is as fragile as a life. Circumstances which would send the works of Baudelaire and Keats to rejoin the works of Menander are no longer in the least inconceivable; they are in all the newspapers...

"Thus the spiritual Persepolis is ravaged equally with the material Susa. All is not lost, but everything has felt itself perish.

"An extraordinary tremor has run through the spinal marrow of Europe. It has felt, in all its thinking substance, that it recognized itself no longer, that it no longer resembled itself, that it was about to lose consciousness - a consciousness acquired by centuries of tolerable disasters, by thousands of men of the first rank, by geographical, racial, historical chances innumerable. . .

"The military crisis is perhaps at an end; the economic crisis is visibly at its zenith; but the intellectual crisis - it is with difficulty that we can seize its true centre, its exact phase. The facts, however, are clear and pitiless: there are thousands of young writers and young artists who are dead. There is the lost illusion of a European culture, and the demonstration of the impotence of knowledge to save anything whatever; there is science, mortally wounded in its moral ambitions, and, as it were, dishonored by its applications; there is idealism, victor with difficulty, grievously mutilated, responsible for its dreams; realism, deceived, beaten, with crimes and misdeeds heaped upon it; covetousness and renunciation equally put out; religions confused among the armies, cross against cross, crescent against crescent; there are the sceptics themselves, disconcerted by events so sudden, so violent, and so moving, which play with our thoughts as a cat with a mouse - the sceptics lose their doubts, rediscover them, lose them again, and can no longer make use of the movements of their minds.

"The rolling of the ship has been so heavy that at the last the best-hung lamps have been upset.

"From an immense terrace of Elsinore which extends from Basle to Cologne, and touches the sands of Nieuport, the marshes of the Somme, the chalk of Champagne, and the granite of Alsace, the Hamlet of Europe now looks upon millions of ghosts." (Quoted from The Living Age, May 10, 1919, pp. 365-368.)

Such is Europe's deplorable condition as she staggers forth from the hideous ordeal of the Great War; her fluid capital dissipated, her fixed capital impaired, her industrial fabric rent and tattered, her finances threatened with bankruptcy, the flower of her manhood dead on the battle-field, her populations devitalized and discouraged, her children stunted by malnutrition. A sombre picture.

And Europe is the white homeland, the heart of the white world. It is Europe that has suffered practically all the losses of Armageddon, which may be considered the white civil war. The colored world remains virtually unscathed.

Here is the truth of the matter: The white world to-day stands at the crossroads of life and death. It stands where the Greek world stood at the close of the Peloponnesian War. A fever has racked the white frame and undermined its constitution. The unsound therapeutics of its diplomatic practitioners retard convalescence and endanger real recovery. Worst of all, the instinct of race-solidarity has partially atrophied.

Grave as is the situation, it is not yet irreparable, any more than Greece's condition was hopeless after Aegospotami. It was not the Peloponnesian War which sealed Hellas's doom, but the cycle of political anarchy and moral chaos of which the Peloponnesian War was merely the opening phase. Our world is too vigorous for even the Great War, of itself, to prove a mortal wound.

The white world thus still has its choice. But it must be a positive choice. Decisions - firm decisions - must be made. Constructive measures - drastic measures - must be taken. Above all: time presses, and drift is fatal. The tide ebbs. The swimmer must put forth strong strokes to reach the shore. Else - swift oblivion in the dark ocean.

CHAPTER IX

THE SHATTERING OF WHITE SOLIDARITY

THE instinctive comity of the white peoples is, as I have already said, perhaps the greatest constant of history. It is the psychological basis of white civilization. Cohesive instinct is as vital to race as gravitation is to matter. Without them, atomic disintegration would alike result. In speaking of race-instinct, I am not referring merely to the ethnic theories that have been elaborated at various times. Those theories were, after all, but attempts to explain intellectually the urge of that profound emotion known to sociologists as the "consciousness of kind."

White race-consciousness has been of course perturbed by numberless internal frictions, which have at times produced partial inhibitions of unitary feeling. Nevertheless, when really faced by non-white opposition, white men have in the past instinctively tended to close their ranks against the common foe. One of the Great War's most deplorable results has been an unprecedented weakening of white solidarity which, if not repaired, may produce the most disastrous consequences.

During the nineteenth century the sentiment of white solidarity was strong. The great explorers and empire-builders who spread white ascendancy to the ends of the earth felt that they were apostles of their race and civilization as well as of a particular country. Rivalries might be keen and colonial boundary questions acute; nevertheless, in their calmer moments, the white peoples felt that the expansion of one white nation buttressed the expansion of all.

Professor Pearson undoubtedly voiced the spirit of the day when he wrote (about 1890) that it would be well "if European statesmen could understand that the wars which carry desolation into civilized countries are allowing the lower races to recruit their numbers and strength. Two centuries hence it may be matter of serious concern to the world if Russia has been displaced by China on the Amoor, if France has not been able to colonize North Africa, or if England is not holding India. For civilized men there can be only one fatherland, and whatever extends the influence of those races that have taken their faith from Palestine, their laws of beauty from Greece, and their civil law from Rome, ought to be matter of rejoicing to Russian, German, Anglo-Saxon, and Frenchman alike." (1 Pearson, pp. 14-15.)

The progress of science also fortified white race-consciousness with its sanctions. The researches of European scholars identified the founders of our civilization with a race of tall, white-skinned barbarians, possessing regular features, brown or blond hair, and light eyes. This was, of course, what we now know as the Nordic type. At first the problem was ill understood, the tests applied being language and culture rather than physical characteristics. For these reasons the early "Caucasian" and "Aryan" hypotheses were self-contradictory and inadequate. Nevertheless, the basis was sound, and the effects on white popular psychology were excellent.

Particularly good were the effects upon the peoples predominantly of Nordic blood. Obviously typifying as they did the prehistoric creators of white civilization, Nordics everywhere were strengthened in consciousness of genetic worth, feeling of responsibility for world-progress, and urge toward fraternal collaboration. The supreme value of Nordic blood was clearly analyzed by the French thinker Count Arthur de Gobineau as early as 1854 (His book "De l'Inégalité des Races Humaines" first appeared at that date.) (albeit Gobineau employed the misleading "Aryan" terminology) and his thesis was subsequently elaborated by many other writers, notably by Englishmen, Germans, and Scandinavians.

The results of all this were plainly apparent by the closing years of the nineteenth century. Quickened Nordic race-consciousnees played an important part in stimulating Anglo-American fraternization , and induced acts like the Oxford Scholarship legacy of Cecil Rhodes. The trend of this movement, though crosscut by nationalistic considerations, was clearly in the direction of a Nordic entente - a Pan-Nordic syndication of power for the safeguarding of the race-heritage and the harmonious evolution of the whole white world. It was a glorious aspiration, which, had it been realized, would have averted Armageddon.

Unfortunately the aspiration remained a dream. The ill-balanced tendencies of the late nineteenth century were against it, and they ultimately prevailed. The abnormal growth of national-imperialism, in particular, wrought fatal havoc. The exponents of imperialistic propagandas like Pan-Germanism and Pan-Slavism put forth literally boundless pretensions, planning the domination of the entire planet by their special brand of national-imperialism. Such men had scant regard for race-lines. All who stood outside their particular nationalistic group were vowed to the same subjection.

Indeed, the national-imperialists presently seized upon race teachings, and prostituted them to their own ends. A notable example of this is the extreme Pan-German propaganda of Houston Stewart Chamberlain (Especially as expounded in Chamberlain's chief work, "Die Grundlagen des neunzehnten Jahrhunderts" ("The Foundations of the Nineteenth Century").) and his fellows. Chamberlain makes two cardinal assumptions: he conceives modern Germany as racially almost purely Nordic; and he regards all Nordics outside the German linguistic-cultural group as either unconscious or renegade Teutons who must at all costs be brought into the German fold. To any one who understands the scientific realities of race, the monstrous absurdity of these assumptions is instantly apparent. The fact is that modern Germany, far from being purely Nordic, is mainly Alpine in race. Nordic blood preponderates only in the northwest, and is merely veneered over the rest of Germany, especially in the upper classes. While the Germania of Roman days was unquestionably a Nordic land, it has been computed that of the 70,000,000 inhabitants of the German Empire in 1914, only 9,000,000 were purely Nordic in character. This displacement of the German Nordics since classic times is chiefly due to Germany's troubled history, especially to the horrible Thirty Years' War which virtually annihilated the Nordics of south Germany. This racial displacement has wrought correspondingly profound changes in the character of the German people.

The truth of the matter is, of course, that the Pan-Germans were thinking in terms of nationality instead of race, and that they were using pseudo-racial arguments as camouflage for essentially political ends. The pity of it is that these arguments have had such disastrous repercussions in the genuine racial sphere. The late war has not only exploded Pan-Germanism, it has also discredited Nordic race-feeling, so unjustly confused by many persons with Pan-German nationalistic propaganda. Such persons should remember that the overwhelming majority of Nordics live outside of Germany, being mainly found in Scandinavia, the Anglo-Saxon countries, northern France, the Netherlands, and Baltic Russia. To let Teuton propaganda gull us into thinking of Germany as the Nordic fatherland is both a danger and an absurdity.

While Pan-Germanism was mainly responsible for precipitating Armageddon with all its disastrous consequences, it was Russian Pan-Slavism which dealt the first shrewd blow to white solidarity. Toward the close of the nineteenth century, Pan-Slavism's "Eastern" wing led by Prince Ukhtomsky and other chauvinists of his ilk, went so far in its imperialistic obsession as actually to deny Russia's white blood. These Pan-Slavists boldly proclaimed the morbid, mystical dogma that Russia was Asiatic, not European, and thereupon attempted to seize China as a lever for upsetting, first the rest of Asia, and then the non-Russian white world - elegantly described as "the rotten west." The white Power immediately menaced was, of course, England, who in acute fear for her Indian Empire, promptly riposted by allying herself with Japan. Russia was diplomatically isolated and militarily beaten in the Russo-Japanese War. Thus the Russo-Japanese War, that destroyer of white prestige whose ominous results we have already noted, was precipitated mainly by the reckless short-sightedness of white men themselves.

A second blow to white solidarity was presently administered - this time by England in concluding her second alliance-treaty with Japan. The original alliance, signed in 1902, was negotiated for a definite, limited objective - the checkmating of Russia's overweening imperialism. Even that instrument was dangerous, but under the circumstances it was justifiable and inevitable. The second alliance-treaty, however, was so general and far-reaching in character that practically all white men in the Far East, including most emphatically Englishmen themselves, pronounced it a great disaster.

Meanwhile, German imperialism was plotting even deadlier strokes at white race-comity, not merely by preparing war against white neighbors in Europe, but also by ingratiating itself with the Moslem East and by toying with schemes for building up a black military empire in central Africa.

Lastly, France was actually recruiting black, brown, and yellow hordes for use on European battle-fields; while Italy, by her buccaneering raid on Tripoli, outraged Islam's sense of justice and strained its patience to the breaking-point.

Thus, in the years preceding Armageddon, all the European Powers displayed a reckless absorption in particularistic ambitions and showed a callous indifference to larger race-interests. The rapid weakening of white solidarity was clearly apparent.

However, white solidarity, though diplomatically compromised, was emotionally not yet really undermined. Those dangerous games above mentioned were largely the work of cynical chancelleries and ultra-imperialist propagandas. The average European, whatever his nationality, still tended to react instinctively against such practices. This was shown by the sharp criticism which arose from the most varied quarters. For example: Russia and Britain were alike sternly taken to task both at home and abroad for their respective Far Eastern policies; proposed German alliances with Pan-Islamism and Japan preached by disciples of Machtpolitik were strenuously opposed as race-treason by powerful sections of German thought; while Italy's Tripolitan imbroglio was generally denounced as the most foolhardy trifling with the common European interest.

A good illustration of instinctive white solidarity in the early years of the twentieth century is a French journalist's description of the attitude of the white spectators (of various nationalities) gathered to watch the landing in Japan of the first Russian prisoners taken in the Russo-Japanese War. This writer depicts in moving language the literally horrifying effect of the spectacle upon himself and his fellows. "What a triumph," he exclaims, "what a revenge for the little Nippons to see thus humiliated these big, splendid men who, for them, represented, not only Russians, but those Europeans whom they so detest! This scene tragic in its simplicity, this grief passing amid joy, these whites, vanquished and captives, defiling before those free and triumphant yellows - this was not Russia beaten by Japan, not the defeat of one nation by another; it was something new, enormous, prodigious; it was the victory of one world over another; it was the revenge which effaced the centuries of humiliations borne by Asia; it was the awakening hope of the Oriental peoples; it was the first blow given to the other race, to that accursed race of the West, which, for so many years, had triumphed without out even having to struggle. And the Japanese crowd felt all this, and the few other Asiatics who found themselves there shared in this triumph. The humiliation of these whites was solemn, frightful. I completely forgot that these captives were Russians, and I would add that the other Europeans there, though anti-Russian, felt the same malaise: they also were forced to feel that these captives were their own kind. When we took the train for Kobe, an instinctive solidarity drove us huddling into the same compartment." (Pinon, "La Lutte pour le Pacifique," p. 165.)

Thus white solidarity, while unquestionably weakened, was still a weighty factor down to August, 1914. But the first shots of

Armageddon saw white solidarity literally blown from the muzzles of the guns. An explosion of internecine hatred burst forth more intense and general than any ever known before. Both sets of combatants proclaimed a duel to the death; both sides vowed the enemy to something near annihilation; while even scientists and litterateurs, disrupting the ancient commonwealths of wisdom and beauty, put one another furiously to the ban.

In their savage death-grapple neither side hesitated for an instant to grasp at any weapon, whatever the ultimate consequences to the race. The Allies poured into white Europe colored hordes of every pigment under the sun; the Teutonic Powers wielded Pan-Islam as a besom of wrath to sweep clean every white foothold in Hither Asia and North Africa; while far and wide over the Dark Continent black armies fought for their respective masters - and learned the hidden weakness of the white man's power. In the Far East, Japan, left to her own devices, bent amorphous China to her imperious will, thereby raising up a potential menace for the entire earth. Every day the tide of intestine hatred within the white world rose higher, until the very concept of a common blood and cultural past seemed in danger of being blotted out.

A symposium of the "hate literature" of the Great War is fortunately no part of my task, but the reader will readily recall both its abysmal fury and its irreconcilable implications. The most appalling feature was the way in which many writers assumed that this state of mind would be permanent; that the end of the Great War might be only the beginning of a war-cycle leading to the utter disruption of white solidarity and civilization. In the spring of 1916, the London Nation remarked gloomily: "Europe is now being mentally conceived as inevitably and permanently dual. We are ceasing to think of Europe. The normal end of war (which is peace) is to be submerged in the idea of a war-series indefinitely prolonged. Soon the entire Continent will have but one longing - the longing for rest. The cup is to be dashed from its lips! For a world steeped in fear and ruled by the barren logomachy of hate, diplomatic intercourse would almost cease to be possible.... In the matter of culture, modern Europe would tend to relapse to a state inferior even to that of mediaeval Europe, and to sink far below that of the Renaissance." (The Nation (London), April 8,1916, pp. 32-33.)

In similar vein, the noted German historian Eduard Meyer (Eduard Meyer, "England: Its Political Organization and Development and the War against Germany" (English translation, Boston, 1916).) predicted that Armageddon was only the first of a long series of Anglo-German "Punic Wars" in which modern civilization would retrograde to a condition of semi-barbarism. Germany, according to this prophecy, would be the victo r- but a Pyrrhic victor, for the colored races, taking advantage of white decadence, would destroy European supremacy and involve all the white nations in a common ruin.

The ulcerated state of European war-psychology did, in fact, lend ominous emphasis to these gloomy prognostications. Before 1914, as we have seen, imperialistic trafficking with common race-interests usually roused wide-spread criticism, while even more, the use of colored troops in white quarrels always roused bitter popular condemnation. In the darkest hours of the Boer War, English public opinion had refused to sanction the use of either black African or brown Indian troops against the white foe, while French plans for raising black armies of African savages for use in Europe were almost universally reprobated. Before Armageddon there thus existed a genuine moral repugnance against settling domestic differences by calling in the alien without the gates.

The Great War, however, sent all such scruples promptly into the discard. Not only did the belligerent governments use all the colored troops they could equip, but the belligerent peoples hailed this action with unqualified approval. The Allies were of course the more successful in practice, but the Germans were just as eager, and the exertions of the Prussian General Liman von Sanders actually got Turkish divisions to the European battle-fronts.

The psychological effect of these colored auxiliaries in deepening the hatred of the white combatants was deplorable. Germany's use of Turks raised among the Allies wrathful emotions reminiscent of the Crusades, while the havoc wrought in the Teutonic ranks by black Senegalese and yellow Gurkhas, together with Allied utterances like Lord Curzon's wish to see Bengal lancers on the Unter den Linden and Gurkhas camping at Sans Souci, so maddened the German people that the very suggestion of white solidarity was jeeringly scoffed at as the most idiotic sentimentality.

Here is a German officer's account of a Senegalese attack on his position, which vividly depicts the mingled horror and fury awakened in German hearts by these black opponents: "They came. First singly, at wide intervals. Feeling their way, like the arms of a horrible cuttlefish. Eager, grasping, like the claws of a mighty monster. Thus they rushed closer, flickering and sometimes disappearing in the cloud. Entire bodies and single limbs, now showing in the harsh glare, now sinking in the shadows, came nearer and nearer. Strong, wild fellows, their log-like, fat, black skulls wrapped in pieces of dirty rags. Showing their grinning teeth like panthers, with their bellies drawn in and their necks stretched forward. Some with bayonets on their rises. Many only armed with knives. Monsters all, in their confused hatred. Frightful their distorted, dark grimaces. Horrible their unnaturally wideopened, burning, bloodshot eyes. Eyes that seem like terrible beings themselves. Like unearthly, hell-born beings. Eyes that seemed to run ahead of their owners, lashed, unchained, no longer to be restrained. On they came like dogs gone mad and cats spitting and yowling, with a burning lust for human blood, with a cruel dissemblance of their beastly malice. Behind them came the first wave of the attackers, in close order, a solid, rolling black wall, rising and falling, swaying and heaving, impenetrable, endless." (Captain Rheinhold Eichacker, "The Blacks Attack!" New York, Times Current History, vol. XI, pp. 110-112, April-June, 1917.)

Here, again, is the proposal of a British officer, to raise a million black savages from England's African colonies for use on the Western Front. Major Stuart-Stephens exults in Britain's "almost unlimited reservoir of African man-power." In northern Nigeria alone, he remarks, there are to-day more than 700,000 warlike tribesmen. "Let them be used!" says the major. "These 'bonny fechters" are now engaged in the pastoral arts of peace. But I would make bold to assert that a couple of hundred thousand could, after six months' training, be usefully employed in daredevil charges into German trenches." Major Stuart-Stephens hopes that at least the Sudanese battalions will be transferred en masse to the Western Front. "This," he concludes, "would mean the placing at once in the trenches of, say, 70,000 big, lusty coal-black devils, the time of whose life is the wielding of the bayonet, and whose advent would not be regarded by the Boches as a pleasing omen of more to come of the same sort." (Major Darnley Stuart-Stephens, "Our Million Black Army,~ English Review, October, 1916.)

The military possibilities are truly engaging! There are literally tens of millions of fighting blacks and scores of millions of fighting Asiatics now living under white rule who could conceivably be armed and shipped to European battle-fields. After which, of course, Europe, the white homeland, would be - a queer place.

Fortunately for our race, the late war did not see this sort of thing carried to its logical conclusion. But the harm done was bad enough. The white world grew accustomed to the use of colored mercenaries and to the contracting of alliances with colored peoples against white opponents as a mere matter of course.

The German war-mind, in particular, teemed with colored alliance-projects. Unable to compete with the Allies in getting colored troops to Europe, Germans planned to revenge themselves in other fields. The Turkish alliance and the resulting "Holy War" proclamation were hailed with delight. "Over there in Turkey," wrote the well-known German publicist Ernst Jaeckh, "stretch Anatolia and Mesopotamia: Anatolia, the 'Land of the Sunrise'; Mesopotamia, the region of ancient paradise. May these names be to us a sign: may this World War bring to Germany and Turkey the sunrise and the paradise of a new time; may it confer upon an assured Turkey and a

Greater Germany the blessing of a fruitful Turco-Teutonic collaboration in peace after a victorious Turco-Teutonic collaboration in war." (Ernst Jaeckh, "Die deutsch-türkische Waffenbruderschaft," p. 30 (Berlin, 1915).)

The scope of Germany's Asiatic aspirations during the war is exemplified by an article from the pen of the learned Orientalist Professor Bernhardt Molden. (Bernhardt Molden, "Die Bedeutung Asiens im Kampf für unsere Zukunft," Preussische Jahrbücher, December, 1914. See also his article "Europa und Asien," Preussische Jahrbücher, October, 1915) Germany's aid to Turkey, contends Professor Molden, is merely symptomatic of her policy to raise the other Asiatic peoples now crushed beneath English and Russian domination. Thus Germany will create puissant allies for the "Second Punic War." Germany must therefore strive to solidify the great Central Asian bloc - Turkey, Persia, Afghanistan, China. Professor Molden urges a "Pan-Asian railroad" from Constantinople to Peking. This should be especially alluring to Afghanistan, which would thereby become one of the great pivots of world-politics and trade. In fine: "Germany must free Asia." As another prominent German writer, Friedrich Delitzsch, wrote in similar vein: "To renovate the East - such is Germany's mission." (Friedrich Delitzsch, "Deutschland und Asien" (pamphlet) (Berlin, 1914).)

In such a mood, Germans hailed Japan's absence of genuine hostility with the greatest satisfaction. The gust of rage which swept Germany at Japan's seizure of Kiao-chao was soon allayed by numerous writers preaching reconciliation and eventual alliance with the mistress of the Far East. Typical of this pro-Japanese propaganda is an article by Herr J. Witte, a former official in the Far East, which appeared in 1915. Herr Witte chides his countrymen for their talk about the Yellow Peril. Such a peril may exist in the future, but it is not pressing at this moment, "at any rate for us Germans, who have no great territorial possessions in the Far East.... We might permit ourselves to speak of a Yellow Peril if there was a white solidarity. This, however, does not exist. We are learning this just now by bitter experience on our own flesh and blood. Our foes have marshalled peoples of all races against us in battle. So long as this helps them, all race-antipathies and race-interests are to them matters of supreme indifference. Under these circumstances, in the midst of a life-and-death struggle against the peoples of the white race, shall we play the role of guardian angel of these peoples against the yellow peoples? For us, as Germans, there is now only one supreme life-interest, to which all other interests must be subordinated: the safety and advancement of Germany and of Deutschtum in the world." Herr Witte therefore advocates a "close political understanding between Germany and Japan. In future we can accomplish nothing in the teeth of Japan. Therefore we must get on good terms with Japan. And we can do it, too. Germany is, in fact, the country above all others who in the future has the best prospect of allying herself advantageously with the Far Eastern peoples." (Lic. Missioninspektor J. Witte, "Deutschland und die Völker Ostasiens im Vergangenheit und Zukunft," Preussische Jahrbücher, May, 1915.)

And so it went throughout the war-years: both sides using all possible colored aid to down the white foe; both sides alike reckless of the ultimate racial consequences.

In fact, leaving ultimate consequences aside, many persons feared during the later phases of the war that Europe might be headed for immediate dissolution. As early as mid-1916, Lord Loreburn expressed apprehension lest the war was entailing general bankruptcy and "such a destruction of the male youth of Europe as will break the thin crust of civilization which has been built up since the Dark Ages." (The Economist (London), June 17, 1916, p. 1134.) These fears were intensified by the Russian revolution of 1917, with its hideous corollary of Bolshevism which definitely triumphed before the close of that year. The Bolshevik triumph evoked despairing predictions like Lord Lansdowne's: "We are not going to lose this war, but its prolongation will spell ruin for the civilized world." (The Literary Digest, December 15, 1917, p. 14.)

Well, the war was prolonged for another year, ending in the triumph of the Allies and America, though leaving Europe in the deplorable condition reviewed in the preceding chapter. The hopes of mankind were now centred on the Peace Conference, but these hopes were oversanguine, for the Versailles "settlement" was riddled with political and economic imperfections from the Saar to Shantung.

This was what a sceptical minority had feared from the first. At the very beginning of the war, for instance, the French publicist Urbain Gohier had predicted that when the diplomats gathered at the end of the conflict they would find the problem of constructive settlement insoluble. (The Literary Digest, December 15, 1914, p. 14.)

Most persons, however, had been more hopeful. Disappointment and disillusionment were therefore correspondingly intense. The majority of liberal-minded, forward-looking men and women throughout the world deplored the Versailles settlement's faulty character, some, however, accepting the situation as the best of a bad business, others entirely repudiating it on the ground that by crystallizing an intolerable status it would entail worse disasters in the near future.

General Smuts, the South African delegate to the Conference, well represents the first attitude. In a formal protest against the Versailles settlement, General Smuts stated: "I have signed the peace treaty, not because I consider it a satisfactory document, but because it is imperatively necessary to close the war; because the world needs peace above all, and nothing could be more fatal than the continuance of the state of suspense between war and peace. The six months since the armistice was signed have, perhaps, been as upsetting, unsettling, and ruinous to Europe as the previous four years of war. I look upon the peace treaty as the close of these two chapters of war and armistice, and only on that ground do I agree to it. I say this now, not in criticism, but in faith; not because I wish to find fault with the work done, but rather because I feel that in the treaty we have not yet achieved the real peace to which our peoples were looking, and because I feel that the real work of making peace will only begin after this treaty has been signed, and a definite halt has thereby been called to the destructive passions that have been desolating Europe for nearly five years." (Official document.)

The English economist J. L. Garvin, who, like General Smuts, accepted the treaty faute de mieux, makes these trenchant comments upon the settlement itself: "Derisive human genius surveying with pity and laughter the present state of mankind and some of the obsolete means adopted at Paris to remedy it, might do most good by another satire like Rabelais, Gulliver, or Candide. But let us put from us here the temptation to conjure up vistas of the grotesque. Let us pursue these plain studies in common sense. A treaty even when signed is paper. It is in itself inoperative without the action or control of living forces which it seeks to express or repress. Treaties not drawn against sound and certain assets may be dishonored in the sequel like bad checks or bills. You do not get peace merely by putting it on paper. And, much more to the point, all that is called peace does not necessarily spell prosperity any more than all that glitters is gold. You can 'make a solitude and call it peace.' The quintessence of death or stupefaction resembles a kind of peace. You can prolong relative stagnation and depression and yet say that it is peace. But that would not be the reconciling and lasting, the constructive and the creative peace, as it was visioned by the Allied peoples in their greatest moments of insight and inspiration during the war. For that higher and wiser thing we lavished our pent-up energies and the accumulated treasure of a hundred years, and sent so many of our best to die." (J. L. Garvin, "The Heritage of Armageddon," The Observer (London). Reprinted in The Living Age, September 6, 1919.)

That veteran student of world-politics Doctor E. J. Dillon put the matter succinctly when he wrote: "The peace is being made not, as originally projected, on the basis of the fourteen points, nor on the lines of territorial equilibrium, but by a compromise which misses the advantage of either, and combines certain evils of both. The treaty has failed to lay the axe to the roots of war, has perhaps increased their number while purporting to destroy them. The germs of future conflicts, not only between the recent belligerents, but also between other groups of states, are numerous, and if present symptoms may be trusted will sprout up in the fulness of time." (In The Daily Telegraph (London). Quoted in The Nation (New York), June 14, 1919, p. 960.)

The badness of the Versailles treaties is nowhere more manifest than in the way they have alienated idealistic support and enthusiasm from the inchoate League of Nations. Multitudes of persons once zealous Leaguers now feel that the League has no moral foundation. Such persons contend that even were the covenant theoretically perfect, the League could no more succeed on the basis of the present peace settlement than a flawlessly designed palace could be erected if superimposed upon a quicksand.

Europe is thus in evil case. Her statesmen have failed to formulate a constructive settlement. Old problems remain unsolved while fresh problems arise. The danger is redoubled by the fact that both Europe and the entire world are faced with a new peril - Bolshevism. The menace of Bolshevism is simply incalculable. Bolshevism is a peril in some ways unprecedented in the world's history. It is not merely a war against a social system, not merely a war against our civilization; it is a war of the hand against the brain. For the first time since man was man there is a definite schism between the hand and the head. Every principle which mankind has thus far evolved: community of interest, the solidarity of civilization and culture, the dignity of labor, of muscle, of brawn, dominated and illumined by intellect and spirit - all these Bolshevism howls down and tramples in the mud.

Bolshevism's cardinal tenets - the dictatorship of the proletariat, and the destruction of the "classes" by social war - are of truly hideous import. The classes," as conceived by Bolshevism, are very numerous.

They comprise not merely the "idle rich," but also the whole of the upper and middle social strata, the landowning country folk, the skilled working men; in short, all except those who work with their

155

untutored hands, plus the elect few who philosophize for those who work with their untutored hands.

The effect of such ideas, if successful, not only on our civilization, but also on the very fibre of the race, can be imagined. The death or degradation of nearly all persons displaying constructive ability, and the tyranny of the ignorant and anti-social elements, would be the most gigantic triumph of disgenics ever seen. Beside it the ill effects of war would pale into insignificance. Civilization would wither like a plant stricken by blight, while the race, summarily drained of its good blood, would sink like lead into the depths of degenerate barbarism.

This is precisely what is occurring in Russia to-day. Bolshevism has ruled Russia less than three years - and Russia is ruined. She ekes out a bare existence on the remains of past accumulations, on the surviving scraps of her material and spiritual capital. Everywhere are hunger, cold, disease, terror, physical and moral death. The "proletariat" is making its "clean sweep." The " classes" are being systematically eliminated by execution, massacre, and starvation. The racial impoverishment is simply incalculable. Meanwhile Lenine, surrounded by his Chinese executioners, sits behind the Kremlin walls, a modern Jenghiz Khan plotting the plunder of a world.

Lenine's Chinese "braves" are merely symptomatic of the intrigues which Bolshevism is carrying on throughout the non-white world. Bolshevism is, in fact, as anti-racial as it is anti-social. To the Bolshevik mind, with its furious hatred of constructive ability and its fanatical determination to enforce levelling, proletarian equality, the very existence of superior biological values is a crime. Bolshevism has vowed the proletarianization of the world, beginning with the white peoples. To this end it not only foments social revolution within the white world itself, but it also seeks to enlist the colored races in its grand assault on civilization. The rulers of Soviet Russia are well aware of the profound ferment now going on in colored lands. They watch this ferment with the same terrible glee that they watched the Great War and the fiasco of Versailles - and they plot to turn it to the same profit.

Accordingly, in every quarter of the globe, in Asia, Africa, Latin America, and the United States, Bolshevik agitators whisper in the ears of discontented colored men their gospel of hatred and revenge. Every nationalist aspiration, every political grievance, every social discrimination, is fuel for Bolshevism's hellish incitement to racial as well as to class war.

And this Bolshevik propaganda has not been in vain. Its results already show in the most diverse quarters, and they are ominous for the future. China, Japan, Afghanistan, India, Java, Persia, Turkey, Egypt, Brazil, Chile, Peru, Mexico, and the "black belts" of our own United States: here is a partial list of the lands where the Bolshevik leaven in color is clearly at work.

Bolshevism thus reveals itself as the arch-enemy of civilization and the race. Bolshevism is the renegade, the traitor within the gates, who would betray the citadel, degrade the very fibre of our being, and ultimately hurl a rebarbarized, racially impoverished world into the most debased and hopeless of mongrelizations.

Therefore, Bolshevism must be crushed out with iron heels, no matter what the cost. If this means more war, let it mean more war. We know only too well war's dreadful toll, particularly on racial values. But what war-losses could compare with the losses inflicted by the living death of Bolshevism? There are some things worse than war, and Bolshevism stands foremost among those dread alternatives.

So ends our survey of the white world as it emerges from the Great War. The prospect is not a brilliant one. Weakened and impoverished by Armageddon, handicapped by an unconstructive peace, and facing internal Bolshevist disaffection which must at all costs be mastered, the white world is ill-prepared to confront - the rising tide of color. What that tide portends will be the subject of the concluding chapters.

157

PART III

THE DELUGE ON THE DIKES

CHAPTER X
THE OUTER DIKES

IN my first chapter I showed that the rising tide of color to-day finds itself confronted by dikes erected by the white race during the centuries of its expansion. The reader will also remember that white expansion has taken two forms: settlement and political control. These two phases differ profoundly in character. Areas of settlement like North America have become integral portions of the white world. On the other hand, regions of political control like India are merely white dependencies, highly valuable perhaps, yet in the last analysis held by title of the sword.

Between these clearly contrasted categories lies an intermediate class of territories typified by South Africa, where whites have settled in large numbers without displacing the native populations. Lastly, there exist certain white territories which may be called "enclaves." These enclaves have become thoroughly white by settlement, yet they are so distant from the main body of the white world and so contiguous to colored race-areas that white tenure does not possess that security which settlement and displacement of the aborigines normally confer. Australia typifies this anomalous class of cases.

The white defenses against the colored tide can be divided into what may be termed the "outer" and the "inner" dikes. The outer dikes (the regions of white political control) contain no settled white population, so that their abandonment, whatever the political or economic loss, would not directly affect white race-integrity. The question of their retention or abandonment should therefore (save in a few exceptional cases) be judged by political, economic, or strategic considerations. The inner dikes (the areas of white settlement), however, are a very different matter. Peopled as they are wholly or largely by whites, they have become parts of the race-heritage, which should be defended to the last extremity no matter if the costs involved are greater than their mere economic value would warrant. They are the true bulwarks of the race, the patrimony of future generations who have a right to demand of us that they shall be born white in a white man's land. Ill will it fare if ever our race should close its ears to this most elemental call of the blood. Then, indeed, would be manifest the writing on the wall.

That issue, however, is reserved for the next chapter. Let us here examine the matter of the outer dikes - the regions of white political control. There, where the white man is not settler but suzerain, his suzerainty should, in the last analysis, depend on the character of the inhabitants.

Right here, let us clear away the doctrinaire pedantry that commonly obscures discussion about the retention or abandonment of white political control over racially non-white regions. Argument usually tends to crystallize around two antitheses. On the one side are the doctrinaire liberals, who maintain the "imprescriptible right" of every human group to attain independence, and of every sovereign state to retain independence. On the opposite side are the doctrinaire imperialists, who maintain the equally imprescriptible right of their particular nation to "vital expansion" regardless of injuries thereby inflicted upon other nations.

Now I submit that both these assumptions are unwarranted. There is no "imprescriptible right" to either independence or empire. It depends on the realities of each particular case. The extreme cases at either end of the scale can be adjudged offhand by ordinary common sense. No one except a doctrinaire liberal would be likely to assert that the Andaman Islanders had an imprescriptible right to independence, or that Haiti, which owed its independence only to a turn in European politics, (Despite the legends which have grown up about the gaining of Haitian independence, such is the fact. Despite the handicap of yellow fever, the French were on the point of stamping out the negro insurgents when the renewal of war with England, in 1803, cut off the French sea-communications. The story of Haiti offers many interesting and instructive points to the student of race-questions. It was the first real shock between the ideals of white supremacy and race-equality; a prologue to the mighty drama of our own day. It also shows what real race-war means. To the historical student I cite my "French Revolution in San Domingo" (Boston, 1914), wherein the entire revolutionary cycle between 1780 and 1804 is described, based largely upon hitherto unexploited archival material.) should forever remain a sovereign-international nuisance. On the other hand, the whole world (with the exception of Teutonic imperialists) denounced Germany's attempt to swallow highly civilized Belgium as a crime against humanity.

In other words: realities, not abstract theories, decide. That does not please the doctrinaires, who insist on setting up Procrustean beds of theory on which realities should be racked or crammed. It does, however, conform to the dictates of nature, which decree that what is attuned shall live while the disharmonic and degenerate shall pass away. And nature usually has the last word.

Surveying the regions of white political control over non-white peoples in this realistic way, thereby avoiding the pitfalls of doctrinaire theory and blind prejudice, we may arrive at a series of conclusions which, though lacking the trim symmetry of the idealogue, will correspond to the facts in the various cases.

One thing is certain: the white man will have to recognize that the practically absolute world-dominion which he exercised during the nineteenth century can no longer be maintained. Largely because of that very dominion, colored races have been drawn out of their traditional isolation and have been quickened by white ideas, while the life-conserving nature of white rule has everywhere favored colored multiplication. These factors have combined to produce a widespread ferment which has been clearly visible for the past two decades, and which is destined to grow more acute in the near future.

This ferment would have developed even if the Great War had never occurred. However, the white world's weakening through Armageddon has immensely accelerated the process and has opened up the possibility of violent "short cuts" which would have mutually disastrous consequences. Especially has it evoked in bellicose and fanatical minds the vision of a "Pan-Colored" alliance for the universal overthrow of white hegemony at a single stroke - a dream which would turn into a nightmare of race-war beside which the late struggle in Europe would seem the veriest child's play.

The effective centres of colored unrest are the brown and yellow worlds of Asia. Both those worlds are not merely in negative opposition to white hegemony, but are experiencing a real renaissance whose genuineness is best attested by the fact that it is a faithful replica of similar movements in past times. White men must get out of their heads the idea that Asiatics are necessarily "inferior." As a matter of fact, while Asiatics do not seem to possess that sustained constructive power with which the whites, particularly the Nordics, are endowed, the browns and yellows are yet gifted peoples who have profoundly influenced human progress in the past and who undoubtedly will contribute much to world-civilization. The Asiatics have by their own efforts built up admirable cultures rooted in remote antiquity and worthy of all respect. They are to-day once more displaying their innate capacity by not merely adopting, but adapting, white ideas and methods. That this profound Asiatic renaissance will eventually result in the substantial elimination of white political control from Anatolia to the Philippines is as natural as it is inevitable.

This does not mean a precipitate white "scuttle" from Asia. Far from it. It does mean, however, a candid facing of realities and a basing of policy on realities rather than on prepossessions or prejudices. Unless the white man does this, he will injure himself more than any one else. If Asia is to-day really renascent, Asia will ultimately reap the political fruits. Men worthy of independence will sooner or later get independence. This is as certain as is the converse truth that men unworthy of independence, though they cry for it never so loudly, will either remain subject or will quickly relapse into subjection should they by some lucky circumstance obtain what they could only misuse.

If, then, Asia deserves to be free, she will be free. The only question is, how she will attain her freedom. Shall it be an evolutionary process, in the main peaceful, based upon mutual respect, with mutual recognition of both increasing Asiatic fitness and white vested interests? Or shall it come through cataclysmic revolution? This is the dilemma which those imperialists should ponder who object to any relaxation of white political control over Asia because of the "value" of the subject regions. That white control over Asiatic lands has been, and still is, immensely profitable, cannot be denied. But what basis for this value is there except lack of effective opposition? If real, sustained opposition now develops, if subject Asia becomes chronically rebellious, if its peoples resolutely boycott white goods - as China and India have shown

Asiatics capable of doing, will not white control be transformed from an asset into a liability? Above all, let us remember that no race-values are involved. No white race-areas would have to be abandoned to nonwhite domination. White control over Asia is political, and can thus be judged by the criteria of material interest undisturbed by the categorical imperative of race-duty.

The need for sympathetic open-mindedness toward awakening Asia if cataclysmic disasters are to be averted becomes all the clearer when we realize that on important issues lying outside Asia the white world must resolutely oppose Asiatic desires. We whites should be the more generous in our attitude toward Asia because imperative reasons of self-protection require us to deny to Asiatics some of their best opportunities in the outer world.

In my opening chapters I discussed the rapid growth of Asiatic populations and the resultant steadily augmenting outward thrust of surplus Asiatics (principally yellow men, but also in lesser degree brown men) from overcrowded homelands toward the less-crowded regions of the earth. It is, in fact, Asiatics, and above all Mongolian Asiatics, who form the first waves of the rising tide of color. Unfortunately, the white world cannot permit this rising tide free scope. White men cannot, under peril of their very race-existence, allow wholesale Asiatic immigration into white race-areas. This prohibition, which will be discussed in the next chapter, is already a serious blow to Asiatic aspirations.

But the matter does not end there. The white world also cannot permit with safety to itself wholesale Asiatic penetration of non-Asiatic colored regions like black Africa and tropical Latin America. To permit Asiatic colonization and ultimate control of these vast territories with their incalculable resources would be to overturn in favor of Asia the political, the economic, and eventually the racial balance of power in the world. At present the white man controls these regions. And he must stand fast. No other course is possible. Neither black Africa nor mongrel-ruled tropical America can stand alone. If the white man goes, the Asiatic comes - browns to Africa, yellows to Latin America. And there is no reason under heaven why we whites should deliberately present Asia with the richest regions of the tropics, to our own impoverishment and probable undoing.

Our race-duty is therefore clear. We must resolutely oppose both Asiatic permeation of white race-areas and Asiatic inundation of those non-white, but equally non-Asiatic, regions inhabited by the really inferior races. But we should also recognize that by taking this attitude we debar Asiatics from golden opportunities and render impossible the realization of aspirations intrinsically just as normal and laudable as our own. And, having closed in their faces so many doors of hope, can we refuse to discuss with gifted and capable Asiatics the problem of turning over to them the keys of their own house without causing festering hatreds whose poison may spread far beyond Asia into other colored lands and possibly into white lands as well? Neither a Pan-Colored nor a Colored-Bolshevist alliance are impossibilities, far-fetched though these terms may sound.

The fact is, we whites are in no position to indulge in the luxury of Bourbonism. Weakened by Armageddon, hampered by Versailles, and harassed by Bolshevism, the white world can ill afford to flout legitimate Asiatic aspirations to independence. Our imperialists may argue that this means abandoning "outer dikes," but I contend that white positions in Asia are not protective dikes but strategic blockhouses, built upon the sands during the long Asiatic ebb-tide, and which the now rising Asiatic waves must ultimately engulf. Is it not the part of wisdom to quit these outposts before they collapse into the swirling waters? Our true "outer dikes" stand, not in Asia, but in Africa and Latin America. Let us not exhaust ourselves by stubborn resistance in Asia which in the end must prove futile. Let us conserve our strength, remembering that by the time Asia has been submerged the flood should have lost much of its pent-up power.

Particularly should this be true of the moral "imponderables." By taking a reasonable, conciliatory attitude toward Asiatic aspirations to independence we would thereby eliminate the moral factors in Asia's present hostility toward ourselves. Many Asiatics would still be our foes from resentment at balked expansion, but we should have separated the sheep from the goats.

And the sheep are the more numerous. There are of course irreconcilables like Japanese imperialists and Pan-Islamic fanatics who would like to upset the whole world. However, taken by and large, Asia is peopled neither by fire-eating jingoes nor howling dervishes. The average Asiatic is by nature less restless, less ambitious, and consequently less aggressive than ourselves. To-day

164

Asiatics are everywhere aroused by a whole complex of stimuli like overcrowding, white domination, and white denial of nationalistic aspirations, to an access of hatred and fury. Those last-mentioned stimuli to anti-white hostility we can remove. The first-mentioned cause of hostility - overpopulation - we cannot remove. Only the Asiatic himself can do that by controlling his reckless procreation. Of course over-population is of itself a sufficiently serious provoker of trouble. There is no more certain breeder of strife than the expansive urge of a fast-breeding people. Nevertheless, this hostile stimulus applies primarily to yellow Asia. Brown Asia, once free or clearly on the road to freedom, would be either satisfied or engrossed in its intestine broils. At any rate, the twin spectres of a Pan-Asian or a Pan-Colored alliance would probably vanish like a mirage of the desert, and the white world would be far better able to deal with yellow pressure on its race frontiers - no light task, weakened and distracted as the white world finds itself to-day.

Unfortunately, no such wise foresight seems to have been vouchsafed our statesmen. Imperialistic secret treaties formed the basis for Versailles's treatment of Asiatic questions, and those treaties were drawn precisely as though Armageddon were a skirmish and Asia the sleeping giant of a century ago. Upon the brown world, in particular, white domination was riveted rather than relaxed.

This amazing disregard of present-day realities augurs ill for the future. Indeed, its evil first-fruits are already apparent. The brown world, convinced that its aspirations can be realized only by force, turns to the yellow world and listens to Bolshevik propaganda, while Pan-Islamism redoubles its efforts in Africa.

Thus is once more manifest the diplomatic bankruptcy of Versailles. The white man, like King Canute, seats himself upon the tidal sands and bids the waves be stayed. He will be lucky if he escapes merely with wet shoes.

CHAPTER XI
THE INNER DIKES

WE come now to the frontiers of the white world - to its true frontiers, marked, not by boundary-stones, but by flesh and blood. These frontiers are not continuous: far from the European homeland, some run in remote quarters of the earth, sundered by vast stretches of ocean and connected only by the slate-gray thread of sea-power - the master-talisman which the white man still grasps firmly in his hand.

But against these race-frontiers - these "inner dikes" - the rising tide of color has for decades been beating, and will beat yet more fiercely as congesting population, quickened self-consciousness, and heightened sense of power impel the colored world to expansion and dominion. Above the eastern horizon the dark storm clouds lower, and the weakened, distracted white world must soon face a colored peril threatening its integrity and perhaps its existence. This colored peril has three facets: the peril of arms, the peril of markets, and the peril of migration. All three contain ominous potentialities, both singly and in combination. Let us review them in turn, to appraise their dynamic possibilities.

First, the peril of arms. The military potencies of the colored races have been the subject of earnest, and frequently alarmist, speculation for the past twenty years, particularly since the Russo-Japanese War. The exciting effects of Pan-Islamism upon the warlike peoples of Asia and Africa have been frequently discussed, while the "Yellow Peril" has long been a journalistic commonplace.

How shall we appraise the colored peril of arms? On the whole, it would appear as though the colored military danger, in its isolated, purely aggressive aspect, had been exaggerated. Visions of a united

Asia, rising suddenly in fanatic frenzy and hurling brown and yellow myriads upon the white West seem to be the products of superheated imaginations. I say "seem," because there are unquestionably mysterious emotional depths in the Asiatic soul which may yet justify the prophets of cataclysmic war. As Hyndman says: "With all the facts before us, and with prejudice thrown aside, we are still unable to lay bare the causes of the gigantic Asian movements of the past. They were certainly not all economic in their origin, unless we stretch the boundaries of theory so far as to include the massacre of whole populations and the destruction of their wealth within the limits of the invaders' desire for material gain. And, whether these movements arose from material or emotional causes, they have been before, and they may occur again. Forecast here is impossible. A new Mohammed is quite as likely to make his appearance as a new Buddha, a reborn Confucius, or a modern Christ.... Asia raided and scourged Europe for more than a thousand years. Now, for five hundred years, the counter-attack of Europe upon Asia has been steadily going on, and it may be that the land of long memories will cherish some desire to avenge this period of wrong and rapine in turn. The seed of hatred has already been but too well sown." (H. M. Hyndman, "The Awakening of Asia," pp. 267-8. (New York, 1919).)

Of course, on this particular point, forecast is, indeed, impossible. Nevertheless, the point should be noted, for Asiatic war-fever may appear, if not in isolation, then in conjunction with other stimuli to warlike action, like population-pressure or imperialistic ambition, which to-day exist and whose amplitude can be approximately gauged. We have already analyzed the military potencies of Pan-Islamism and Japan, and China also should not be forgotten. Pacifist though China has long been, she has had her bellicose moments in the past and may have them in the future. Should this occur, China, as the world's greatest reservoir of intelligent man-power, would be immensely formidable. Pearson visualizes a China "become an aggressive military power, sending out her armies in millions to cross the Himalayas and traverse the Steppes, or occupying the islands and the northern parts of Australia, by pouring in immigrants protected by fleets. Luther's old name for the Turks, that they were 'the people of the wrath of God,' may receive a new and terrible application." (Pearson, pp. 140-1.)

Granted that the Chinese will never become the fighting equals of the world's warrior races, their incredible numbers combined with their tenacious vitality might overcome opponents individually their superiors. Says Professor Ross: "To the West the toughness of the Chinese physique may have a sinister military significance. Nobody fears lest in a stand-up fight Chinese troops could whip an equal number of well-conditioned white troops. But few battles are fought by men fresh from tent and mess. In the course of a prolonged campaign involving irregular provisioning, bad drinking-water, lying out, loss of sleep, exhausting marches, exposure, excitement, and anxiety, it may be that the white soldiers would be worn down worse than the yellow soldiers. In that case the hardier men with less of the martial spirit might in the closing grapple beat the better fighters with the less endurance." (Edward Alsworth Ross, "The Changing Chinese," pp. 46-47 (New York, 1911).)

The potentialities of the Chinese soldier would acquire vastly greater significance if China should be thoroughly subjugated by, or solidly leagued to, ambitious and militaristic Japan. The combined military energies of the Far East, welded into an aggressive unity, would be a weapon of tremendous striking-power.

The colored peril of arms may thus be summarized: The brown and yellow races possess great military potentialities. These (barring the action of certain ill understood emotional stimuli) are unlikely to flame out in spontaneous fanaticism; but, on the other hand, they are very likely to be mobilized for political reasons like revolt against white dominion or for social reasons like over-population. The black race offers no real danger except as the tool of Pan-Islamism. As for the red men of the Americas, they are of merely local significance.

We are now ready to examine the economic facet of the colored peril: the industrial-mercantile phase. In the second part of this volume I showed the profound effect of the "industrial revolution" in furthering white world-supremacy, and I pointed out the tremendous advantages accruing to the white world from exploitation of undeveloped colored lands and from exports of manufactured goods to colored markets. The prodigious wealth thereby amassed has been a prime cause of white prosperity, has buttressed the maintenance of white world-hegemony, and has made possible much of the prodigious increase of white population.

We little realize what the loss of these advantages would mean. As a matter of fact, it would mean throughout the white world diminished prosperity, lessened political and military strength, and such relative economic and social stagnation as would depress national vigor and check population. It is even possible to visualize a white world reverting to the condition of Europe in the fifteenth century - thrown back upon itself, on the defensive, and with a static rather than a progressive civilization. Such conditions could of course occur only as the result of colored military and industrial triumphs of the most sweeping character. But the possibility exists, nevertheless, as I shall endeavor to show.

Down to the close of the nineteenth century white supremacy was as absolute in industry as it was in politics and war. Even the civilized brown and yellow peoples were negligible from the industrial point of view. Asia was economically on an agricultural basis. Such industries as she possessed were still in the "house-industry" stage, and her products, while often exquisite in quality, were produced by such slow, antiquated methods that their quantity was limited and their market-price relatively high. Despite very low wages, Asiatic products not only could not compete in the world-market with European and American machine made, mass-produced articles, but were hard hit in their home-markets as well. The way in which an ancient Asiatic handicraft like the Indian textiles was literally annihilated by the destructive competition of Lancashire cottons is only one of many similar instances.

With the beginning of the twentieth century, however, Asia began to show signs of an economic activity as striking in its way as the activity which Asia was displaying in idealistic and political fields. Japan had already laid the foundations of her flourishing industrial life based on the most up-to-date Western models, while in other Asiatic lands, notably in China and India, the whir of machinery and the smoke of tall factory chimneys proclaimed that the East was fathoming the industrial secrets of the West.

What Asiatics were seeking in their industrial revival was well expressed a decade ago by a Hindu, who wrote in a leading Indian periodical: "In one respect the Orient is really menacing the West, and so earnest and open-minded is Asia that no pretense or apology whatever is made about it. The Easterner has thrown down the industrial gauntlet, and from now on Asia is destined to witness a progressively intense trade warfare, the Occidental scrambling to retain his hold on the markets of the East, and the Oriental endeavoring to beat him in a battle in which heretofore he has been an easy victor.... In competing with the Occidental commercialists, the Oriental has awakened to a dynamic realization of the futility of pitting unimproved machinery and methods against modern methods and appliances. Casting aside his former sense of self-complacency, he is studying the sciences and arts that have given the West its material prosperity. He is putting the results of his investigations to practical use, as a rule, recasting the Occidental methods and tools to suit his peculiar needs, and in some instances improving upon them." (The Literary Digest, November 5, 1910, p. 786 (from The Indian Review, Madras).)

The accuracy of this Hindu statement of Asia's industrial awakening is endorsed by the statements of white observers. At the very moment when the above article was penned, an American economic writer, Clarence Poe, was making a study tour of the Orient, from which he brought back the following report: "The real cause of Asia's poverty lies in just two things: the failure of Asiatic governments to educate their people, and the failure of the people to increase their productive capacity by the use of machinery. Ignorance and lack of machinery are responsible for Asia's poverty;

knowledge and modern tools are responsible for America's prosperity." But, continues Mr. Poe, we must watch out. Asia now realizes these things and is doing much to remedy the situation. Hence, "we must face in ever-increasing degree the rivalry of awakening peoples who are strong with the strength that comes from struggle with poverty and hardship, and who have set themselves to master and apply all our secrets in the coming world-struggle for industrial supremacy and for racial readjustment." (Clarence Poe, "What the Orient Can Teach Us," World's Work, July, 1911.) And more recently another American observer of Asiatic economic conditions reports: "All Asia is being permeated with modern industry and present-day mechanical progress." (Clayton S. Cooper, "The Modernizing of the Orient," p. 5 (New York, 1914).)

Take, for example, the momentous possibilities involved in the industrial awakening of China. China is not merely the most populous of lands, containing as it does nearly one-fourth of all the human beings on earth, but it is also cowered with immense natural resources, notably coal and iron - the prime requisites of modern industrial life. Hitherto China has been on an agricultural basis, with virtually no exploitation of her mineral wealth and with no industry in the modern sense. But the day when any considerable fraction of China's laborious millions turn from the plough and handicrafts to the factory must see a portentous reaction in the most distant markets.

Thirty years ago, Professor Pearson forecast China's imminent industrial transformation. "Does any one doubt," he asks, "that the day is at hand when China will have cheap fuel from her coal-mines, cheap transport by railways and steamers, and will have founded technical schools to develop her industries? Whenever that day comes, she may wrest the control of the world's markets, especially throughout Asia, from England and Germany." (Pearson, p. 133.)

Much of what Professor Pearson prophesied has already come to pass, for China to-day has the beginnings of a promising industrial life. Even a decade ago Professor Ross wrote of industrial conditions there.

"Assuredly the cheapness of Chinese labor is something to make a factory owner's mouth water. The women reelers in the silk filatures of Shanghai get from eight to eleven cents for eleven hours of work. But Shanghai is dear; and, besides, everybody there complains that the laborers are knowing and spoiled. In the steel works at Hanyang common labor gets three dollars a month, just a tenth of what raw Slavs command in the South Chicago iron-works. Skilled mechanics get from eight to twelve dollars. In a coalmine near Ichang a thousand miles up the Yangtse the coolie receives one cent for carrying a 400-pound load of coal on his back down to the river a mile and a half away. He averages ten loads a day but must rest every other week. The miners get seven cents a day and food; that is, a cent's worth of rice and meal. They work eleven hours a day up to their knees in water, and all have swollen legs. After a week of it they have to lie off a couple of days. No wonder the cost of this coal (semi-bituminous) at the pit's mouth is only thirty-five cents a ton. At Chengtu servants get a dollar and a half a month and find themselves. Across Szechuan lusty coolies were glad to carry our chairs half a day for four cents each. In Sianfu the common coolie gets three cents a day and feeds himself, or eighty cents a month. Through Shansi roving harvesters were earning from four to twelve cents a day, and farm-hands got five or six dollars a year and their keep. Speaking broadly, in any part of the empire, willing laborers of fair intelligence may be had in any number at from eight to fifteen cents a day.

"With an ocean of such labor power to draw on, China would appear to be on the eve of a manufacturing development that will act like a continental upheaval in changing the trade map of the world. The impression is deepened by the tale of industries that have already sprung up." (Ross, pp. 117-118.)

Of course there is another side to the story. Low wages alone do not insure cheap production. As Professor Ross remarks: "For all his native capacity, the coolie will need a long course of schooling, industrial training, and factory atmosphere before he inches up abreast of the German or American working man." (Ross, p. 119.) In

172

the technical and directing staffs there is the same absence of the modern industrial spirit, resulting in chronic mismanagement, while Chinese industry is further handicapped by traditional evils like "squeeze," nepotism, lust for quick profits, and incapacity for sustained business team-play. These failings are not peculiar to China; they hamper the industrial development of other Asiatic countries, notably India. Still, the way in which Japanese industry, with all its faults, is perfecting both its technic and its methods shows that these failings will be gradually overcome and indicates that within a generation Asiatic industry will probably be sufficiently advanced to supply at least the Asiatic home-markets with most of the staple manufactures.

Thus it looks as though white manufactures will tend to be progressively eliminated from Asiatic markets, even under conditions of absolutely free competition. But it is a very moot point whether competition will remain free - whether, on the contrary, white wares will not be increasingly penalized. The Asiatic takes a keen interest in his industrial development and consciously favors it even where whites are in political control. The "swadeshi" movement in India is a good example, while the Chinese and Egyptian boycotts of foreign as against native goods are further instances in point. The Japanese have supplemented these spontaneous popular movements by systematic governmental discrimination in favor of Japanese products and the elimination of white competition from Japan and its dependencies. This Japanese policy has been markedly successful, and should Japan's present hegemony over China be perpetuated the white man may soon find himself economically as well as politically expelled from the whole Far East.

A decade ago Putnam Weale wrote warningly: "If China is forced, owing to the short-sighted diplomacy of those for whom the question has really supreme importance, to make common cause with Japan as a pis aller, then it may be accepted as inevitable that in the course of time there will be created a mare clausum, which will extend from the island of Saghalien down to Cochin-China and

Siam, including all the island-groups, and the shores of which will be openly hostile to the white man....

"And since there will be no danger from the competition of white workmen, but rather from the white man's ships, the white man's merchants, his inventions, his produce - it will be these which will be subJected to humiliating conditions.... It is not a very far cry from tariffs on goods to tariffs and restrictions on foreign shipping, on foreign merchants, on everything foreign - restrictions which by imposing vast and unequal burdens on the activities of aliens will soon totally destroy such activities.... What can very easily happen is that the federation of eastern Asia and the yellow races will be finally arranged in such a manner as to exclude the white man and his commerce more completely than any one yet dreams of." (B.L. Putnam Weale, "The Conflict of Color," pp. 179-181.)

This latter misfortune may be averted by concerted white action, but it is difficult to see how the gradual elimination of white goods from Asiatic markets as the result of successful Asiatic competition can be averted. Certainly the stubborn maintenance of white political domination over a rebellious Asia would be no remedy. That would merely intensify swadeshi boycotts in the subject regions, while in the lands freed from white political control it would further Japan's policy of excluding everything white. If Asiatics resolve to buy their own products instead of ours we may as well reconcile ourselves to the loss. Here again frank recognition of the inevitable will enable us to take a much stronger and more justifiable position on the larger world-aspects of the problem.

For Asia's industrial transformation is destined to cause momentous reactions in other parts of the globe. If Asiatic industry really does get on an efficient basis, its potentialities are so tremendous that it must presently not only monopolize the home-markets but also seek to invade white markets as well, thus presenting the white world with commercial and economic problems as unwelcome as they will be novel.

Again, industrialization will in some respects aggravate Asiatic longings for migration and dominion.

In my opening pages I mentioned industrialization as a probable reliever of population-pressure in Asiatic countries by affording new livelihoods to the congested masses. This is true. But, looking a trifle farther, we can also see that industrialization would stimulate a further prodigious increase of population. Consider the growth of Europe's population during the nineteenth century under the stimulus of the industrial revolution, making possible the existence in our industrialized Europe of three times as many people as existed in the agricultural Europe of a hundred years ago. Why should not a similar development occur in Asia? To-day Asia, though still upon a basis as agricultural as eighteenth-century Europe, contains fully 900,000,000 people. That even a partially industrialized Asia might support twice that number would (judging by the European precedent) be far from improbable.

But this would mean vastly increased incentives to expansion - commercial, political, racial- beyond the bounds of Asia. It would mean intensified encroachments, not only upon areas of white settlement, but perhaps even more upon non-Asiatic colored regions of white political control like Africa and tropical America. Here again we see why the white man, however conciliatory in Asia, must stand like flint in Africa and Latin America. To allow the whole tropic belt clear round the world to pass into Asiatic hands would practically spell white race-suicide.

Professor Pearson paints a truly terrible picture of the stagnation and hopelessness which would ensue. "Let us conceive," he writes, "the leading European nations to be stationary, while the black and yellow belt, including China, Malaysia, India, central Africa, and tropical America, is all teeming with life, developed by industrial enterprise, fairly well administered by native governments, and owning the better part of the carrying trade of the world. Can any one suppose that, in such a condition of political society, the habitual temper of mind in Europe would not be profoundly

175

changed? Depression, hopelessness, a disregard of invention and improvement, would replace the sanguine confidence of races that at present are always panting for new worlds to conquer. Here and there, it may be, the more adventurous would profit by the traditions of old supremacy to get their services accepted in the new nations, but as a rule there would be no outlet for energy, no future for statesmanship. The despondency of the English people, when their dream of conquest in France was dissipated, was attended with a complete decay of thought, with civil war, and with a standing still, or perhaps a decline of population, and to a less degree of wealth.... It is conceivable that our later world may find itself deprived of all that is valued on earth, of the pageantry of subject provinces and the reality of commerce, while it has neither a disinterred literature to amuse it nor a vitalized religion to give it spiritual strength." (Pearson, pp. 138, 139.)

To sum up: The economic phase of the colored peril, though not yet a major factor, must still be seriously reckoned with by forward-looking statesmanship as something which will increasingly complicate the relations of the white and non-white worlds. In fact, even to-day it tends to intensify Asiatic desires for expansion, and thus exacerbates the third, or migratory, phase of the colored peril, which is already upon us.

The question of Asiatic immigration is incomparably the greatest external problem which faces the white world. Supreme phase of the colored peril, it already presses, and is destined to press harder in the near future. It infinitely transcends the peril of arms or markets, since it threatens not merely our supremacy or prosperity but our very race-existence, the wellsprings of being, the sacred heritage of our children.

That this is no overstatement of the issue, a bare recital of a few biological axioms will show. We have already seen that nothing is more unstable than the racial make-up of a people, while, conversely, nothing is more unchanging than the racial divisions of mankind. We have seen that true amalgamation is possible only between members of the same race stock, while in crossings between stocks even as relatively near together as the main divisions of the white species, the race-characters do not really fuse but remain distinct in the mixed offspring and tend constantly to resort themselves as pure types by Mendelian inheritance. Thus a country inhabited by a mixed population is really inhabited by different races, one of which always tends to dominate and breed the other out - the outbred strains being lost to the world forever.

Now, since the various human stocks differ widely in genetic worth, nothing should be more carefully studied than the relative values of the different strains in a population, and nothing should be more rigidly scrutinized than new strains seeking to add themselves to a population, because such new strains may hold simply incalculable potentialities for good or for evil. The potential reproductive powers of any stock are almost unlimited. Therefore the introduction of even a small group of prolific and adaptable but racially undesirable aliens may result in their subsequent prodigious multiplication, thereby either replacing better native stocks or degrading these by the injection of inferior blood.

The admission of aliens should, indeed, be regarded just as solemnly as the begetting of children, for the racial effect is essentially the same. There is no more damning indictment of our lopsided, materialistic civilization than the way in which, throughout the nineteenth century, immigration was almost universally regarded, not from the racial, but from the material point of view, the immigrant being viewed not as a creator of race-values but as a mere vocal tool for the production of material wealth.

Immigration is thus, from the racial standpoint, a form of procreation, and like the more immediate form of procreation it may be either the greatest blessing or the greatest curse. Human history is largely the story of migrations, making now for good and now for ill. Migration peopled Europe with superior white stocks displacing ape-like aborigines, and settled North America with

Nordics instead of nomad redskins. But migration also bastardized the Roman world with Levantine mongrels, drowned the West Indies under a black tide, and is filling our own land with the sweepings of the European east and south.

Migration, like other natural movements, is of itself a blind force. It is man's divine privilege as well as duty, having been vouchsafed knowledge of the laws of life, to direct these blind forces, rejecting the bad and selecting the good for the evolution of higher and nobler destinies.

Colored immigration is merely the most extreme phase of a phenomenon which has already moulded prodigiously the development of the white world. In fact, before discussing the specific problems of colored immigration, it would be well to survey the effects of the immigration of various white stocks. When we have grasped the momentous changes wrought by the introduction of even relatively near-related and hence relatively assimilable strains, we will be better able to realize the far more momentous consequences which the introduction of colored stocks into white lands would entail.

The racial effects of immigration are ably summarized by that lifelong student of immigration problems, Prescott F. Hall. These effects are, he truly remarks, "more far-reaching and potent than all others. The government, the state, society, industry, the political party, social and political ideals, all are concepts and conventions created by individual men; and when individuals change these change with them. Recent discoveries in biology show that in the long run heredity is far more important than environment or education; for though the latter can develop, it cannot create. They also show what can be done in a few years in altering species, and in producing new ones with qualities hitherto unknown, or unknown in combination." (Prescott F. Hall, "Immigration," p. 99 (New York, 1907).)

The way in which admixture of alien blood can modify or even

178

destroy the very soul of a people have been fully analyzed both by biologists and by social psychologists like Doctor Gustave Le Bon. (See especially his "Psychology of Peoples" (London, 1898, English translation).) The way in which wholesale immigration, even though mainly white, has already profoundly modified American national character is succinctly stated by Mr. Eliot Norton. "If," he writes, "one considers the American people from, say, 1775 to 1860, it is clear that a well defined national character was in process of formation. What variations there were, were all of the same type, and these variations would have slowly grown less and less marked. It needs little study to see of what great value to any body of men, women, and children a national or racial type is. It furnishes a standard of conduct by which any one can set his course. The world is a difficult place in which to live, and to establish moral standards has been one of the chief occupations of mankind. Without such standards, man feels as a mariner without a compass. Religions, rules, Iaws, and customs are only the national character in the form of standards of conduct. Now national character can be formed only in a population which is stable. The repeated introduction into a body of men of other men of different type or types cannot but tend to prevent its formation. Thus the 19,000,000 of immigrants that have landed have tended to break up the type which was forming, and to make the formation of any other type difficult. Every million more will only intensify this result, and the absence of a national character is a loss to every man, woman, and child. It will show itself in our religions, rules of conduct, in our laws, in our customs." (Eliot Norton, in Annals of the American Academy of Political and Social Science, vol. XXIV, p. 163, July, 1904. Of course, since Mr. Norton wrote, millions more aliens have entered the United States, and the situation is much worse.)

The vital necessity of restriction and selection in immigration to conserve and build race-values is thus set forth by Mr. Hall:

"There is one aspect of immigration restriction in the various countries which does not often receive much attention; namely, the possibility of its use as a method of world-eugenics. Most persons think of migration in terms of space - as the moving of a certain number of people from one part of the earth's surface to another. Whereas the much more important aspect of it is that of a functioning in time.

"This comes from two facts. The first is that the vacuum left in any country by emigration is rapidly filled up through a rise in the birth-rate.... The second fact is that immigration to any country of a given stratum of population tends to sterilize all strata of higher social and economic levels already in that country. So true is this that nearly all students of the matter are agreed that the United States would have a larger population to-day if there had been no immigration since 1820, and, it is needless to add, a much more homogeneous population. As long as the people of any community are relatively homogeneous, what differences of wealth and social position there may be do not affect the birth-rate, or do so only after a considerable time. But put into that community a number of immigrants, inferior mentally, socially, and economically, and the natives are unwilling to have their children associate with them in work or social life. They then limit the number of their children in order to give them the capital or education to enter occupations in which they will not be brought into contact with the new arrivals. This result is quite apparent in New England, where successive waves of immigration from lower and lower levels have been coming in for eighty years. In the West, the same New England stock has a much higher birth-rate, showing that its fertility is in no way diminished. In the South, where until very recently there was no immigration at all, and the only socially inferior race was clearly separated by the accident of color, the birth rate has remained very high, and the very large families of the colonial period are even now not uncommon.

"This is not to say that other causes do not contribute to lower the birth-rate of a country, for that is an almost world-wide phenomenon. But the desire to be separated from inferiors is as strong a motive to birth-control as the desire for luxury or to ape one's economic superiors. Races follow Gresham's law as to money:

the poorer of two kinds in the same place tends to supplant the better. Mark you, supplant not drive out. One of the most common fallacies is the idea that the natives whose places are taken by the lower immigrants are 'driven up' to more responsible positions. A few may be pushed up; more are driven to a new locality, as happened in the mining regions; but most are prevented from coming into existence at all.

"What is the result, then, of the migration of 1,000,000 persons of lower level into a country where the average is of a higher level? Considering the world as a whole, there are, after a few years, 2,000,000 persons of the lower type in the world, and probably from 500,000 to 1,000,000 less of the higher type. The proportion of lower to higher in the country from which the migration goes may remain the same; but in the country receiving it, it has risen. Is the world as a whole the gainer?

"Of course the euthenist (I.e., a person believing in the preponderance of environment rather than heredity) says at once that these immigrants are improved. We may grant that, although the improvement is probably much exaggerated. You cannot make bad stock into good by changing its meridian, any more than you can turn a cart-horse into a hunter by putting it into a fine stable, or make a mongrel into a fine dog by teaching it tricks. But such improvement as there is involves time, expense, and trouble; and, when it is done, has anything been gained? Will any one say that the races that have supplanted the old Nordic stock in New England are any better, or as good, as the descendants of that stock would have been if their birth-rate had not been lowered?

"Further, in addition to the purely biological aspects of the matter, there are certain psychological ones. Although a cosmopolitan atmosphere furnishes a certain freedom in which strong congenital talents can develop, it is a question whether as many are not injured as helped by this. Indeed, there is considerable evidence to show that for the production of great men, a certain homogeneity of environment is necessary. The reason of this is very simple. In a homogeneous community, opinions on a large number of matters are fixed. The individual does not have to attend to such things, but is free to go ahead on some special line of his own, to concentrate to his limit on his work, even though that work be fighting the common opinions.

"But in a community of many races, there is either cross-breeding or there is not. If there is, the children of such cross-breeding are liable to inherit two souls, two temperaments, two sets of opinions, with the result in many cases that they are unable to think or act strongly and consistently in any direction. The classic examples are Cuba, Mexico, and Brazil. On the other hand, if there is no cross-breeding, the diversity exists in the original races, and in a community full of diverse ideals of all kinds much of the energy of the higher type of man is dissipated in two ways. First, in the intellectual field there is much more doubt about everything, and he tends to weigh, discuss, and agitate many more subjects, in order to arrive at a conclusion amid the opposing views. Second, in practical affairs, much time and strength have to be devoted to keeping things going along old lines, which could have been spent in new research and development. In how many of our large cities to-day are men of the highest type spending their whole time fighting, often in vain, to maintain standards of honesty, decency, and order, and in trying to compose the various ethnic elements, who should be free to build new structures upon the old!

"The moral seems to be this: Eugenics among individuals is encouraging the propagation of the fit, and limiting or preventing the multiplication of the unfit. World-eugenics is doing precisely the same thing as to races considered as wholes. Immigration restriction is a species of segregation on a large scale, by which inferior stocks can be prevented from both diluting and supplanting good stocks. Just as we isolate bacterial invasions, and starve out the bacteria by limiting the area and amount of their food-supply, so we can compel an inferior race to remain in its native habitat, where its own multiplication in a limited area will, as with all organisms, eventually limit its numbers and therefore its influence. On the other hand, the superior races, more self-limiting than the others, with the benefits of more space and nourishment will tend to still higher levels.

"This result is not merely a selfish benefit to the higher races, but a good to the world as a whole. The object is to produce the greatest number of those fittest not 'for survival' merely, but fittest for all purposes. The lower types among men progress, so far as their racial inheritance allows them to, chiefly by imitation and emulation. The presence of the highest development and the highest institutions among any race is a distinct benefit to all the others. It is a gift of psychological environment to any one capable of appreciation." (Prescott F. Hall, "Immigration Restriction and World Eugenics," The Journal of Heredity, March, 1919.)

The impossibility of any advanced and prosperous community maintaining its social standards and handing them down to its posterity in these days of cheap and rapid transportation except by restrictions upon immigrations is thus explained by Professor Ross: "Now that cheap travel stirs the social deeps and far-beckoning opportunity fills the steerage, immigration becomes ever more serious to the people that hopes to rid itself at least of slums, 'masses,' and 'submerged.' What is the good of practicing prudence in the family if hungry strangers may crowd in and occupy at the banquet table of life the places reserved for its children? Shall it, in order to relieve the teeming lands of their unemployed, abide in the pit of wolfish competition and renounce the fair prospect of growth in suavity, comfort, and refinement? If not, then the low-pressure society must not only slam its doors upon the indraft, but must double-lock them with forts and iron-clads, lest they be burst open by assault from some quarter where 'cannon food' is cheap." (Edward Alsworth Ross, "Changing America," pp.. 45-46 (New York, 1912).)

These admirable summaries of the immigration problem in its world-aspect are strikingly illustrated by our own country, which may be considered as the leading, if not the "horrible," example.

Probably few persons fully appreciate what magnificent racial treasures America possessed at the beginning of the nineteenth century. The colonial stock was perhaps the finest that nature had evolved since the classic Greeks. It was the very pick of the Nordics of the British Isles and adjacent regions of the European continent - picked at a time when those countries were more Nordic than now, since the industrial revolution had not yet begun and the consequent resurgence of the Mediterranean and Alpine elements had not taken place.

The immigrants of colonial times were largely exiles for conscience's sake, while the very process of migration was so difficult and hazardous that only persons of courage, initiative, and strong will-power would voluntarily face the long voyage overseas to a life of struggle in an untamed wilderness haunted by ferocious savages.

Thus the entire process of colonial settlement was one continuous, drastic cycle of eugenic selection. Only the racially fit ordinarily came, while the few unfit who did come were mostly weeded out by the exacting requirements of early American life.

The eugenic results were magnificent. As Madison Grant well says: "Nature had vouchsafed to the Americans of a century ago the greatest opportunity in recorded history to produce in the isolation of a continent a powerful and racially homogeneous people, and had provided for the experiment a pure race of one of the most gifted and vigorous stocks on earth, a stock free from the diseases, physical and moral, which have again and again sapped the vigor of the older lands. Our grandfathers threw away this opportunity in the blissful ignorance of national childhood and inexperience." (Madison Grant, "The Passing of the Great Race," p. 90.) The number of great names which America produced at the beginning of its national life shows the high level of ability possessed by this relatively small people (only about 3,000,000 whites in 1790). With our hundred-odd millions we have no such output of genius to-day.

The opening decades of the nineteenth century seemed to portend for America the most glorious of futures. For nearly seventy years after the Revolution, immigration was small, and during that long period of ethnic isolation the colonial stock, unperturbed by alien influences, adjusted its cultural differences and began to display the traits of a genuine new type, harmonious in basic homogeneity and incalculably rich in racial promise. The general level of ability continued high and the output of talent remained extraordinarily large. Perhaps the best feature of the nascent "native American" race was its strong idealism. Despite the materialistic blight which was then creeping over the white world, the native American displayed characteristics more reminiscent of his Elizabethan forebears than of the materialistic Hanoverian Englishman. It was a wonderful time and it was only the dawn!

But the full day of that wondrous dawning never came. In the late forties of the nineteenth century the first waves of the modern immigrant tide began breaking on our shores, and the tide swelled to a veritable deluge which never slackened till temporarily restrained by the late war. This immigration, to be sure, first came mainly from northern Europe, was thus largely composed of kindred stocks, and contributed many valuable elements. Only during the last thirty years have we been deluged by the truly alien hordes of the European east and south. But, even at its best, the immigrant tide could not measure up to the colonial stock which it displaced, not reinforced, while latterly it became a menace to the very existence of our race, ideals, and institutions. All our slowly acquired balance - physical, mental, and spiritual - has been upset, and we to-day flounder in a veritable Serbonian bog, painfully trying to regain the solid ground on which our grandsires confidently stood.

The dangerous fallacy in that short-sighted idealism which seeks to make America the haven of refuge for the poor and oppressed of all lands, and its evil effects not only on America but on the rest of the world as well, has been convincingly exposed by Professor Ross. He has scant patience with those social "uplifters" whose sympathy with the visible alien at the gate is so keen that they have no feeling for the invisible children of our poor who will find the chances gone, nor for those at the gate of the to-be, who might have been born, but will not be.

"I am not of those," he writes, "who consider humanity and forget the nation, who pity the living but not the unborn. To me, those who are to come after us stretch forth beseeching hands as well as do the masses on the other side of the globe. Nor do I regard America as something to be spent quickly and cheerfully for the benefit of pent-up millions in the backward lands. What if we become crowded without their ceasing to be so? I regard it (America) as a nation whose future may be of unspeakable value to the rest of mankind, provided that the easier conditions of life here be made permanent by high standards of living, institutions, and ideals, which finally may be appropriated by all men. We could have helped the Chinese a little by letting their surplus millions swarm in upon us a generation ago; but we have helped them infinitely more by protecting our standards and having something worth their copying when the time came." (Edward Alsworth Ross, "The Old World in the New," Preface, p. 2 (New York, 1914).)

The perturbing influence of recent immigration must vex American life for many decades. Even if laws are passed to-morrow so drastic as to shut out permanently the influx of undesirable elements, it will yet take several generations before the combined action of assimilation and elimination shall have restabilized our population and evolved a new type-norm approaching in fixity that which was on the point of crystallizing three-quarters of a century ago.

The biologist Humphrey thus punctures the "melting-pot" delusion: "Our 'melting-pot,'" he writes, "would not give us in a thousand years what enthusiasts expect of it - a fusing of all our various racial elements into a new type which shall be the true American. It will give us for many generations a perplexing diversity in ancestry, and since our successors must reach back into their ancestry for characteristics, this diversity will increase the uncertainty of their inheritances. They will inherit no stable blended character, because there is no such thing. They will inherit from a mixture of unlike characteristics contributed by unlike peoples, and in their inheritance they will have certain of these characteristics in full identity, while certain others they will not have at all." (S. K. Humphrey, "Mankind: Racial Values and the Racial Prospect," p. 155.)

Thus, under even the most favorable circumstances, we are in for generations of racial readjustment - an immense travail, essentially needless, since the final product will probably not measure up to the colonial standard. We will probably never (unless we adopt positive eugenic measures) be the race we might have been if America had been reserved for the descendants of the picked Nordics of colonial times.

But that is no reason for folding our hands in despairing inaction. On the contrary, we should be up and doing, for though some of our race-heritage has been lost, more yet remains. We can still be a very great people - if we will it so. Heaven be praised, the colonial stock was immensely prolific before the alien tide wrought its sterilizing havoc. Even to-day nearly one-half of our population is of the old blood, while many millions of the immigrant stock are sound in quality and assimilable in kind. Only the immigrant tide must at all costs be stopped and America given a chance to stabilize her ethnic being. It is the old story of the sibylline books. Some, to be sure, are ashes of the dead past; all the more should we conserve the precious volumes which remain.

One fact should be clearly understood: If America is not true to her own race-soul, she will inevitably lose it, and the brightest star that has appeared since Hellas will fall like a meteor from the human sky, its brilliant radiance fading into the night. "We Americans," says Madison Grant, "must realize that the altruistic ideals which have controlled our social development during the past century and the maudlin sentimentalism that has made America 'an asylum for the oppressed,' are sweeping the nation toward a racial abyss. If the melting-pot is allowed to boil without control and we continue to follow our national motto and deliberately blind ourselves to 'all distinctions of race, creed, or color,' the type of native American of colonial descent will become as extinct as the Athenian of the age of Pericles and the Viking of the days of Rollo." (Grant, p. 263.)

And let us not lay any sacrificial unction to our souls. If we cheat our country and the world of the splendid promise of American life, we shall have no one to blame but ourselves, and we shall deserve, not pity, but contempt. As Professor Ross well puts it: "A people that has no more respect for its ancestors and no more pride of race than this deserves the extinction that surely awaits it." (Ross, "The Old World in the New," p. 304.)

This extended discussion of the evil effects of even white immigration has, in my opinion, been necessary in order to get a proper perspective for viewing the problem of colored immigration. For it is perfectly obvious that if the influx of inferior kindred stocks is bad, the influx of wholly alien stocks is infinitely worse. When we see the damage wrought in America, for example, by the coming of persons who, after all, belong mostly to branches of the white race and who nearly all possess the basic ideals of white civilization, we can grasp the incalculably greater damage which would be wrought by the coming of persons wholly alien in blood and possessed of idealistic and cultural backgrounds absolutely different from ours. If the white immigrant can gravely disorder the national life, it is not too much to say that the colored immigrant would doom it to certain death.

This doom would be all the more certain because of the enormous potential volume of colored immigration. Beside it, the white immigrant tide of the past century would pale into insignificance. Leaving all other parts of the colored world out of the present discussion, three Asiatic countries - China, Japan, and India - together have a population of nearly 800,000,000. That is practically twice the population of Europe - the source of white immigration. And the vast majority of these 800,000,000 Asiatics are potential immigrants into white territories. Their standards of living are so inconceivably low, their congestion is so painful, and their consequent desire for relief so keen that the high-standard, relatively empty white world seems to them a perfect paradise. Only the barrier of the white man's veto has prevented a perfect deluge of colored men into white lands, and even as it is the desperate seekers after fuller life have crept and crawled through every crevice in that barrier, until even these advance-guards to-day constitute serious local problems along the white world's race-frontiers.

The simple truth of the matter is this: A mighty problem - a planet-wide problem - confronts us today and will increasingly confront us in the days to come. Says Putnam Weale: "A struggle has begun between the white man and all the other men of the world to decide whether non-white men - that is, yellow men, or brown men, or black men - may or may not invade the white man's countries in order there to gain their livelihood. The standard of living being low in the lands of colored men and high in the lands of the white man, it has naturally followed that it has been in the highest degree attractive for men of color during the past few decades to proceed to regions where their labor is rewarded on a scale far above their actual requirements - that is, on the white man's scale. This simple economic truth creates the inevitable contest which has for years filled all the countries bordering on the Pacific with great dread; and which, in spite of the temporary truce which the so-called 'Exclusion Policy' has now enforced, will go much farther than it has yet gone." (Putnam Weale, "The Conflict of Color," pp. 98-99.)

The world-wide significance of colored immigration and the momentous conflicts which it will probably provoke are ably visualized by Professor Ross.

"The rush of developments," he writes, "makes it certain that the vision of a globe 'lapped in universal law' is premature. If the seers of the mid-century who looked for the speedy triumph of free trade had read their Malthus aright, they might have anticipated the tariff barriers that have arisen on all hands within the last thirty years. So, to-day one needs no prophet's mantle to foresee that presently the world will be cut up with immigration barriers which will never be levelled until the intelligent accommodation of numbers to resources has greatly equalized population-pressure an over the globe.... Dams against the color races, with spillways of course for students, merchants, and travellers, will presently enclose the white man's world. Within this area minor dams will protect the high wages of the less prolific peoples against the surplus labor of the more prolific.

"Assuredly, every small-family nation will try to raise such a dam, and every big-family nation will try to break it down. The outlook for peace and disarmament is, therefore, far from bright. One needs but compare the population-pressures in France, Germany, Russia, and Japan to realize that, even to-day, the real enemy of the dove of peace is not the eagle of pride or the vulture of greed, but the stork!

"The great point of doubt in birth restriction is the ability of the Western nations to retain control of the vast African, Australasian, and South American areas they have staked out as preserves to be peopled at their leisure with the diminishing overflow of their population. If underbreeding should leave them without the military strength that alone can defend their far-flung frontiers in the southern hemisphere, those huge underdeveloped regions will assuredly be filled with the children of the brown and the yellow races." (Ross, "Changing America," pp. 46-48.)

Thus, white men, of whatever country and however far removed from personal contact with colored competitors, must realize that the question of colored immigration vitally concerns every white man, woman, and child; because nowhere - absolutely nowhere - can white labor compete on equal terms with colored immigrant labor. The grim truth is that there are enough hard-working colored men to swamp the whole white world.

No palliatives will serve to mitigate the ultimate issue, for if the white race should to-day surrender enough of its frontiers to ease the existing colored population-pressure, so quickly would these surrendered regions be swamped, and so rapidly would the fast-breeding colored races fill the homeland gaps, that in a very short time the diminished white world would be faced with an even louder colored clamor for admittance - backed by an increased power to enforce the colored will.

The profoundly destructive effects of colored competition upon white standards of labor and living has long been admitted by all candid students of the problem. So warm a champion of Asiatics as Mr. Hyndman acknowledges that "the white workers cannot hold their own permanently against Chinese competition in the labor market. The lower standard of life, the greater persistence, the superior education of the Chinese will beat them, and will continue to beat them." (Hyndman, "The Awakening of Asia," p. 180.)

Wherever the white man has been exposed to colored competition, particularly Asiatic competition, the story is the same. Says the Australian Professor Pearson: "No one in California or Australia, where the effects of Chinese competition have been studied, has, I believe, the smallest doubt that Chinese laborers, if allowed to come in freely, could starve all the white men in either country out of it, or force them to submit to harder work and a much lower standard of wages." (Pearson, p. 132.)

And a South African, writing of the effects of Hindu immigration into Natal, remarks in similar vein: "The condition of South Africa - especially of Natal - is a warning to other lands to bar Asiatic immigrants.... Both economically and socially the presence of a large Oriental population is bad. The Asiatics either force out the white workers, or compel the latter to live down to the Asiatic level. There must be a marked deterioration amongst the white working classes, which renders useless a great deal of the effort made in educational work. The white population is educated and trained according to the best ideas of the highest form of Western civilization - and has to compete for a livelihood against Asiatics! In South Africa this competition is driving out the white working class, because the average European cannot live down to the Asiatic level -

and if it is essential that the European must do so, for the sake of his own happiness, do not educate him up to better things. If cheapness is the only consideration, if low wages are to come before everything else, then it is not only waste of money, but absolute cruelty, to inspire in the white working classes tastes and aspirations which it is impossible for them to realize. To meet Asiatic competition squarely, it would be necessary to train the white children to be Asiatics. Even the pro-Orientals would hardly advocate this." (L. E. Neame, "Oriental Labor in South Africa," Annals of the American Academy of Political and Social Science, vol. XXXIV, pp. 179-180, September, 1909.)

The lines just quoted squarely counter the "survival of the fittest " plea so often made by Asiatic propagandists for colored immigration. The argument runs that, since the Oriental laborer is able to underbid the white laborer, the Oriental is the "fittest" and should therefore be allowed to supplant the white man in the interests of human progress. This is of course merely clever use of the well-known fallacy which confuses the terms "fittest" and "best." The idea that, because a certain human type "fits" in certain ways a particular environment (often an unhealthy, man-made social environment), it should be allowed to drive out another type endowed with much richer potentialities for the highest forms of human evolution, is a sophistry as absurd as it is dangerous.

Professor Ross puts the matter very aptly when he remarks concerning Chinese immigration: "The competition of white laborer and yellow is not so simple a test of human worth as some may imagine. Under good conditions the white man can best the yellow man in turning off work. But under bad conditions the yellow man can best the white man, because he can better endure spoiled food, poor clothing, foul air, noise, heat, dirt, discomfort, and microbes. Reilly can outdo Ah-San, but Ah-San can underlive Reilly. Ah-San cannot take away Reilly's job as being a better workman; but because he can live and do some work at a wage on which Reilly cannot keep himself fit to work at all, three or four Ah-Sans can take Reilly's job from him. And they will do it, too, unless they are barred out of the market where Reilly is selling his labor. Reilly's endeavor to exclude Ah-San from his labor market is not the case of a man dreading to pit himself on equal terms against a better man. Indeed, it is not quite so simple and selfish and narrow-minded as all that. It is a case of a man fitted to get the most out of good conditions refusing to yield his place to a weaker man able to withstand bad conditions." (Ross, "The Changing Chinese," pp. 47-48.)

All this is no disparagement of the Asiatic. He is perfectly justified in trying to win broader opportunities in white lands. But we whites are equally justified in keeping these opportunities for ourselves and our children. The hard facts are that there is not enough for both; that when the enormous outward thrust of colored population-pressure bursts into a white land it cannot let live, but automatically crushes the white man out - first the white laborer, then the white merchant, lastly the white aristocrat; until every vestige of white has gone from that land forever.

This inexorable process is thus described by an Australian: "The colored races become agencies of economic disturbance and social degradation. They sap and destroy the upward tendencies of the poorer whites. The latter, instead of always having something better to look at and strive after, have a lower standard of living, health, and cleanliness set before them, and the results are disastrous. They sink to the lower level of the Asiatics, and the degrading tendency proceeds upward by saturation, affecting several grades of society.... There is an insidious, yet irresistible, process of social degradation. The colored race does not intentionally, or even consciously, lower the European; it simply happens so, by virtue of a natural law which neither race can control. As debased coinage will drive out good currency, so a lowered standard of living will inexorably spread until its effects are universally felt." (J. Liddell Kelly, "What Is the Matter with the Asiatic?" Westminster Review, September, 1910.)

It all comes down to a question of self-preservation. And, despite what sentimentalists may say, self-preservation is the first law of nature. To love one's cultural, idealistic, and racial heritage; to swear to pass that heritage unimpaired to one's children; to fight, and, if need be, to die in its defense: all this is eternally right and proper, and no amount of casuistry or sentimentality can alter that unalterable truth. An Englishman put the thing in a nutshell when he wrote: "Asiatic immigration is not a question of sentiment, but of sheer existence. The whole problem is summed up in Lafcadio Hearn's pregnant phrase: 'The East can underlive the West." (From an article in The Pall Mall Gazette (London). Quoted in The Literary Digest, May 31, 1913, pp. 1215-16.)

Rigorous exclusion of colored immigrants is thus vitally necessary for the white peoples. Unfortunately, this exclusion policy will not be easily maintained. Colored population-pressure is insistent and increasing, while the matter is still further complicated by the fact that, while no white community can gain by colored immigration, white individual employers of labor may be great gainers and hence often tend to put private interest above racial duty. Barring a handful of sincere but misguided cosmopolitan enthusiasts, it is unscrupulous business interests which are behind every white proposal to relax the exclusion laws protecting white areas.

In fairness to these business interests, however, let us realize their great temptations. To the average employer, especially in the newer areas of white settlement where white labor is scarce and dictatorial, what could be more enticing than the vision of a boundless supply of cheap and eager colored labor?

Consider this Californian appraisement of the Chinese coolie: "The Chinese coolie is the ideal industrial machine, the perfect human ox. He will transform less food into more work, with less administrative friction, than any other creature. Even now, when the scarcity of Chinese labor and the consequent rise in wages have eliminated the question of cheapness, the Chinese have still the advantage over all other servile labor in convenience and efficiency. They are patient, docile, industrious, and above all 'honest' in the business sense that they keep their contracts. Also, they cost nothing but money. Any other sort of labor costs human effort and worry, in addition to the money. But Chinese labor can be bought like any other commodity, at so much a dozen or a hundred. The Chinese contractor delivers the agreed number of men, at the agreed time and place, for the agreed price, and if any one should drop out he finds another in his place. The men board and lodge themselves, and when the work is done they disappear from the employer's ken until again needed. The entire transaction consists in paying the Chinese contractor an agreed number of dollars for an agreed result. This elimination of the human element reduces the labor problem to something the employer can understand. The Chinese labor-machine, from his standpoint, is perfect." (Chester H. Rowell, "Chinese and Japanese Immigrants," Annals of the American Academy, vol. XXXIV, p. 4, September, 1909.)

What is true of the Chinese is true to a somewhat lesser extent of all "coolie" labor. Hence, once introduced into a white country, it becomes immensely popular - among employers. How it was working out in South Africa, before the exclusion acts there, is clearly explained in the following lines: "The experience of South Africa is that when once Asiatic labor is admitted, the tendency is for it to grow. One manufacturer secures it and is able to cut prices to such an extent that the other manufacturers are forced either to employ Asiatics also or to reduce white wages to the Asiatic level. Oriental labor is something which does not stand still. The taste for it grows. A party springs up financially interested in increasing it. In Natal to-day the suggestion that Indian labor should no longer be imported is met by an outcry from the planters, the farmers, and landowners, and a certain number of manufacturers, that industries and agriculture will be ruined. So the coolie ships continue to arrive at Durban, and Natal becomes more and more a land of black and brown people and less a land of white people. Instead of becoming a Canada or New Zealand, it is becoming a Trinidad or Cuba. Instead of white settlers, there are brown settlers.... The working-class white population has to go, as it is going in Natal. The country becomes a country of white landlords and supervisors controlling a horde of Asiatics. It does not produce a nation or a free people. It becomes what in the old days of English colonization was called a 'plantation.'" (Neame, "Oriental Labor in South Africa," Annals of the American Academy, vol. XXXIV, p. 181.)

All this gives a clearer idea of the difficulties involved in a successful guarding of the gates. But it also confirms the conviction that the gates must be strictly guarded. If anything further were needed to reinforce that conviction it should be the present state of those white outposts where the gates have been left ajar.

Hawaii is a good example. This mid-Pacific archipelago was brought under white control by masterful American Nordics, who established Anglo-Saxon institutions and taught the natives the rudiments of Anglo-Saxon civilization. The native Hawaiians' like the other Polynesian races, could not stand the pressure of white civilization, and withered away. But the white oligarchy which controlled the islands determined to turn their marvellous fertility to immediate profit. Labor was imported from the ends of the earth, the sole test being working ability without regard to race or color. There followed a great influx of Asiatic labor - at first Chinese until annexation to the United States brought Hawaii under our Chinese exclusion laws; later on Filipinos, Koreans, and, above all, Japanese.

The results are highly instructive. These Asiatics arrived as agricultural laborers to work on the plantations. But they did not stay there. Saving their wages, they pushed vigorously into all the middle walks of life. The Hawaiian fisherman and the American artisan or shopkeeper were alike ousted by ruthless undercutting. To-day the American mechanic, the American storekeeper, the American farmer, even the American contractor, is a rare bird indeed, while Japanese corporations are buying up the finest plantations and growing the finest pineapples and sugar. Fully half the population of the islands is Japanese, while the Americans are being literally encysted as a small and dwindling aristocracy. In 1917 the births of the two races were: American, 295; Japanese, 5,000 ! Comment is superfluous.

Clear round the globe, the island of Mauritius, the half-way house between Asia and Africa, tells the same tale. Originally settled by Europeans, mostly French, Mauritius imported negroes from Africa to work its rich soil. This at once made impossible the existence of a white laboring class, though the upper, middle, and artisan classes remained unaffected by the economically backward blacks. A hundred years ago one-third of the population were whites. But after the abolition of slavery the negroes quit work, and Asiatics were imported to take their place. The upshot was that the whites were presently swamped beneath the Asiatic tide here mostly Hindus. To-day the Hindus alone form more than two-thirds of the whole population, the whites numbering less than one-tenth. Indeed, the very outward aspect of the island is changing. The old French landmarks are going, and the fabled land of "Paul and Virginia" is becoming a bit of Hindustan, with a Chinese fringe. Even Port Louis, the capital town, has mostly passed from white to Indian or Chinese hands.

Now what do these two world-sundered cases mean? They mean, as an English writer justly remarks, "that under the British flag Mauritius has become an outpost of Asia, just as Hawaii is another such and under the Stars and Stripes." (Viator, "Asia contra Mundum," Fortnightly Review, February, 1908.) And, of course, there is Natal, already mentioned, which, at the moment when the recent South African Exclusion Act stayed the Hindu tide, had not only been partially transformed into an Asiatic land, but was fast becoming a centre of Asiatic radiation all over South Africa.

With such grim warnings before their eyes, it is not strange that the lusty young Anglo-Saxon communities bordering the Pacific-Australia, New Zealand, British Columbia, and our own "coast" have one and all set their faces like flint against the Oriental and have emblazoned across their portals the legend: "All White." Nothing is more striking than the instinctive and instantaneous solidarity which binds together Australians and Afrikanders, Californians and Canadians, into a "sacred union" at the mere whisper of Asiatic immigration.

Everywhere the slogan is the same. "The 'White Australia' idea," cries an antipodean writer, "is not a political theory. It is a gospel. It counts for more than religion; for more than flag, because the flag waves over all kinds of races; for more than the empire, for the empire is mostly black, or brown or yellow; is largely heathen, largely polygamous, partly cannibal. In fact, the White Australia doctrine is based on the necessity for choosing between national existence and national suicide." (Quoted by J. F. Abbott, "Japanese Expansion and American Policies" p. 154 (New York, 1916).) "White Australia!" writes another Australian in similar vein. "Australians of all classes and political affiliations regard the policy much as Americans regard the Constitution. It is their most articulate article of faith. The reason is not far to seek.... Australian civilization is little more than a partial fringe round the continental coastline of 12,210 miles. The coast and its hinterlands are settled and developed, although not completely for the entire circumference; in the centre of the country lie the apparently illimitable wastes of the Never-Never Land, occupied entirely by scrub, snakes, sand, and blackfellows. The almost manless regions of the island-continent are a terrible menace. It is impossible to police at all adequately such an enormous area. And the peoples of Asia, beating at the bars that confine them, rousing at last from their age-long slumber, are chafing at the restraints imposed upon their free entry into and settlement of such uninhabited, undeveloped lands." (H. C. Douglas, "What May Happen in the Pacific," American Review of Reviews, April, 1917.)

So the Australians, 5,000,000 whites in a far-off continent as large as the United States, defy clamoring Asia and swear to keep Australia a white man's land. Says Professor Pearson: "We are guarding the last part of the world in which the higher races can increase and live freely, for the higher civilization. We are denying the yellow race nothing but what it can find in the home of its birth, or in countries like the Indian Archipelago, where the white man can never live except as an exotic." (Pearson, p. 17.)

So Australia has raised drastic immigration barriers conceived on the lines laid down by Sir Henry Parkes many years ago: "It is our duty to preserve the type of the British nation, and we ought not for any consideration whatever to admit any element that would detract from, or in any appreciable degree lower, that admirable type of nationality. We should not encourage or admit amongst us any class of persons whatever whom we are not prepared to advance to all our franchises, to all our privileges as citizens, and all our social rights, including the right of marriage. I maintain that no class of persons should be admitted here who cannot come amongst us, take up all our rights, perform on a ground of equality all our duties, and share in our august and lofty work of founding a free nation." (Neame, op. cit., Annals of the American Acadeemy, vol. XXXIV, pp. 181-2.)

From Canada rises an equally uncompromising determination. Listen to Mr. Vrooman, a high official of British Columbia: "Our province is becoming Orientalized, and one of our most important questions is whether it is to remain a British province or become an Oriental colony - for we have three races demanding seats in our drawing-room, as well as places at our board - the Japanese, Chinese, and East Indian." (Quoted by Archibald Hurd, "The Racial War in the Pacific," Fortnightly Review, June, 1913.) And a well-known Canadian writer, Miss Laut, thus defines the issue: " If the resident Hindu had a vote - and as a British subject, why not? - and if he could break down the immigration exclusion act, he could outvote the native-born Canadian in ten years. In Canada are 5,500,000 native-born, 2,000,000 aliens. In India are hundreds of millions breaking the dikes of their own natural barriers and ready to flood any open land. Take down the barriers on the Pacific coast, and there would be 10,000,000 Hindus in Canada in ten years." (Agnes C. Laut, "The Canadian Commonwealth," p. 146 (Indianapolis, 1915).)

Our Pacific coast takes precisely the same attitude. Says Chester H. Rowell, a California writer: "There is no right way to solve a race problem except to stop it before it begins.... The Pacific coast is the frontier of the white man's world, the culmination of the westward migration which is the white man's whole history. It will remain the frontier so long as we regard it as such; no longer. Unless it is

199

maintained there, there is no other line at which it can be maintained without more effort than American government and American civilization are able to sustain. The multitudes of Asia are awake, after their long sleep, as the multitudes of Europe were when our present flood of immigration began. We know what could happen, on the Asiatic side, by what did happen and is happening on the European side. On that side we have survived.... But against Asiatic immigration we could not survive. The numbers who would come would be greater than we could encyst, and the races who would come are those which we could never absorb. The permanence not merely of American civilization, but of the white race on this continent, depends on our not doing on the Pacific side what we have done on the Atlantic coast." (Rowell, op. cit., Annals of the American Academy, vol. XXXIV, p. 10.

Says another Californian, Justice Burnett: "The Pacific States comprise an empire of vast potentialities and capable of supporting a population of many millions. Those now living there propose that it shall continue to be a home for them and their children, and that they shall not be overwhelmed and driven eastward by an ever-increasing yellow and brown flood." (Honorable A. G. Burnett, "Misunderstanding of Eastern and Western States Regarding Oriental Immigration," Annals of the American Academy, vol. XXXIV, p. 41.)

All " economic" arguments are summarily put aside. "They say," writes another Californian, "that our fruit-orchards, mines, and seed-farms cannot be worked without them (Oriental laborers). It were better that they never be developed than that our white laborers be degraded and driven from the soil. The same arguments were used a century and more ago to justify the importation of African labor.... As it is now, no self-respecting white laborer will work beside the Mongolian upon any terms. The proposition, whether we shall have white or yellow labor on the Pacific coast, must soon be settled, for we cannot have both. If the Mongolian is permitted to occupy the land, the white laborer from east of the Rockies will not come here - he will shun California as he would a pestilence. And who can blame him?" (A. E. Yoell, "Oriental versus American Labor," Annals of the American Academy, vol. XXXIV, p. 36.)

The middle as well as the working class is imperilled by any large number of Orientals, for "The presence of the Japanese trader means that the white man must either go out of business or abandon his standard of comfort and sink to the level of the Asiatic, who will sleep under his counter and subsist upon food that would mean starvation to his white rival." (S. G. P. Coryn, "The Japanese Problem in California," Annals of the American Academy, vol. XXXIV, pp. 43-44.)

Indeed, Californian assertions that Oriental immigration menaces, not merely the coast, but the whole continent, seem well taken. This view was officially indorsed by Mr. Caminetti, Commissioner-General of Immigration, who testified before a Congressional committee some years ago: "Asiatic immigration is a menace to the whole country, and particularly to the Pacific coast. The danger is general. No part of the United States is immune. The Chinese are now spread over the entire country, and the Japanese want to encroach. The Chinese have become so acclimated that they can prosper in any part of our country.... I would have a law to register the Asiatic laborers who come into the country. It is impossible to protect ourselves from persons who come in surreptitiously." (Quoted by J. D. Whelpley, "Japan and the United States," Fortnightly Review, May, 1914.)

Fortunately, the majority of thinking Americans are to-day convinced that Oriental immigration must not be tolerated. Most of our leading men have so expressed themselves. For example, Woodrow Wilson, during his first presidential campaign, declared on May 3, 1912: "In the matter of Chinese and Japanese coolie immigration, I stand for the national policy of exclusion. The whole question is one of assimilation of diverse races. We cannot make a homogeneous population of a people who do not blend with the Caucasian race. Their lower standard of living as laborers will crowd out the white agriculturist and is in other fields a most serious industrial menace. The success of free democratic institutions demands of our people education, intelligence, and patriotism, and the State should protect them against unjust and impossible competition. Remunerative labor is the basis of contentment. Democracy rests on the equality of the citizen. Oriental coolieism will give us another race-problem to solve and surely we have had our lesson." (Quoted by Montaville Flowers, "The Japanese Conquest of American Opinion," p. 23 (New York, 1917).)

The necessity for rigid Oriental exclusion is nowhere better exemplified than by the alarm felt to-day in California by the extraordinarily high birth-rate of its Japanese residents. There are probably not over 150,000 Japanese in the whole United States, their numbers being kept down by the "Gentlemen's Agreement" entered into by the Japanese and American Governments. But, few though they are, they bring in their women - and these women bring many children into the world. The California Japanese settle in compact agricultural colonies, which so teem with babies that a leading California organ, the Los Angeles Times, thus seriously discusses the matter:

"There may have been a time when an anti-Japanese land bill would have limited Japanese immigration. But such a law would be impotent now to keep native Japanese from possessing themselves of the choicest agricultural and horticultural land in California. For there are now more than 30,000 children in the State of Japanese parentage, native-born; they possess all the rights of leasing and ownership held by white children born here.... The birth statistics seem to prove that the danger is not from the Japanese soldiers, but from the picture brides. The fruitfulness of those brides is almost uncanny.... Here is a Japanese problem of sufficient gravity to merit serious consideration. We are threatened with an over-production of Japanese children. First come the men, then the picture brides, then the families. If California is to be preserved for the next generation as a 'white man's country' there must be some movement started that will restrict the Japanese birth-rate in

202

California. When a condition is reached in which two children of Japanese parentage are born in some districts for every white child, it is about time something else was done than making speeches about it in the American Senate.... If the same present birth-ratio were maintained for the next ten years, there would be 150,000 children of Japanese descent born in California in 1929 and but 40,000 white children. And in 1949 the majority of the population of California would be Japanese, ruling the State." (The Literary Digest, August 9, 1919, p. 53.)

The alarm of our California contemporary may, in this particular instance, be exaggerated. Nevertheless, when we remember the practically unlimited expansive possibilities of even small human groups under favorable conditions, the picture drawn contains no features inherently impossible of realization. What is absolutely certain is that any wholesale Oriental influx would inevitably doom the whites, first of the Pacific coast, and later of the whole United States, to social sterilization and ultimate racial extinction.

Thus all those newer regions of the white world won by the white expansion of the last four centuries are alike menaced by the colored migration peril; whether these regions be under-developed, under-populated frontier marches like Australia and British Columbia, or older and better-populated countries like the United States.

And let not Europe, the white brood-land, the heart of the white world, think itself immune. In the last analysis, the self-same peril menaces it too. This has long been recognized by far-sighted men. For many years economists and sociologists have discussed the possibility of Asiatic immigration into Europe. Low as wages and living standards are in many European countries, they are yet far higher than in the congested East, while the rapid progress of social betterment throughout Europe must further widen the gap and make the white continent seem a more and more desirable haven for the swarming, black-haired bread-seekers of China, India, and Japan.

Indeed, a few observers of modern conditions have come to the conclusion that this invasion of Europe by Asiatic labor is unescapable, and they have drawn the most pessimistic conclusions. For example, more than a decade ago an English writer asserted gloomily: "No level-headed thinker can imagine that it will always be possible to prevent the free migration of intelligent races, representing in the aggregate half the peoples of the world, should those peoples actively conceive that their welfare demands that they should seek employment in Europe. In these days of rapid transit, of aviation, such a measure of repression is impossible.... We shall not be destroyed, perhaps, by the sudden onrush of invaders, as Rome was overwhelmed by the northern hordes; we shall be gradually subdued and absorbed by the 'peaceful penetration' of more virile races." (J. S. Little, "The Doom of Western Civilization," pp. 56 and 63 (London, 1907).)

Now, mark you! All that I have thus far written, concerning colored immigration has been written without reference to the late war. In other words, the colored-migration peril would have been just as grave as I have described it even if the white world were still as strong as in the years before 1914.

But the war has of course immensely aggravated an already critical situation. The war has shaken both the material and psychological bases of white resistance to colored infiltration, while it has correspondingly strengthened Asiatic hopes and hardened Asiatic determination to break down the barriers debarring colored men from white lands.

Asia's perception of what the war signified in this respect was instantaneous. The war was not a month old before Japanese Journals were suggesting a relaxation of Asiatic exclusion laws in the British colonies as a natural corollary to the Anglo-Japanese Alliance and Anglo-Japanese comradeship in arms. Said the Tokio Mainichi Deupo in August, 1914: "We are convinced that it is a matter of the utmost importance that Britons beyond the seas should make a better attempt at fraternizing with Japan, as better relations between the English-speaking races and Japan will have a vital bearing on the destiny of the empire. There is no reason why the British colonies fronting on the Pacific should not actively participate in the Anglo-Japanese Alliance. Britain needs population for her surplus land and Japan needs land for her surplus population. This fact alone should draw the two races closer together. Moreover, the British people have ample capital but deficiency of labor, while it is the reverse with Japan.... The harmonious co-operation of Britain and her colonies with Japan insures safety to British and Japanese interests alike. Without such co-operation, Japan and Great Britain are both unsafe." (The Literary Digest, August 29, 1914, p. 337.)

What this "co-operation" implies was very frankly stated by The Japan Magazine at about the same date: "There is nothing that would do so much to bind East and West firmly together as the opening of the British colonies to Japanese immigration. Then, indeed,

Britain would be a lion endowed with wings. Large numbers of Japanese in the British colonies would mean that Britain would have the assistance of Japan in the protection of her colonies. But if an anti-Japanese agitation is permitted, both countries will be making the worst instead of the best of the Anglo-Japanese Alliance. Thus it would be allowed to make Japan an enemy instead of a friend. It seems that the British people both at home and in the colonies are not yet alive to the importance of the policy suggested, and it is, therefore, pointed out and emphasized before it is too late." (The Literary Digest, August 29, 1914, pp. 337-8.)

The covert threat embodied in those last lines was a forerunner of the storm of anti-white abuse which rose from the more bellicose sections of the Japanese press as soon as it became evident that neither the British Dominions nor the United States were going to relax their immigration laws. Some of this anti-white comment, directed particularly against the Anglo-Saxon peoples, I have already noted in the second chapter of this book, but such comment as bears directly on immigration matters I have reserved for discussion at this point.

For example, the Tokio Yorodzu wrote early in 1916: "Japan has been most faithful to the requirements of the Anglo-Japanese Alliance, and yet the treatment meted out to our countrymen in Canada, Australia, and other British colonies has been a glaring insult to us." (Ibid., April 22, 1916, p. 1138.)

A year later a writer in The Japan Magazine declared: "The agitation against Japanese in foreign countries must cease, even if Japan has to take up arms to stop it. She should not allow her immigration to be treated as a race-question." (Quoted in The Review of Reviews (London), February, 1917, p. 174.) And in 1919 the Yorodzu thus paid its respects to the exclusionist activity of our Pacific coast States: "Whatever may be their object, their actions are more despicable than those of the Germans whose barbarities they attacked as worthy of Huns. At least, these Americans are barbarians who are on a lower plane of civilization than the Japanese." (The Literary Digest, July 5, 1919, p. 31.)

The war produced no letting down of immigration barriers along the white world's exposed frontiers, where men are fully alive to the peril. But the war did produce temporary waverings of sentiment in the United States, while in Europe colored labor was imported wholesale in ways which may have ominous consequences.

Our own acute labor shortage during the war, particularly in agriculture, led many Americans, especially employers, to cast longing eyes at the tempting reservoirs of Asia. Typical of this attitude is an article by Hudson Maxim in the spring of 1918. Mr Maxim urged the importation of a million Chinese to solve our farming and domestic-service problems.

"If it is possible," he wrote, "by the employment of Chinese methods of intensive farming, to increase the production of our lands to such an extent, how stupendous would be the benefit of wide

206

introduction of such methods. The exhausted lands of New England could be made to produce like a tropical garden. The vast areas of the great West that are to-day not producing 10 per cent of what they ought to produce could be made to produce the other 90 per cent by the introduction of Chinese labor.... The average American does not like farming. The sons of the prosperous farmers do not take kindly to the tilling of the soil with their own hands. They prefer the excitement and the diversions and stimulus of the life of city and town, and they leave the farm for the office and factory....

"Chinese, imported as agricultural laborers and household servants, would solve the agricultural labor problem and the servant problem, and we should have the best agricultural workers in the world and the best household servants in the world, in unlimited numbers." (Leslie's Weekly, May 4, 1918.)

Now I submit that such arguments, however well-intentioned, are nothing short of race-treason. If there be one truth which history has proved, it is the solemn truth that those who work the land will ultimately own the land.

Furthermore, the countryside is the seed-bed from which the city populations are normally recruited. The one bright spot in our otherwise dubious ethnic future is the fact that most of our unassimilable aliens have stopped in the towns, while many of the most assimilable immigrants have settled in the country, thus reinforcing rather than replacing our native American rural population. Any suggestion which advocates the settlement of our countryside by Asiatics and the deliberate driving of our native stocks to the towns, there to be sterilized and eliminated, is simply unspeakable.

Fortunately, such fatal counsels were with us never acted upon, albeit they should be remembered as lurking perils which will probably be urged again in future times of stress. But during Europe's war-agony, yellow, brown, and black men were imported wholesale, not only for the armies, but also for the factories and fields. These colored aliens have mostly been shipped back to their homes. Nevertheless, they have carried with them vivid recollections of the marvellous West, and the tale will spread to the remotest corners of the colored world, stirring hard-pressed colored breadseekers to distant ventures. Furthermore, Europe has had a practical demonstration of the colored alien's manifold usefulness, and if Europe's troubles are prolonged, the colored man may be increasingly employed there both in peace and war.

Even during the war the French and English working classes felt the pressure of colored competition. Race-feeling grew strained, and presently both England and France witnessed the (to them) unwonted spectacles of race-riots in their port-towns where the colored aliens were most thickly gathered. An American observer thus describes the "breaking of the exclusion walls erected against the Chinese ":

"In London, one Wednesday evening, twenty-four months ago (i. e., in 1916), there was a mass-meeting held on the corner of Piggot Street, Limehouse, to protest against the influx of John Chinaman into bonny old England.... The London navvies that night heard a protest against 'the Chinese invasion' of Britain. They knew that down on the London docks there were two Chinamen to every white man since the coming of war. They knew that many of these yellow aliens were married. They knew, too, that a big Chinese restaurant had just opened down the West India Dock Road.

"The Sailors' and Firemen's Union - one of the most powerful in England - carried the protest into the Trades-Union Congress held at Birmingham. There, alarm was voiced at the steady increase in the number of Chinese hands on Britain's ships. It was an increase, true, since the stress of war-times had begun to try Britain. But what England's sons of the seven seas wanted to know was: when is 'this Orientalizing' of the British marine to stop ? . . . The seamen's unions were willing to do their bit for John Bull, but they wondered what was going to happen after the coming of peace. Would the Chinese continue to man John Bull's ships?

"Such is one manifestation of the decisive lifting of gates and barriers that has taken place since the white world went to war. To-day the Chinese - for decades finding a wall in every white man's country - are numbered by the tens of thousands in the service of the Allies. They have made good. They are a war-factor.... All told, 200,000 Chinese are 'carrying on' in the war-zone, laboring behind the lines, in munition-works and factories, manning ships...

"What will happen when peace comes upon this red world - a world turned topsyturvy by the white man's Great War, which has taken John Chinaman from Shantung, Chilhi, and Kwangtung to that battleground in France? . . . That makes the drafting of China's man-power one of the most supremely important events in the Great War. The family of nations is taking on a new meaning - John Chinaman overseas has a place in it. As Italian harvest-labor before the war went to and from Argentina for a few months' work, so the Chinese have gone to Europe under contract and go home again. Perhaps this action will have a bearing on the solution of the Far West's agricultural labor problem.

"Do not believe for a moment that the armies of Chinese in Europe will forget the lessons taught them in the West. When these sons of Han come home, the Great War will be found to have given birth to a new East." (G. C. Hodges in The Sunset Magazine. Quoted by The Literary Digest, September 14, 1918, pp. 40-42.)

So ends our survey. It has girdled the globe. And the lesson is always the same: Colored migration is a universal peril, menacing every part of the white world.

Nowhere can the white man endure colored competition; everywhere "the East can underlive the West." The grim truth of the matter is this: The whole white race is exposed, immediately or ultimately, to the possibility of social sterilization and final replacement or absorption by the teeming colored races.

What this unspeakable catastrophe would mean for the future of the planet, and how the peril may be averted, will form the subject of my concluding pages.

CHAPTER XII
THE CRISIS OF THE AGES

OURS is a solemn moment. We stand at a crisis - the supreme crisis of the ages. For unnumbered millenniums man has toiled upward from the dank jungles of savagery toward glorious heights which his mental and spiritual potentialities give promise that he shall attain. His path has been slow and wavering. Time and again he has lost his way and plunged into deep valleys. Man's trail is littered with the wrecks of dead civilizations and dotted with the graves of promising peoples stricken by an untimely end.

Humanity has thus suffered many a disaster. Yet none of these disasters were fatal, because they were merely local. Those wrecked civilizations and blighted peoples were only parts of a larger whole. Always some strong barbarians, endowed with rich, unspoiled heredities, caught the falling torch and bore it onward flaming high once more.

Out of the prehistoric shadows the white races pressed to the front and proved in a myriad ways their fitness for the hegemony of mankind. Gradually they forged a common civilization; then, when vouchsafed their unique opportunity of oceanic mastery four centuries ago, they spread over the earth, filling its empty spaces with their superior breeds and assuring to themselves an unparalleled paramountcy of numbers and dominion.

Three centuries later the whites took a fresh leap forward. The nineteenth century was a new age of discovery - this time into the realms of science. The hidden powers of nature were unveiled, incalculable energies were tamed to human use, terrestrial distance was abridged, and at last the planet was integrated under the hegemony of a single race with a common civilization.

The prospects were magnificent, the potentialities of progress apparently unlimited. Yet there were commensurate perils. Towering heights mean abysmal depths, while the very possibility of supreme success implies the possibility of supreme failure. All these marvellous achievements were due solely to superior heredity, and the mere maintenance of what had been won depended absolutely upon the prior maintenance of race-values. Civilization of itself means nothing. It is merely an effect, whose cause is the creative urge of superior germ-plasm. Civilization is the body; the race is the soul. Let the soul vanish, and the body moulders into the inanimate dust from which it came.

Two things are necessary for the continued existence of a race: it must remain itself, and it must breed its best. Every race is the result of ages of development which evolves specialized capacities that make the race what it is and render it capable of creative achievement. These specialized capacities (which particularly mark the superior races), being relatively recent developments, are highly unstable. They are what biologists call "recessive" characters; that is, they are not nearly so "dominant" as the older, generalized characters which races inherit from remote ages and which have therefore been more firmly stamped upon the germ-plasm. Hence, when a highly specialized stock interbreeds with a different stock, the newer, less stable, specialized characters are bred out, the variation, no matter how great its potential value to human evolution, being irretrievably lost. This occurs even in the mating of two superior stocks if these stocks are widely dissimilar in character. The valuable specializations of both breeds cancel out, and the mixed offspring tend strongly to revert to generalized mediocrity.

And, of course, the more primitive a type is, the more prepotent it is. This is why crossings with the negro are uniformly fatal. Whites, Amerindians, or Asiatics - all are alike vanquished by the invincible prepotency of the more primitive, generalized, and lower negro blood.

There is no immediate danger of the world being swamped by black blood. But there is a very imminent danger that the white stocks may be swamped by Asiatic blood.

The white man's very triumphs have evoked this danger. His virtual abolition of distance has destroyed the protection which nature once conferred. Formerly mankind dwelt in such dispersed isolation that wholesale contact of distant, diverse stocks was practically impossible. But with the development of cheap and rapid transportation, nature's barriers are down. Unless man erects and maintains artificial barriers the various races will increasingly mingle, and the inevitable result will be the supplanting or absorption of the higher by the lower types.

We can see this process working out in almost every phase of modern migration. The white immigration into Latin America is the exception which proves the rule. That particular migration is, of course, beneficent, since it means the influx of relatively high types into undeveloped lands, sparsely populated by types either no higher or much lower than the new arrivals. But almost everywhere else, whether we consider interwhite migrations or colored encroachments on white lands, the net result is an expansion of lower and a contraction of higher stocks, the process being thus a disgenic one. Even in Asia the evils of modern migration are beginning to show. The Japanese Government has been obliged to prohibit the influx of Chinese and Korean coolies who were undercutting Japanese labor and thus undermining the economic bases of Japanese life.

Furthermore, modern migration is itself only one aspect of a still more fundamental disgenic trend. The whole course of modern urban and industrial life is disgenic. Over and above immigration, the tendency is toward a replacement of the more valuable by the less valuable elements of the population. All over the civilized world racial values are diminishing, and the logical end of this disgenic process is racial bankruptcy and the collapse of civilization.

Now why is all this? It is primarily because we have not yet adjusted ourselves to the radically new environment into which our epochal scientific discoveries led us a century ago. Such adaptation as we have effected has been almost wholly on the material side. The no less sweeping idealistic adaptations which the situation calls for have not been made. Hence, modern civilization has been one-sided, abnormal, unhealthy - and nature is exacting penalties which will increase in severity until we either fully adapt or finally perish.

"Finally perish!" That is the exact alternative which confronts the white race. For white civilization is to-day conterminous with the white race. The civilizations of the past were local. They were confined to a particular people or group of peoples. If they failed, there were always some unspoiled, well-endowed barbarians to step forward and "carry on." But today there are no more white barbarians. The earth has grown small, and men are everywhere in close touch. If white civilization goes down, the white race is irretrievably ruined. It will be swamped by the triumphant colored races, who will obliterate the white man by elimination or absorption. What has taken place in Central Asia, once a white and now a brown or yellow land, will take place in Australasia, Europe, and America. Not to-day, nor yet to-morrow; perhaps not for generations; but surely in the end. If the present drift be not changed, we whites are all ultimately doomed. Unless we set our house in order, the doom will sooner or later overtake us all.

And that would mean that the race obviously endowed with the greatest creative ability, the race which had achieved most in the past and which gave the richer promise for the future, had passed away, carrying with it to the grave those potencies upon which the realization of man's highest hopes depends. A million years of human evolution might go uncrowned, and earth's supreme life-product, man, might never fulfil his potential destiny. This is why we today face "The Crisis of the Ages."

To many minds the mere possibility of such a catastrophe may seem unthinkable. Yet a dispassionate survey of the past shows that it is not only possible but probable if present conditions go on unchanged. The whole history of life, both human and subhuman, teaches us that nature will not condone disobedience; that, as I have already phrased it, "no living being stands above her law, and protozoon or demigod, if they transgress, alike must die."

Now we have transgressed; grievously transgressed - and we are suffering grievous penalties. But pain is really kind. Pain is the importunate tocsin which rouses to dangerous realities and spurs to the seeking of a cure.

As a matter of fact we are confusedly aware of our evil plight, and legion are the remedies to-day proposed.

Some of these are mere quack nostrums. Others contain valuable remedial properties. To be sure, there is probably no one curative agent, since our troubles are complex and magic elixirs heal only in the realm of dreams. But one element should be fundamental to all the compoundings of the social pharmacopoeia. That element is blood.

It is clean, virile, genius-bearing blood, streaming down the ages through the unerring action of heredity, which, in anything like a favorable environment, will multiply itself, solve our problems, and sweep us on to higher and nobler destinies. What we to-day need above all else is a changed attitude of mind - a recognition of the supreme importance of heredity, not merely in scientific treatises but in the practical ordering of the world's affairs. We are where we are today primarily because we have neglected this vital principle; because we have concerned ourselves with dead things instead of with living beings.

This disregard of heredity is perhaps not strange. It is barely a generation since its fundamental importance was scientifically established, and the world's conversion to even the most vital truth takes time. In fact, we also have much to unlearn. A little while ago we were taught that all men were equal and that good conditions could, of themselves, quickly perfect mankind. The seductive charm of these dangerous fallacies lingers and makes us loath to put them resolutely aside.

Fortunately, we now know the truth. At last we have been vouchsafed clear insight into the laws of life. We now know that men are not, and never will be, equal. We know that environment and education can develop only what heredity brings. We know that the acquirements of individuals are either not inherited at all or are inherited in so slight a degree as to make no perceptible difference from generation to generation. In other words: we now know that heredity is paramount in human evolution, all other things being secondary factors.

This basic truth is already accepted by large numbers of thinking men and women all over the civilized world, and if it becomes firmly fixed in the popular consciousness it will work nothing short of a revolution in the ordering of the world's affairs.

For race-betterment is such an intensely practical matter! When peoples come to realize that the QUALITY of the population is the source of all their prosperity, progress, security, and even existence; when they realize that a single genius may be worth more in actual dollars than a dozen gold-mines, while, conversely, racial decline spells material impoverishment and decay; when such things are really believed, we shall see much-abused "eugenics" actually moulding social programmes and political policies. Were the white world to-day really convinced of the supreme importance of race-values, how long would it take to stop debasing immigration, reform social abuses that are killing out the fittest strains, and put an end to the feuds which have just sent us through hell and threaten to send us promptly back again?

Well, perhaps our change of heart may come sooner than now appears. The horrors of the war, the disappointment of the peace, the terror of Bolshevism, and the rising tide of color have knocked a good deal of the nonsense out of us, and have given multitudes a hunger for realities who were before content with a diet of phrases.

Said wise old Benjamin Franklin: "Dame Experience sets a dear school, but fools will have no other." Our course at the dame's school is already well under way and promises to be exceeding dear.

Only, it is to be hoped our education will be rapid, for time presses and the hour is grave. If certain lessons are not learned and acted upon shortly, we may be overwhelmed by irreparable disasters and all our dear schooling will go for naught.

What are the things we must do promptly if we would avert the worst? This "irreducible minimum" runs about as follows:

First and foremost, the wretched Versailles business will have to be thoroughly revised. As it stands, dragon's teeth have been sown over both Europe and Asia, and unless they be plucked up they will presently grow a crop of cataclysms which will seal the white world's doom.

Secondly, some sort of provisional understanding must be arrived at between the white world and renascent Asia.

We whites will have to abandon our tacit assumption of permanent domination over Asia, while Asiatics will have to forego their dreams of migration to white lands and penetration of Africa and Latin America. Unless some such understanding is arrived at, the world will drift into a gigantic race-war - and genuine race-war means war to the knife. Such a hideous catastrophe should be abhorrent to both sides. Nevertheless, Asia should be given clearly to understand that we cannot permit either migration to white lands or penetration of the non-Asiatic tropics, and that for these matters we prefer to fight to a finish rather than yield to a finish - because our "finish" is precisely what surrender on these points would mean.

Thirdly, even within the white world, migrations of lower human types like those which have worked such havoc in the United States must be rigorously curtailed. Such migrations upset standards, sterilize better stocks, increase low types, and compromise national futures more than war, revolutions, or native deterioration.

Such are the things which simply must be done if we are to get through the next few decades without convulsions which may render impossible the white world's recovery.

These things will not bring in the millennium. Far from it. Our ills are so deep-seated that in nearly every civilized country racial values would continue to depreciate even if all three were carried into effect.

But they will at least give our wounds a chance to heal, and they will give the new biological revelation time to permeate the popular consciousness and transfuse with a new idealism our materialistic age. As the years pass, the supreme importance of heredity and the supreme value of superior stocks will sink into our being, and we will acquire a true race-consciousness (as opposed to national or cultural consciousness) which will bridge political gulfs, remedy social abuses, and exorcise the lurking spectre of miscegenation.

In those better days, we or the next generation will take in hand the problem of race-depreciation, and segregation of defectives and abolition of handicaps penalizing the better stocks will put an end to our present racial decline. By that time biological knowledge will have so increased and the popular philosophy of life will have been so idealized that it will be possible to inaugurate positive measures of race-betterment which will unquestionably yield the most wonderful results.

Those splendid tasks are probably not ours. They are for our successors in a happier age. But we have our task, and God knows it is a hard one the salvage of a shipwrecked world! Ours it is to make possible that happier age, whose full-fruits we shall never see.

Well, what of it? Does not the new idealism teach us that we are links in a vital chain, charged with high duties both to the dead and the unborn? In very truth we are at once sons of sires who sleep in calm assurance that we will not betray the trust they confided to our hands, and sires of sons who in the Beyond wait confident that we shall not cheat them of their birthright.

218

Let us, then, act in the spirit of Kipling's immortal lines:

"Our Fathers in a wondrous age,
Ere yet the Earth was small,
Ensured to us an heritage,
And doubted not at all
That we, the children of their heart,
Which then did beat so high,
In later time should play like part
For our posterity.

Then, fretful, murmur not they gave
So great a charge to keep,
Nor dream that awestruck Time shall save
Their labor while we sleep.
Dear-bought and clear, a thousand year
Our fathers' title runs.
Make we likewise their sacrifice,
Defrauding not our sons. "

(Rudyard Kipling, "The Heritage." Dedicatory poem to the volume entitled "The Empire and the Century" (London, 1905), the volume being a collaboration by prominent British writers.)